D0645316

Medieval Academy Reprints for Teaching

EDITORIAL BOARD

Photograph (× 5) by the late Charles Rosser of a plaster cast made from an impression, now in the Ashmolean Museum, Oxford, of the seal-ring (no longer extant) of King Childeric I (died 481/2) found in his grave at Tournai in 1653. It has recently been discussed and its authenticity defended in P. E. Schramm, *Herrschaftszeichen und Staatssymbolik*, I (1954), pp. 213 ff.

J.M. WALLACE-HADRILL

# The
# Long-Haired
# Kings

Published by University of Toronto Press
Toronto  Buffalo  London
in association with the Medieval Academy of America

© Medieval Academy of America 1982
Printed in USA
ISBN 0-8020-6500-7



First published by Methuen and Company Ltd 1962
This edition is reprinted by arrangement with Professor J.M. Wallace-Hadrill

TO
MY MOTHER

# Contents

*

# *Preface*

\*

The essay from which this book takes its title is a study of a particular kind of barbarian kingship. It is in no way intended as a political history of the Merovingian kings. Some of the matters to which it refers I had already written about in papers published elsewhere. I therefore thought that it might be a convenience to reprint six of these papers, even at the risk of a certain amount of repetition, and, it may be, of change in viewpoint. They have been revised, some extensively.

For permission to reprint, I have to thank the Governors of the John Rylands Library, Manchester (chapters II, IV and VI); the Council of the Royal Historical Society (chapter III); the Direction of the *Revue d'histoire du droit* (chapter V); and Messrs Methuen and Co. Ltd (chapter 1). I have also to thank the Ashmolean Museum, Oxford, for permission to reproduce as frontispiece the photograph of the seal-ring of King Childeric, taken for me by the late Mr Charles Rosser.

J. M. W-H.

Merton College, Oxford
October 1961

CHAPTER ONE

# Frankish Gaul[1]

*

The Franks who reached Gaul in the fifth century were a group of West German tribes from across the Rhine; tribes that had been in contact with Roman civilization for generations, the trusted soldiers of successive emperors. They were good soldiers, especially on foot, and clever in making and using arms (we know exactly what sort); they were good husbandmen, too; in brief, they were a long way from their nomadic origins. The only strange thing about them might seem to be that they were not Christians years before they set foot in Gaul; but such is the fact, and familiarity is not always the key to conversion. Further, it may be noticed that even combined with all the Visigoths and other barbarians, their numbers can have been only a fraction of the total population of Gaul; and that they had neither the desire nor the means to resist the process of romanization. They wanted to be Gallo-Romans, though in actual fact they became French; not, however, overnight, for what follows Gaul is not immediately France but sub-Roman Gaul, and sub-Roman it remains throughout certainly the first 150 years of Merovingian rule, and perhaps beyond. It is a society to which, a century after the coming of Clovis and his Franks, Gregory of Tours does not deem it necessary to explain what he means by *civitas, pagus, territorium, vicus, villa, exactor, fiscus, indiculus, privilegium, rescriptum testamentum*: the administrative shape of Frankish Gaul is for the most part sub-Roman and the men who run it use the old Latin terms, sometimes inaccurately but never with any sense of constraint. In the words of Einar Löfstedt, speaking of Merovingian Gaul, 'before 600 the popular speech may be called Latin,

<hr/>

[1] From *France, Government and Society*, edited by J. M. Wallace-Hadrill and J. McManners (Methuen, 1957).

I

after 800 Romance. For the intervening period either name will serve.' And what is true of Frankish Gaul in the narrow sense (the greater part, that is, of old *Gallia Comata*) is true also of Burgundian Gaul and Visigothic Gaul. All three are sub-Roman and the differences between them have more to do with degrees of romanization than of barbarization. All three, moreover, are held together, however loosely, by common experience of the forms of Roman rule, most particularly as expressed by Roman Law. For this reason, and because it is too often neglected, this paper pays rather more attention to Gallo-Frankish law and its social implications than a balanced survey would require. It should, however, be emphasized that the society over which the Merovingian kings ruled was no more 'Roman' than it was 'Germanic'. It was something new.

We can look quite deep into this Gallo-Frankish society as it appears in its most famous legal pronouncement, *Lex Salica*, the Salic Law. This Law is transmitted to us in no very good shape, but it is more than a fair guess that it gives a true, if partial, picture of how the Salian Franks ordered their lives in sixth-century Gaul. (The Law does not apply only to northern Gaul, but is binding on Salian Franks wherever they may live in the *Regnum Francorum*, by the banks of the Loire or deep in the Ardennes, as well as in the Paris basin.)

*Lex Salica* reveals not a mobile, pastoral but a settled, agricultural society, far advanced from the Germanic world of Tacitus. The Franks are farmers. They are not simple cattle-raisers but owners of orchards, cornfields, beanfields, lentil-fields, vineyards. They are concerned about the inviolability of standing corn, about the cutting of hay and rights over fishing, and they know something about what medievalists would call 'vert and venison'; they have adapted themselves to the *villa*-economy of a Roman province, and that over a wide area. We can no longer mean by this the static and classic *villa* championed by Fustel. It is rather an adaptation. Nevertheless, though fragmented and under new management, the Gallo-Roman *villa* survives in a sense in which the Romano-British does not. What consequences may not flow from this vital distinction? But to return to law, the assumptions of *Lex Salica* are peaceful, not warlike. Nor is this surprising when we remember that, for all their paganism, the Franks were no savages; they were *foederati* with a long experience of Roman ways and a taste for Roman things. The grave of their chieftain Childeric, buried at Tournai in 482, contained possessions that suggest the successful business man as much as the ruthless warrior. His followers were not wild horsemen, like Attila's Huns, but for the most part plodding foot-soldiers. We have their graves by the score, where they lie quite often cheek by jowl with Gallo-Romans. It is difficult, at this remove of time, to appreciate that vendetta (the normal Germanic way of settling differences arising from bloodshed) was not the law of the jungle but a duty regulated by custom that one owed to the community for maintenance of order (the phrase is Miss Whitelock's). It was sometimes bloodthirsty and even rather wasteful; but it was all that the Germanic tribesmen had till, as in the case of those who settled in Gaul, they had had time to learn other and better ways from their hosts. But if the first Franks were rather tamer than Gregory of Tours believed, on the other hand the Gallo-Romans were not all aristocrats like Sidonius. We use the term 'Gallo-Roman' to describe a mixed society already highly barbarized before the Franks arrived in Gaul. Their *villae* and their *vici*, to say nothing of their towns, had long been crying out for more men, more labour, and there cannot have been much forcible dispossession of Gallo-Roman gentry to make room for the Franks. One reason for accepting the social implications of *Lex Salica* is that they are also the implications of archaeology and of place-name study. They all three point to the peaceful absorption into the countryside (the Celtic, Roman countryside) of one more group of tribes, soldiers at a pinch and better led than the Goths south of the Loire, but essentially farmers.

Yet there is more to *Lex Salica* than this. It is full, too, of assumptions about government. Of these, one, though not perhaps the first, is that there is a king, the *Rex Francorum* (*caput populi*, Avitus called him), the ruler of all free men who acknowledge him, whether of German or Latin stock. He is still a war-leader who keeps about him a devoted body of henchmen, his antrustions. These not only protect him with their lives but are the nucleus of his field-force. In return for their devotion, he

3

provides for their upkeep and protects their lives with a specially heavy *wergild*, or man-price. In one form or another, the antrustions remain at the king's side to the end of this period. However, the kings who sanctioned *Lex Salica* liked Gallo-Romans as well as Franks, for their company also included a type of antrustion classified as *Romanus homo, conviva regis*. The Frankish king's authority as a judge is direct and far-reaching; non-attendance at his court, or at the courts of his officials, is a serious matter – it costs 15 *solidi*; his officials (laymen, as under the Empire) issue *cartae de rege* for those who wish to move from their land; before him come those who have accusations to make against their fellows, and it proves expensive if the accusation is false; before the king, freedom is bought; a count who fails in his duty to those he governs will be punished, unless excused on the ground of royal business. Moreover, the king can delegate his authority to counts and other officials who rule, much as in Roman times over the *civitates* and districts (*pagi*), but he is clearly expected to resume that authority as and when he wishes. What is the basis of all this power? It is, quite simply, wealth – and wealth far in excess of any rival's. It is both landed wealth and wealth in the form of movable treasure, amassed by taxation, confiscation, subsidies, bribes and plain loot. Numismatists tell us that the gold coinage of the earlier Merovingians is of excellent quality. The landed wealth is the old imperial fisc in Gaul, an enormous area of scattered estates that only centuries of alienation in the shape of lavish gifts seriously reduced. But the point is this: the distinctive features of royal Frankish power, as they are revealed or implied in *Lex Salica*, do not come direct from the forests of Germany but are for the most part indigenous to Late Roman Gaul. Here is no mystique of barbarian kingship. It is improbable that Clovis knew his own genealogy further back than his great-grandfather, if so far. His prestige rested on his unique achievement of seizing the kingdoms of Syagrius and Alaric, northern and southern Gaul, and then ruling them much in the way they were used to. *Lex Salica* is not a piece of Roman Law, but it is unthinkable without a Roman background.

In the course of the seventh century, and probably in its first half, a certain Marculf, who labels himself 'least and vilest of all monks', made a collection of documents, royal and other, and presented the resulting formulary to a bishop Landericus. He did not mean it to be useful for scribes nor, he says, was it meant for clever men, skilled in composition; it was merely *ad exercenda initia puerorum*. Marculf clearly had access to important deposits of documents, perhaps in the Paris region. There is no evidence that he had access to the Merovingian court itself and he certainly did not regard his collection as in any sense officially sponsored; and this makes it the more remarkable as evidence of royal authority in the century after Clovis' death. Marculf divides his ninety-two documents into two books, which he calls *cartae regales* and *cartae pagenses*. The former, taken as a whole, leaves the impression that the Merovingian kings were even stronger than they had formerly been. They corroborate the picture that the historian Fredegar gives of King Dagobert on one of his great tours of justice; his coming into Burgundy, writes the historian, caused profound alarm among the bishops and magnates, though his justice brought joy to the poor; neither bribes nor respect of persons influenced him, and for a time he neither ate nor slept lest anyone, rich or poor, should leave his presence without having obtained justice. Fredegar did not love Dagobert and must be supposed not to exaggerate common report here. But to return to Marculf, the tone as well as the format of his *cartae regales* is Roman, not Germanic. We learn from them how a duke or patrician or count was appointed; what provision was to be made for royal agents on the king's business; how a *beneficium* was granted, under the royal hand; how a man became an antrustion; how royal permission was given for receiving the clerical tonsure; the conditions under which royal *missi* were sent to supervise the division of land; how slaves were freed in the royal presence; how royal protection or *mundeburdium* was granted to those who sought it (specially important for foreigners and travellers); how a bishop could be ordered to give up property to which he had no right; how a count could be ordered to enforce the restoration of lands unjustly seized; how a rebel was deprived of his possessions and pursued; and how the count assembled all free men from his *civitates*, *vici* and *castella* to swear fidelity, before the Merovingian *missi*, to a new royal prince. Certain cases could be terminated by oath in the royal chapel, on St Martin's *cappa* (the greatest Christian relic of Roman Gaul appropriated by the Frankish kings); and we are given the prologue, very grandiloquent, to a royal judgement. Throughout, the accent is on judgement, decision, action; the king, *in palatio nostro*, is a very busy man, constantly being sought out by suitors from all over his kingdom. 'Le roi, lorsqu'il juge', wrote Fustel, 'est toujours chez lui', and it would be equally true to say that when a weakling or a minor reigned, there was still this need for royal action that somehow or other went on being expressed in legal forms and official documents. Perhaps the most characteristic sort of Merovingian document is the concession or the confirmation issued in the form of a judgement. Landowners of all kinds will come to the king and beg him to confirm in writing his gift, or that of his ancestors, or even that of a third party; and this is done because it is worth doing. The power of the royal *palatium* is a reality that can be made to be felt through its writing-office and through its control over royal officers everywhere. One may recall the words of Isidore (*Etymol.*, I, iii, 1): *litterae autem sunt indices rerum, signa verborum, quibus tanta vis est, ut nobis dicta absentium sine voce loquantur*. There is no count and no bishop who may not find himself summoned to explain his conduct to the king personally or to surrender to the king in his court a case, civil or criminal, in which the king has decided to show interest. All this, however, takes place against a background of the steady giving-away of royal estates to the Church and other beneficiaries that increases snowball-wise as the centuries pass. Lands so given remained as a rule directly under royal protection; the count and his officers were excluded from them; they enjoyed, in brief, immunity. Judicially, and often fiscally, the immunist is himself the substitute of the count, though not of the king. From the king's point of view, his *fideles*, Roman or Frankish in origin, lay or clerical, were receiving at his hands not so much a privilege as an obligation: the obligation, namely, to assume the responsibilities and costs of royal administration within their own properties. It was one way of getting the work done. But not all royal gifts were grants of Roman *villae* and the like to churches; a smaller, but very significant, kind of gift, made in lieu of a stipend, was a direct descendant of the old Roman

6

concession of land made for the same reason. A landowner – it might be a king or a church or a lay magnate – would make a grant of land to a follower (a *miles* or *bucellarius*, perhaps, or a *fidelis* or *amicus*). The grant was freely bestowed without any sort of contract; it was revocable and lasted just so long as the service of which it was payment lasted. Strictly speaking, it was a benefice in return for service, the beneficiary being further tied to the donor by the personal bond of fidelity. That there is little written evidence of these concessions *in stipendio* is probably to be explained by the fact that they would as a rule have been bestowed verbally. But here at all events seems to lie one root of that union of land-as-salary with faithful service in return that a later age was to generalize in use. It is incipient feudalism – but of a kind that only increases the power of the king, who can pay his bodyguard or *amici* in land, and can, and does, get it back again. His estates are not necessarily the poorer.

It would be wrong to give the impression that Merovingian Gaul was a close-knit administrative or political unit, or that its kings ever commanded sufficient resources to enforce their will everywhere at the same time; it is the lack of efficient administration rather than the presence of it that first strikes historians. Undeniably the Merovingians could never have run Gaul at all without leaning heavily, like their Roman predecessors, on the local authority of magnates, lay and ecclesiastical; and there was always a tendency for local families to assume local public office if possible, and to make it hereditary. But a tendency is only a tendency, and when all is said and done, one must take account of Merovingian success, not simply in settling a shattered Roman province but in quietly assuming so many of its forms of government: the *palatium* and its officials, including the *maior domus*, are Roman; and so are the form and language of the documents they issue, the *civitas* and *pagus* and their officers, the occasional municipal *curia* with its senators, the taxation they vainly try to perpetuate, and much of the justice they mete out. ('The judicial system of the Merovingians', writes Dill, 'paid slight heed to old German ideas of justice.') But above all, the Merovingian church is Roman; its diocesan boundaries, coterminous with the *civitates*, have been disturbed hardly at all by the Germanic settlers; its

B

7

bishops, so far from disappearing like those of the Romano-British church, remain to deepen their control over provincial administration (many a Merovingian bishop's *Vita* could be cited in illustration); and if, on the one hand, the Merovingians will stand no nonsense from men they have appointed to positions of power, on the other hand the smooth transition from Gaul to France owes infinitely much to their encouragement of unbroken episcopal rule. The Gallo-Roman episcopate, without entering into the inmost recesses of the Frankish *comitatus*, does share with its lay brethren, lawyers especially, the task of grooming the new barbarians for their rôle of underwriters of Gallo-Roman civilization; and in return, to its enormous landed possessions the Merovingians are willing to make additions for nearly three centuries. Only towards the end of this long time do they find it necessary to take back something of what they had given, by regranting church lands to their warriors – a makeshift that the early Carolingians were greatly to develop. Unlike the Carolingians, however, the Merovingians did safeguard some of their rights over churches, and what affords them a certain independence of the Church is not barbarian aloofness or vestigial heathenism but a sense of being heirs to a Roman administration still run by secular officials and backed by the resources of rich estates.

The legal assumptions of *Lex Salica* and, still more, of Marculf's formulary, were Roman. But in what way were they Roman? They plainly have nothing in common with classical Roman Law, the Law of the Republic and of the Empire in its prime. Their background is Vulgar, not classical, Law, but it is still inescapably Roman. For example, the barbarian law of possession or seisin can now be shown to be derived from the Vulgar Roman law of *possessio*, and this is only one of many instances within the Law of Property where what was once thought Germanic, just because it was not classical Roman, can now be proved to be not Germanic at all. The idea of unrestricted donation is Roman and so, too, is the structure of the transaction for the transfer of property. Something of all this the Franks must have absorbed when they first settled as neighbours of the *coloni* on the Roman *villae* north of the Loire, if they had not already done so much earlier; but one obvious effect of the conquest of Visigothic Gaul by Clovis and his sons was to open the north more fully to the Roman legal usages of the south. Roman Law schools still existed in Aquitaine (the Clermont school still flourished in the seventh century) and their resources had enabled Alaric II to produce a Roman law-book with some claim to style and subtlety. It is real law-making. Alaric's book lies behind the law-giving of the Burgundians in eastern Gaul, and it was known and used by Romans in the north. Even as early as 596, the Frankish King Childebert II is borrowing from the *Lex Romana Burgundionum* for a famous decree that survives as an addendum to *Lex Salica*. This may serve as a warning against putting trust in the theory of a sharp break with the Roman background of Frankish Gaul. The Franks may well have misunderstood and failed to use much of what they found of government and administration in Gaul, but they certainly brought no alternative with them. Their rule was Roman-derivative.

Some notable changes occur in the years that follow the death of the great King Dagobert. From the late seventh century onwards we are among the 'rois fainéants' who, for one reason and another, can no longer make their power felt practically, although it is still often expressed theoretically in traditional forms. Family degeneracy may have played its part in the failure of the Merovingians, but the historian will do better to focus his attention on their lack of means. For one thing, the giving away of royal estates was beginning to tell, and, for another, the *teloneum*, the Roman tax on commerce that made the early Merovingians so rich in movable wealth, was drying up with the Mediterranean trade that fed it. The later Merovingians had less land and less money than had their predecessors and consequently their power was less felt and less relied on. What were the consequences? The prestige of kingship suffered, but, much more, the prestige of the Merovingians themselves, until the point was reached when even the Church that had done so much for them saw that it would be safe, as well as desirable, to liberate Frankish kingship from their weakness and to entrust it, instead, to new men – men with lands unimpaired, loyal followers and new ideas. Furthermore, the later Merovingians had to face the drying-up of the supply of trained officials, secular and ecclesiastical, and the consequent need of their masters, the mayors of the palace, to take emergency

9

measures to ensure any sort of administration. But here we should be on our guard against making too much of the initiative of the early Carolingians, even including Charlemagne, in over-hauling and centralizing Frankish government. They were men of personal authority and power rather than of administrative genius; in most respects Charlemagne's reign marks no sharp break in the story of the development of Frankish government within Francia. The significant domestic achievement of the early Carolingians was the reduction of the Roman Midi, a world of which the Frank had hitherto had only occasional direct experi-ence. This reduction cannot be laid wholly at the door of the Arab invaders from Spain, for one has only to turn to Fredegar to read of repeated raids by Charles Martel and Pippin III into the Midi, when towns were sacked, walls demolished, people driven away and the vineyards and countryside laid waste. Nothing approach-ing this systematic penetration had ever been undertaken by the Merovingians, who were generally content with control of those Mediterranean *civitates* from which came wealth and the good things of life. The reduction, however, was economic rather than political (though there were administrative changes). No bar-barian ruler, whether Merovingian or Carolingian, could have de-vised a means of keeping the men of the Midi under permanent control; they lived, as they had always lived, their own lives under the forms largely bequeathed to them by Rome.

The mid-ninth century is the time of great change. About the year 843, a lady named Dhuoda, wife of Bernard, marquis of Septimania, addressed a letter to her son William, urging on him the importance of fidelity towards his lord the king, to whom he had, or should have, commended himself. It is an enlightening document. The following is part of it (the translation is Philip Grierson's):

An admonition relating to your lord.
Since God, as I believe, and your father Bernard have chosen you, in the flower of your youth, to serve Charles as your lord, I urge you ever to remember the record of your family, illus-trious on both sides, and not to serve your master simply to satisfy him outwardly, but to maintain towards him and his ser-

vice in all things a devoted and certain fealty both of body and soul. . . . That is why, my son, I exhort you to maintain faithfully all that is in your charge, with all your strength of body and soul, as long as your life shall last. . . . May the madness of infidelity be ever far from you; may evil never find such a place in your heart as to render you unfaithful to your lord in any matter whatsoever. . . . But I do not fear this on your part or on the part of those that serve with you. . . . Therefore, my son William, you who are of our blood, show yourself towards your lord, as I have already urged, true, vigilant, useful and most prompt to his service. In every matter which concerns the power and welfare of the King, both within the kingdom and without, show that wisdom with which God has plentifully endowed you. Read the lives and words of the holy men of former times, and you will find there how to serve your lord and be faithful to him in all things. And when you receive his commands, apply yourself faithfully to execute them. Observe also and regard carefully those who show the greatest fidelity and assiduity in his service, and learn of them the way in which to act.

It has been said that the interesting things about this letter are the religious character of the vassal's oath of fealty (or fidelity) to his lord, and the fact that the lady is only urging her son to behave to the king exactly as any vassal would behave to any *senior* (or lord). What, perhaps, is stranger is the possibility, rather harped on, of unfealty, *infidelitas* (the word is used more than once); a great man's son needs such a warning at the outset of his career. We can compare this with a letter, some two centuries earlier, from a Merovingian lady to her son, the future Desiderius of Cahors: 'be faithful to the king, cherish your companions, always love and fear the Lord'. There is nothing here about the madness of infidelity. The emphasis of Dhuoda is different. Fidelity can be dug out of the lives and words of the old holy men: infidelity, not fidelity, is the new general feature of social relationships under the Carolingians. So much so, that the word even comes to be used of offences against canon law or the Ten Commandments (e.g. theft). How did this come about?

The late eighth and ninth centuries are the era of Viking attacks along the entire length of the Frankish coastline and deep into the interior, up the rivers. The people of Gaul had always been sensitive about attack from the sea; Sidonius was most perturbed about the Saxon sea-pirates and thought that even the Visigothic settlers in Aquitaine were better than no protection. But the Viking danger was more formidable, because more continuous. We know in some detail of monastic communities uprooted or destroyed by the plunderers, but the monkish historians were not concerned to explain what became of the countryside and of its villages and manors. Yet there is enough evidence to let us guess at widespread local dislocation. For example, in the Toulonnais the old boundaries between properties were no longer recognizable; at Vontes, in Touraine, five men of servile rank 'could have the land if there were peace'; at Martigny, many men were recorded as having neither wives nor families; in the Limousin and Burgundy, whole villages were abandoned by people seeking safety in the hills. The fear of destruction seems to have been almost as devastating as destruction itself. At all events, the effect of the two was to depopulate the countryside and allow good agricultural land to lapse; and to these should be added the effects of what looks, now and again, like scorched-earth policy. Small wonder that Marc Bloch sums up the demographic problems of the age in the phrase 'absence de densité'. For at the very time when, because of disruption of trade in the Mediterranean, land was becoming increasingly the one possession worth having, its defence and its upkeep became more difficult than before. More men than ever were seeing the necessity of seeking a lord's protection, not, as in Roman times, against an exacting State but against attack and insecurity; and this protection, in its turn, was seen as part of a contract (since free men were involved) highly personal in its nature and based on the working and protection of land. Nothing is implied as to the relations of either lord or man to the king; it is simply the natural drawing-together and extension of two things that have been known since Roman times: the lord-man relationship and the holding of land in return for service. The king can do little, for he lacks the means to defend all his people everywhere at the same time; they must look after themselves against a menace the chief characteristic of which is that it is irregular, unpredictable. The king has enough to do looking after his own without bothering about other people's property. As the West is attacked, so it becomes intensely local in its outlook. The attacks of the ninth century did not unite Frankish Gaul; by their very nature they dissipated effort and compelled men to concentrate on the local, not on the national, aspects of their tribulations. There was no continental King Alfred.

Though the Carolingians took more notice of the general peril and more steps to combat it than is sometimes thought, their chief concern was a weakness that had nothing to do with the Vikings: namely, the dispersal of royal estates by the later Merovingians, the virtual impossibility of reclaiming them and the difficulty of adding to them. These estates, the fisc, were not primarily a source of movable wealth to the kings; much, we know, was rough and uncultivated land. The great value of the fisc was as a reservoir for the rewarding of followers and for the endowment of churches. The crown generally lost nothing tangible when an alienation was made; but what it did do, apart from lowering the reservoir, was in effect to invite the recipient to extend the privileges of his new immunity over all his other possessions; and this did involve loss to the crown. When the later Merovingians made presents of domains of the fisc, mostly to churches, they did so unconditionally. The gifts were absolute even when the kings still kept some kind of judicial control within them. The Carolingians had more trouble in keeping such control and failed to keep clear the distinction between land given as a personal reward and land given as salary for public office held temporarily; the two kinds tended to be fused, and here was the basis of the great territorial principalities of the Middle Ages. This last, perhaps, more than outweighs the benefit of the Carolingian resolve never, if they could help it, to grant away their lands unconditionally but always to leave a loophole for reclaiming them as royal.

The Carolingians started their career in possession not only of the rump of the Merovingian fisc but also of their own huge estates in north-east Francia and the Rhineland. Together, these constituted a formidable property – formidable not only in extent but in wealth: no estates were better worth having than those of the Meuse and Moselle valleys, to say nothing of the Rhine. So long as the Carolingians could hold this nucleus together they were safe, if not very safe. They had not the vast landed superiority of the earlier Merovingians but they were better off than anyone else, except the Church. (The Church had been despoiled by Charles Martel and others who needed land quickly for their armed retainers, but it was still richer than any layman.) The first two Carolingian kings succeeded in keeping intact their estates north of the Loire, and indeed added to them by a policy of conquest and clearings. In Alamannia, Thuringia, Frisia, and Saxony we read of the estates of defeated kings or magnates *fisci ditionibus redactae*. This was not the purpose of the foreign expeditions of Pippin III and Charlemagne, but it was one outcome of them. Constant exertion and vigilance (the hall-mark of the Carolingians) kept these new estates under royal control; but it was a struggle. When we reach Louis the Pious, the struggle is abandoned. Louis adds nothing by conquest to the patrimony, though, on the other hand, he is notoriously generous and willing to grant away property with inadequate safeguards for its return; this is the beginning of the end of Carolingian power, such as it was, and we can watch it happening. Thegan, one of Louis's biographers, writes that the emperor was generous to the point that 'he would give outright to his faithful men royal *villae* that had been his, his father's and his grandfather's'; and, what is more, he actually restored the properties that his father had confiscated from the Frisians and Saxons. Finally, he renounced all claims on Church lands as a means of endowing his vassals. In reversing the domanial policy of his dynasty he was, very largely, following the behests of the Church, and his action should not be condemned outright as a piece of lunacy; his is a difficult reign to understand and much work remains to be done on it and him. Nonetheless, his contemporaries recognized that, from reasons however pressing, Louis the Pious had seriously reduced his territorial heritage, had renounced the obvious means of increasing it, and had, at a time of mounting social crisis, increased tension and instability. He had done more: by reducing his means of action, he had reduced his capacity to intervene as a matter of course in the affairs of what may be called provincial France. Stability, the assurance of unbroken control and of unchanging lordship, was the backbone of fidelity, the bond that really held men together; and this the emperor seriously weakened. And so we get back to the problem that worried the lady Dhuoda: why were men less faithful than they had once been?

How to ensure fidelity had been Charlemagne's principal worry, no less vital than the problem of holding together the royal estates; and the same problem of fidelity was becoming the principal worry of all landowners, great and small, throughout the Carolingian world. Uprooted communities, dispossession, insecurity, all tended to make men (armed men and men who could work land) worth more to the landowner than ever before; lordship had to be made attractive; yet a bond that could so easily and so eagerly be entered upon, with whatever public solemnity, could equally be broken by the forces that brought it into being. The lord whose protection was worth having one day might look less formidable than his neighbour not long after; and there might be better land to work and better terms of service somewhere else. This made for social instability and also, increasingly, instability in government. It has often, and rightly, been said that the apex of the Carolingian social structure, the makeshift structure that faced the Vikings and Magyars and Arabs, was the bond of personal service and fidelity, particularly as developed in the *vassi dominici*, the vassals of the lord king and of nobody else, devoted fighting men who looked for a homestead (*casa*) as their pay, and who, if they did not get it, would look elsewhere. More and more reliable fighting men on horseback were needed, and this was the only way of getting them and holding them: they had to be *casati*, given homesteads, settled. Once they were installed and had their land, and knew the terms of their military service, and had expressed their allegiance contractually in the most binding of oaths, the assumption was that the bond so established would never be broken; in fact, of course, it often was. But Charlemagne did more than bind men to himself in this way and use them everywhere on his service; he recognized the existence of the same bond of lord and vassal throughout society, and he encouraged it so long as it made for more obedience to him. The last clause of a famous capitulary (no. 64) reads: 'Concerning ordinary folk (*de vulgari populo*), let each man so control his dependants that they shall the better obey and accept the imperial orders and decrees.' Once again, in the good Roman tradition, those with actual power over the countryside are being dragooned into responsibility for the public duties and burdens of those who follow them. There is not yet much risk from that infinite shifting-off of responsibility and multiplication of loyalties that marked the advent of sub-infeudation. The king knew where power lay and could still, by vigilance, control it reasonably well. Again and again his capitularies insist on the need for fidelity, especially to him; again and again his *missi* or special agents go out into the countryside to take the oaths of all free men. It is still possible to insist that all free men stand in a personal relationship to their king, and there is no provincial dynasty great enough to prevent this for long; but it is becoming more and more difficult to assert.

It is unnecessary to attempt a definition of the various terms in which this age expressed its social obligations and rights; they change and shift and will not be pinned down; but one, at least, cannot be avoided – vassalage. Anyone commended to his lord for the purpose of fighting is, by the ninth century, a *vassus* or vassal; the word, originally Celtic, had long since lost its pejorative sense of humble domestic service, but vassalage could still seem very burdensome and unwelcome to some great men. The best way of getting the feel of the word to the Carolingians is to take an example. A good one is provided in a letter from Archbishop Hincmar of Rheims to the future Emperor Louis the German. (Hincmar was an acute and powerful man with an inventive mind, but in this case there is no cause to suspect him.) The letter is the outcome of Louis's decision to invade France and supplant his brother, Charles the Bald. This was frustrated largely through the resistance of the French bishops, led by Hincmar, and in this masterly letter Hincmar explains why they feel no compulsion to answer his summons; they have, he pleads, too little notice to foregather and, anyway, it is nearly Christmas-time. Instead of coming personally, however, they will send him some advice. First, he should remember that one day he will have to face the Lord's judgement, and in the meantime it would be as well to attack the pagans who are devastating Christian lands (and not, by implication, attack his brother). Then follows some very interesting advice on how a good ruler should act, and how to protect his subjects and the Church; he should only employ God-fearing men, and those who defy law and justice should look to themselves. In particular, there should be good administration of the royal *villae*. Much of this is general advice that would have benefited any ninth-century king. But finally there comes this (Odegaard's translation):

> We ought and wish to believe you such that you would not wish to increase your realm at the cost of your soul, nor to receive us as helpers in ecclesiastical affairs and government if we were dishonoured with the loss of the priesthood, as would be the case if, against God and the authority of reason, we should be zealous in commending ourselves and our churches to you – the churches entrusted to us by God are not benefices or property of the king of a kind that he can give them away out of mere whim and without advice – and we bishops consecrated to God are not men of such a kind that we should commend ourselves into vassalage like secular men – we ought not in any way to swear an oath which evangelical and apostolic and canonical authority forbids.

In other words, Hincmar will not have it that by oath or by any other means bishops or their churches are compelled to serve their kings like other men, because they cannot be vassals in the ordinary sense. They commend themselves and their churches in order to help govern ecclesiastical affairs, and that is all: 'sed ad defensionem et adjutorium gubernationis in ecclesiastico regimine nos ecclesiasque nostras committere'. In this case, no military help was forthcoming – which is what Louis really wanted. Hincmar seems to have got away with it, though other churchmen, before as well as after, were less lucky, and he himself seemed later to withdraw his definition. The point is, that vassalage is seen as the vital relationship in a landed society geared to battle, though it is still fluid enough for a bishop to give a public lesson to a king on what it does and does not imply. Reading between the lines of the letter, it can be seen that royal vassals, whether or not Hincmar was right about the bishops, are important men who can legitimately be called on to bring armed help to the king, for they have formidable followings of their own. Military service is mediatized.

It would be wrong to give the impression that the Carolingians (at least to Charles the Bald) were so taken up with the implications of vassalage, to say nothing of worries over their fisc, that they had no time or strength for the traditional public duties of their office. This is a field in which they are less strong than some Merovingians; but their writ does, so to say, run. The doing of justice is still a main concern of the earlier Carolingians. *Magna* or *alta justitia*, the major pleas or pleas of blood, are still reserved for the count in his court and, under Charlemagne at least, are not granted to the count as a personal reward; nor, as an immunist in his own right, would a count hold these pleas. It is for the immunist, whoever he is, to present persons involved in major pleas to the count in his court, though he will keep the minor pleas for himself. In distinguishing so clearly between major and minor pleas (and indeed in somewhat rearranging local courts to take account of this) the early Carolingians were delimiting what rights of justice the crown must expect to surrender to immunists and what rights were to be retained if at all possible. The distinction lasts through the Middle Ages. The practical difficulty was to keep any sort of control over the count himself. Charlemagne leaned heavily on the services of friends and relations from Austrasian Francia, though even these proved hard to handle and harder to replace; an official could not be prevented from identifying himself and his family with the locality where his work lay. This, the control of counts, is the true measure of the power of government under the Carolingians; it is much more important than the high-sounding terms of the Carolingian capitularies or the antiquarian zest of the age for writing-up and misunderstanding the old barbarian laws. The Carolingians really end with a burst of Byzantine splendour at the court of Charles the Bald in the mid-ninth century; but outside that court circle (which certainly satisfied one of the contemporary requirements of kingship) there was not much left.

Two great partition-treaties in the ninth century, Verdun and

Meersen, dealt the final blow to the royal Frankish fisc. Their principal object was to provide a share of fiscal territory for each of the Carolingian brothers with a claim to any. To do such a thing was to carry out a major operation on the great Austrasian nucleus of fiscal lands that still survived; it was necessary, but there was no other justification for it. The commissioners entrusted with the division went about their work with very great care and only after much preparation; it was not the extent of the lands (and the dioceses) they were splitting that worried them, but their value. When the partitions had taken place, Austrasia was destroyed and Lorraine artificially created. The brothers had their shares, and out of them had to satisfy the demands of their supporters for rewards and restitutions; but the economic power of the Carolingians was split and ruined for ever. Thereafter, the fiscal lands of Lorraine become the chief bone of contention between the East and West Frankish Carolingians, for in Lorraine lay the only reserve of lands rich enough to solve their problem of how and where to enfeoff their followers and recoup their losses. It was not the *kingdom* or *duchy* of Lorraine that mattered but the *estates* of Lorraine, from which the first Carolingians had drawn strength.

How did society meet this collapse of kingly power? In the first place, it is plain that no one welcomed it. Nobody wanted to smash kingship, though some did want to displace the Carolingians, and in course of time succeeded. Too much is written of the 'greed' of magnates whose incessant demands increased Carolingian worries and distracted attention from the Vikings, for the magnates were placed in much the same position as their kings; they, too, had followers clamouring for land, and not enough land to give them. Nor should we be surprised at the great areas of land thought necessary to sustain comparatively few people, when we remember what the fate of that land for several generations had been; as always, it was its actual yield that men had to take into account, not acreage. So, all down the social scale men bargained and fought for land. Probably the most successful bargainers were the men who managed to establish their dynasties in what, in effect, were independent territorial principalities; their growth, and the decline of royal power, are the most obvious features of French society in the late ninth and tenth centuries.

A territorial principality in this sense has been defined as a place where the king intervenes only by permission, or from which, in other words, the immunist has power to exclude the king when he wishes. This may place too much emphasis on the will of the immunist whose first object, after all, was not insubordination; it might be better to say that the king was generally content, in such cases, to leave the immunist free to run his principality as best he could on his own resources. If the king gained no prestige from this exclusion he clearly gained in several practical ways. But in any case the phenomenon of the practical exclusion of the state from the affairs of a great immunity was not new to the ninth century; it is a commonplace of the Later Empire. More interesting is surely the emergence of new families, sustained by these immunities and destined to run France for generations. Great families do not, on the whole, have much luck in permanently establishing themselves before the late ninth century. Not even the royal families of the Dark Ages succeeded in persuading men that they had an inalienable right to go on ruling because some bogus genealogy linked them with Woden or Julius Caesar. The truth, perhaps, about the Merovingians is that they actually succeeded in doing this for two and a half centuries, because that was as long as their wealth lasted, and as long as the glamour of their name sustained them in the good opinion of sensible men. In every other case it was strength and wealth alone, not blood at all, that decided the issue of survival, usually in a matter of two or three generations. There was, it has been said, no aristocracy of blood in the Dark Ages, and hence no ancient families. Written genealogies are a game of a later age. Under Charlemagne and Louis the Pious, in the ninth century, a very few such families do succeed in establishing themselves. As a rule they are Frankish intimates of the king, who are sent off to govern some March of the Empire with viceregal powers, and there establish themselves. The dynasty of St William of Toulouse, surrounded with its colonies of Aquitanian vassals, is a case in point. But these are rare. By the middle of the ninth century family succession to official appointments, especially that of count, becomes fairly widespread. Even

if a son does not succeed his father, the succession may be restricted within a group of local families. This happened at Autun.
Charles the Bald lost some ground in this way and had to admit
the practical claims of heredity in the matter; but he was still
strong enough to displace a comital family on occasion with
brutal severity, and would never have admitted that he had no
business to interfere in the appointment of counts and bishops. To
the end of his life his *missi* continue to inspect and visit his *pagi*.
By then, eight great principalities had been established in France
through the accumulation of *honores*, though some of these did
not last for long. Among those that did last were the dynasties
of Robert the Strong, who held the counties of Angers, Blois,
Touraine, Autun, Auxerre and Nevers, and Baldwin who was
count of Ghent, Waas, Ternois, and Flanders. These multiple
counties, and a consequent reduction in the total number of
counts, worked well so long as the fidelity of the few great
families could be relied on. Charles the Bald seemed to have no
doubt; he was put under no pressure, other than military need, to
establish these principalities and did not consider that the crown
lost anything in the process. They were a frank acceptance of his
own limitations in skilled manpower and resources and a falling-
back upon the ancient divisions of Gaul – Aquitaine, Burgundy
and Neustria.

Charles's death altered all this, for with him died stability. For
a century at least, it is the great marcher dynasties who settle the
affairs of the kingdom and dispose of the crown. The accession of
the Robertinian Odo marks the first break in the Carolingian succession. The facts are not in dispute; it has always been clear that
tenth-century kingship was a hazardous business. But what does
this mean? What is the difference between Charles the Bald, the
last effective Carolingian, and his successors? It is not that they
are much weaker in a material sense, though it is interesting that
the wretched Odo found it necessary to spend most of his time
in cities and monasteries, because his *villae* could not sustain him.
It is rather that men have lost confidence in what the king can
do; there is no basis for fidelity, no assurance of continuity. The
last Carolingians exercise continuous authority in northern France
only, and then not everywhere. Their poverty is seen for what it

is; and no king ever commanded fidelity for long without the means of rewarding it. Thus it is something negative, not positive, not, above all, the wicked planning of the territorial magnates, that ruins Carolingian monarchy and the last shreds of public administration. Against this tendency the magnates themselves sometimes try to react. Public instruments are still issued by the last Carolingians in the conventional form, and royal charters of attestation, though rare, continue to look impressive; the reason is that the recipients like and value them. But royal rights are slipping away all the time, more and more royal functions are exercised discontinuously or not at all; and once such functions are discontinued they are nearly impossible to resume. It is fair to add that the trouble was not with the personalities of these last Carolingians: they were really quite impressive people. It took some resolution for them to turn once more, against French advice, and in the teeth of German opposition, to the traditional task of winning back the Lotharingian fisc, though it was too late. Also it took resolution to concentrate attention and resources, as they did, on the control of the key-bishopric of Rheims. Readers of Flodoard's *History of the Church of Rheims* will remember that hardly any king of the ninth and early tenth centuries, Carolingian or Robertinian, failed to grasp the tactical importance of Rheims or failed to do all he could to control it.

That vassalage on which Charlemagne had rested his hopes had long since ceased to hold society to its king. Mixed and rapidly changing loyalties, and the stress now laid on the contractual aspect of kingship, acted together to alienate men from the king; between him and them stood the territorial princes and others who had land to give. By the tenth century it is the feoff, the benefice, that looms large in every sort of contract. In practice, the *petit seigneur* no longer thinks of the king as the war-leader, the law-giver or the enforcer of justice; someone much nearer at hand fills these rôles. The local comital dynasties are as secure as the marcher-princes above them. None of this comes about through anyone's planning it, and few indeed could have seen precisely what was happening. No one would have thought – or should have – that vassalage itself had undermined the state; rather it was all that was left when the state disintegrated for the reasons that have been suggested. Odo of Cluny tells how one royal vassal in Auvergne, Gerald of Aurillac, obstinately refused to become a vassal of the duke of Aquitaine because of the faith he owed the king; but even here, in the end, a compromise had to be reached and Gerald, in effect, surrendered.

The vital strand running through Gallo-Frankish society from the fifth to the tenth centuries is *seigneurie*, lordship. We start with the Gallo-Roman *seigneurs*, the *potentes* of the age of Sidonius Apollinaris, living on their estates among their *coloni*, some of them great landlords, others quite small. These are joined by barbarian landlords, Visigoths, Burgundians, and finally Franks. Whatever the fate of the *colonus*, the cultivator, and whatever his mother-tongue, he will generally be the man of a lord. In due course, the lord of the sub-Roman colonate will give place to the lord of the Merovingian and the Carolingian immunity (Marc Bloch and others have shown how this happened). The *seigneurie* remains the effective world of the peasant-cultivator, free or unfree. The problem is, how does the state – that is, the king – come into contact with the *seigneurie*? He does so, most obviously, through the count and the officials of the *civitas* and the *pagi*. As time passes, the count may find it harder to exercise his judicial and other rights within every *seigneurie* of his area; but that will be nothing to the difficulty of the king in keeping control of the count, especially after the count has ceased to be a mere royal official and has become, instead, the local dynast. It is then that loyalties are strained, and while the crown binds men to itself afresh in vassalage and fidelity, these same men expose themselves daily to the charge made by the lady Dhuoda. Fidelity is not easy. All the links of control are weak, but none is weaker than the link between count and king. Royal power disintegrated; that is clear; but paradoxically it did so just when it was most needed. There never was any desire to weaken kingship; usurpations of royal authority are the assumption of what the king himself can no longer manage; acts of insubordination are personal, not institutional. Royal power disintegrates not because it is attacked but because it lacks the material means to continue. As it stands on the brink, men of the ability of Hincmar, Jonas of Orleans, Kathwulf, Sedulius Scotus, reflect upon the theory of government

C

and write treatises upon the nature of rule and the exercise of authority in church and state.

No Englishman will make the mistake of underrating the bigness of France; it is a country at all times impatient of centralized control, and geography has not a little to do with it. When to this is added the absence of any conception of centralization as a political or administrative good to be pursued for its own sake, we begin to see how hard it is to fathom the intentions of those who governed France in the Dark Ages.

Huns, Saxons, Franks, Visigoths, Burgundians, Arabs, Vikings: is it not altogether remarkable that France, when she emerged, could still claim to be in so many ways recognizably Roman? Her rulers could not do much; the rule of a Charlemagne, even, was a fragile, personal thing bearing little resemblance to that of a Caesar or a Napoleon; but by taking account of the Celtic and Roman shape of Gaul they perpetuated it where it most mattered, at the level of the *civitas* (or bishopric) and the estate. Their decisions, as recorded by the narrative writers of their time and enshrined often enough in their diplomas, charters and edicts, reflect their acknowledgement that the life of the *civitas* and the *villa* was the life of Gaul.

# CHAPTER TWO

# Gothia and Romania [1]

*

In his more relaxed moments, the Visigothic chieftain Athaulf used to say that he had had the idea to obliterate the 'nomen Romanum' and to substitute a Gothic state, with himself as its Caesar Augustus; which was as much as to say – 'ut vulgariter loquar' in Orosius' words – that *Gothia* should succeed *Romania*. However, long experience had taught him that his Goths were too barbarous ever to live under law; and since, without law, you cannot have a state, he had decided to leave things as they were and to support the 'nomen Romanum' with Gothic arms.[2] What I would like to do is to see, in the light of this curious jest, whether any of Athaulf's successors as kings of Toulouse came within measurable distance of taking seriously that *Gothia* which Athaulf abandoned; for, like many jests, it had something behind it.

It is easy to connect Athaulf's decision in favour of *Romania* with his marriage with Galla Placidia,[3] though Orosius does not put the matter quite in this way. He merely says that she helped him – 'ad omnia bonarum ordinationum opera persuasu et con-

---

[1] *Bulletin of the John Rylands Library*, vol. 44, no. 1 (September 1961). A lecture delivered in the John Rylands Library, Manchester. I wish to thank Professor E. A. Thompson, Professor R. E. Keller and Dr Arnold Ehrhardt for help in its preparation, and friends in Oxford for stimulating me to think again about what I had written.

[2] Orosius, *Hist.*, vii, 43.

[3] Ludwig Schmidt, *Geschichte der deutschen Stämme bis zum Ausgang der Völkerwanderung: die Ostgermanen* (2nd ed., 1941), p. 457; J. B. Bury, *History of the Later Roman Empire* (1923), i, 197; F. Lot, C. Pfister and F. L. Ganshof, *Les destinées de l'empire en occident* (1940), p. 45; and P. Courcelle, *Histoire littéraire des grandes invasions germaniques* (1948), p. 69, who goes so far as to connect the remark with an alleged design of Athaulf's that Theodosius, his son by Galla Placidia, should one day become emperor. But if Theodosius had lived, and had become emperor, this need have had no effect on the status of the Visigoths.

silio temperatus'; at most, helped him to see what long experience of his own people's limitations already pointed to. I think we must take the story as it stands. Athaulf knew that he could not subvert Roman authority, even though he entered Gaul without imperial sanction: he could not turn *Romania* into *Gothia*. Equally, he is not reported to have envisaged the absorption of *Gothia* into *Romania*. The Goths were to act, if Orosius is right, as *Romania's* shield, whether in Gaul or in Spain. In fact, a kingdom based on Toulouse was not the end of Athaulf's ambition. His successor, Wallia, reluctantly abandoned an attempt to cross from Spain to Africa, and returned to Gaul to negotiate with the patrician Constantius because he could not help it. The most solid achievements of Euric were to be in Spain, not Gaul. This following in the path of the Vandals, not always with hostile intent, is a recurrent theme of Visigothic history for the entire century of their residence in Gaul; the Visigoths were both attracted to and frightened by them. They were not so very distantly related and had much in common. Despite their long contact with the Empire, I do not think that the Visigoths had been any more romanized than had the Vandals, though they may have been tamer. They were homeless cultivators, roaming armed and in search of food, and denied the outlet to Africa which had first been sought through Italy by their leader, Alaric. Two years later, they were brought back from Spain to Gaul in a hurry, to be allotted a settlement-area on the Atlantic seaboard and a guarantee of 600,000 measures of grain. Their need for land and food was met; though the prospect of Spain was still there to haunt them. But what was gained by the Romans, with whom the initiative clearly lay? For it was they who would have drawn up the terms of the subsequent *foedus*.[1]

The settlement of upwards of 100,000 Goths (men, women and children) upon Roman land and at the expense of landlords' rents would be unwelcome, unless there was some threat that the movement of the Goths might counter.[2] One such threat may

[1] Prosper, *Chron.*, s.a., 419 and Hydatius, *Chron.*, chap. 69, provide some facts about the *foedus*, and others may be inferred from subsequent events; but its terms and their implementation are not clear in detail.

[2] In what follows I am heavily indebted to Professor E. A. Thompson, and notably to his article 'The settlement of the barbarians in southern Gaul', *Journal of*

have been the power of the Goths themselves in Spain; this has been inferred from the report of Hydatius;[1] the Romans believed them safer in Gaul than in Spain; in Gaul they could at least be stopped from moving about. They may also, once settled, have been more useful there. Professor Thompson believes that the Roman authorities really wished to take precautionary measures against the Gallic Bacaudae. He argues that the senatorial estates taken over by the Goths were not tucked away upon some remote frontier but lay deep in the heart of Aquitaine; in other words, they lay among, and not in front of, the lands the Goths were meant to defend. Following good Roman practice, the Goths were being entrusted with the defence of their own interests. Just how far we know about this settlement I shall consider shortly; but Thompson's idea has its attractions. A principal seat of Bacaudic activity lay immediately north of the original area of Visigothic settlement – namely, in the region of the Loire.[2] The Aquitanian senators might not anticipate a frontal attack, but the danger of disaffection spreading among their own peasantry was something more than academic. The enslavement of masters by their own slaves in open revolt was not unknown.[3] The entry in

---

*Roman Studies*, vol. xlvi (1956). Though he goes further than I would in detecting a Bacaudic threat behind the Germanic settlements, his work still marks a new departure in our understanding of the subject.

[1] By L. Schmidt, op. cit. p. 461; but Hydatius' words are 'ad Gallias revocati sedes in Aquitanica a Tolosa usque ad Oceanum acceperunt'.

[2] We may look upon these Bacaudae as the entire peasant population of western Gaul in a state of chronic revolt, or as such parts of the Armorican population as were, at any one time, in active revolt. In my view, Armoricans are one thing and Bacaudae another, and I would distinguish Bacaudic activities from the endemic banditry from which the Later Empire suffered. Nor can I think that the *Tractus Armoricanus* was a vast fifth-column area that worked in collaboration with the barbarians to overthrow Roman rule in Gaul. I do not distrust Jordanes' statement (*Getica*, xxxvi, 191) that Armoricans helped Aetius to save Gaul from the Huns, or Sidonius' recollection that they had been roused to battle by his father-in-law, Avitus (*Carmina*, vii, 547). While accepting a good deal of Thompson's case against the landlords (see also his *History of Attila and the Huns*, 1948, *passim*), I believe he overlooks the grim truth that extortion and corruption are often the price of protection, and that many are willing to pay that price. Authority may gain in attraction where the possibility of its withdrawal has once been contemplated. For all his tyranny, Aetius represented in Gaul, and not only to senators, an active ideal of authority, of *imperium*, such as we can still see operative in Orosius, Ambrosiaster and the *Actus Sylvestri*.

[3] Rutilius Namatianus, *De Reditu Suo*, i, 216.

the *Chronica Gallica* for the year 435 is explicit: 'Gallica ulterior Tibattonem principem rebellionis secuta a Romana societate discessit, a quo tracto initio omnia paene Galliarum servitia in Bacaudam conspiravere.'

A local rising, that is, under a rebel leader named Tibatto wins the sympathy of a large part of the slave-population of Gaul.[1] This is not very surprising and perhaps not as alarming as it sounds. But these risings do seem to coincide with the Visigothic settlement of Gaul. If the Bacaudae and the Visigoths ever came to blows, we do not know of it, though Constantius tells us that Goar's Alans, settled near Orleans, did take the field against the Bacaudae.[2] Perhaps the Bacaudae and their sympathizers were frightened by the presence of the Goths into leaving the Aquitanian landlords in peace. But this is conjecture. We do not know why the Visigoths were settled in Aquitaine, any more than we know why the Burgundians were admitted to Savoy by Aetius in 443. Indeed, Savoy does not itself seem to have been subject to any social disturbance at the time of settlement, though it had once been so. It does not follow that the landowners of Savoy were being protected against social unrest within their own borders. If the Alamans were too far away from Savoy to constitute an immediate threat, it must still be allowed that as soon as they did move into Alsace in 455 the senators of Lyons at once permitted an extension of Burgundian territory in that direction, to counter the danger. So that the Burgundians, though settled on the land, were still expected to take the field and to meet an external threat. The same may have been true of the Visigoths, whose first assignment in the Prefecture of the Gauls had, after all, been to fight not Bacaudae but Vandals in the name of the Empire.

Another approach is to see the Visigothic *foedus* is a measure designed to keep Saxon and Frankish sea-pirates at bay. There is no evidence of any relevant operations of Saxon pirates in the first half of the fifth century, but there were Saxons in the estuary

[1] Thompson appears to translate 'conspiravere' when he writes 'Soon after he rose, [Tibatto] was joined by practically every slave in Gaul' (*History of Attila*, p. 69). This is modified to 'conspired with' in *J.R.S.*, xlvi, 73, n. 43; but even this seems to be going too far.

[2] Constantius, *Vita Germani*, 28, 40.

of the Loire in the sixties;[1] and in or about 480 Sidonius writes
to Namatius that news has just come of his weighing anchor and
being on patrol along the Atlantic coast, on the lookout for the
curved ships of the Saxon *archipiratas*. He goes on to beg his
friend to have a care, for the Saxons are skilful and daring, and
think nothing of rough seas and a dangerous coast: 'si sequatur
intercipit, si fugiat evadit.' [2] The danger is sufficiently real, and
fits the well-authenticated background of more general Roman
preparations to meet pirates along the entire length of the *Litus
Saxonicum*. This was a planned defence of a coast, of harbours and
of rivers – notably the Garonne and the Dordogne with their
tributaries, and to some extent the Charente also. Should not the
Visigothic settlements be seen in terms of the defence of properties against attack from the rivers? Would not this equally well
account for their dispersal over the richer properties? Defence
against the Bacaudae can be imagined as rather differently de-
ployed; but defence against tip-and-run raiding from the estuaries
can hardly be envisaged in any other way. When Rutilius tells
us that his kinsman Exuperantius has been restoring law and
order in Armorica, he refers specifically to 'Armoricas oras'.[3]
The coastline was claiming his attention, not the huge inland
area of the *Tractus*, two of the five provinces of which (*Aquitanica*
I and *Lugdunensis* IV) had no coastline at all.[4] In fact, however,
we do not have to choose between Saxons and Bacaudae. The
Romans' chief gain may have been neither more nor less than
the drawing-off of the principal Goths from Spain and their pinning-down in a manageable area of Gaul that was probably over-
due for a little rough treatment. If, in addition, there was a danger
against which the Goths could defend Gallo-Roman interests, this
cannot be identified; nor can we be sure how they were to defend
them, since we cannot tell whether the Visigoths were settled in
dense masses or were uniformly spread out over the countryside.
Either way, they left little enough trace in the soil or in toponymy
when their time came to go.

[1] Gregory of Tours, *Hist.*, ii, 18.

[2] *Epist.*, viii, 6, 13–17. The story in the *Vita* of St Vivian of Saintonges (*Monumenta
Germaniae Historica, Scriptores Rerum Merovingicarum*, iii, 98) seems to be an echo of
this.

[3] *De Reditu Suo*, i, 213–16.        [4] *Notitia Dignitatum*, Occ. XXXVII.

In Aquitaine, place-names terminating once in *-ingos* and now in *-ens* can hardly be taken as an undifferentiated class, as Gamill-scheg[1] and others have taken them, and referred to Gothic occu-pation alone. Virtually no such place-names occur in heavily gothicized Septimania and Spain, and out of a total of some 300 in Aquitaine, only twenty-nine contain a demonstrably Gothic root; that is, are associated with names as Gothic as Andila, Mundila, Wulfila, Swinthila and Thrasila. The rest are almost all West Germanic, with Frankish and Alamannic predominating. Furthermore, they belong to those parts of Aquitaine conquered by Euric, not by Athaulf, and thus rather briefly occupied. Place-name study does not seem to reveal overwhelming Germanic (let alone Visigothic) settlement among the Gallo-Roman *villae* of the Aquitanian river-basins; it points to a few, and to a few also on the fringes of the forested areas, where the Goths in particular could indulge their love of hunting and of the breeding of horses. Athaulf was assassinated while attending to his own horses. If we take into account all Germanic forms of place-names, they are few and far between in relation to the total toponymy of Aquitaine. We can infer from them nothing whatever as to numbers. We do not really know how many Goths entered Gaul with Athaulf (100,000 is a guess), or whether they increased or diminished in the years between Athaulf and Euric, or even whether by Goths we should mean Goths only or assorted camp-followers as well.[2] However, these place-names in Aquitaine with their West Germanic roots receive a little elucidation in written sources. Gregory of Tours is silent here, but Isidore says that, after the battle of Vouillé, the *Regnum Tolosanum* was destroyed, 'occupantibus Francis'.[3] A later chronicler adds, in reference to

[1] *Romania Germania*, i, 330 ff. Cf. M. Broëns, 'Le Peuplement germanique de la Gaule entre la Méditerranée et l'Océan', *Annales du Midi*, lxviii, 1956, whose re-searches I summarize here, and the same author's 'Anthroponymie Germanique du VIᵉ au XIIᵉ siècle dans le pays soumis au rayonnement de Toulouse', *Revue Inter-nationale d'Onomastique*, October 1955.

[2] W. Reinhart, 'Germanische Reichsgründungen auf der Iberischen Halbinsel', *Germanen Erbe*, 1942, fasc. 3 and 4, has argued that many lowly cultivators would have been left behind in Aquitaine by the fleeing Goths. But are we to count these as Goths? It could be argued, as Mr J. N. L. Myres has pointed out to me, that a genuine *tertiatio*, settling Goths within the framework of the old estates, might leave few place-name traces; but we know almost nothing of this settlement.

[3] *Historia Gothorum*, M.G.H., *Chron. Min.*, ii, 282.

Clovis: 'in Santonico vel Burdigalense Francos praecepit manere';[1]
and a second chronicler, after the tale of destruction: 'electos
milites atque fortissimos, cum parvulis atque mulieribus, ad per-
vasas civitates custodiendas et ad reprimendam Gothorum saevi-
tiam dereliquit'.[2] Do not these three report some memory of a
permanent Frankish occupation, military and civil, of the *civitates*
abandoned by the Goths? The temporary recovery of part of
Aquitaine by the Goths in 510 shows the reason for these Frankish
precautions. Reinforcement of the West Germanic settlements –
Frankish and other – must account for the surprising fact that in
542, the kings Childebert and Chlotar led a kind of colonizing
movement from Aquitaine into Spain, and ultimately to Lusitania.[3]
What is more, the picture suggested by these writers and by
place-name study is the picture presented by archaeology. Gothic
cemeteries of the fifth century in Aquitaine are hard to distinguish
and Gothic grave-goods still, after years of work, hard to interpret.
There are no Germanic 'Reihengräber', as in the north-east. But
this much may be said: the large silver riveted fibulae characteristic
of Gothic graves in fifth-century Spain are nowhere to be found
in Aquitaine, except at Herpes, most notoriously complex of sites;
and even the bronze fibulae common in sixth-century Septimania
are, outside, confined to regions immediately bordering Septimania. Hispano-Gothic buckles of the sixth and seventh centuries
are unknown outside Gothic territories of that period. On the
other hand, the grave-goods of the Aquitanian cemeteries that have
been called Visigothic – there are some eighty of them – yield
arms, scramasaxes, franciscas and vases that are highly characteristic of Frankish grave-goods of the early sixth century but
not in the least of recognizably Gothic grave-goods.[4] I conclude

[1] *Liber Historiae Francorum*, chap. 17 (*M.G.H., S.R.M.*, ii, 270).
[2] Roric, *Gesta Francorum, Patrologia Latina*, 139, col. 614. The work of Roric, who
wrote in the eleventh century, is treated with more scepticism than it has been proved
to deserve. It preserves curious points of detail that merit attention.
[3] Cf. Isidore, loc. cit. p. 284 and the case argued by Broëns.
[4] Cf. E. Salin, *La civilization mérovingienne*, i, esp. pp. 387–406, and E. A. Thompson
in *Past and Present*, xiv (November 1958), 25, n. 40. A Gothic cemetery outside
Aquitaine that has been properly investigated is that of Estagel (Pyrénées Orientales),
though even here, according to R. Lantier, it is hard to tell Goths from autoch-
thonous tribesmen (*Gallia*, vol. i, 1942, and in the comptes-rendus of the *Académie
des Inscriptions*, 1947 and 1948).

that, making every allowance, place-names, grave-goods and written testimony do not yield any clear picture of a Visigothic settlement of southern Gaul, excluding Septimania. They suggest to me that military occupation was one thing, and settlement another. Perhaps many warriors of the original settlement may have been kept in cantonments in or around the principal cities surrendered to the Goths, and have drawn rents from, without taking up residence on, the estates allotted for their upkeep.[1] This is particularly suggested by the case of Toulouse, their capital. The court of the Visigothic kings found its normal home there, and the Roman notaries and other civil officials for whom they had a use retained offices and perhaps schools there, much as was later to happen in Lombardic Pavia.[2] But the presence of a few notaries and other Romans anxious to be at the centre of things will not explain why, perhaps alone of Gallo-Roman cities, the walled enceinte of Toulouse expanded in the course of the fifth century. Unless we take account of the need of six successive Visigothic kings to have extensive followings quartered within the city walls, we shall be hard put to it to explain this expansion of a Roman city that hitherto had been of no special commercial or strategic importance.[3] The *trustis* or *comitatus* of a powerful barbarian chieftain may have been rather more of an army than a bodyguard. Quartering on a smaller scale, calling for no extension of walls, may have been the fate of other cities at one time or another in Visigothic hands, such as Bordeaux, Tours, Narbonne, Arles, Clermont, Carcassonne, and, farther south, Barcelona

[1] Plainly *some* Goths lived on their estates or it would have been unnecessary for their kings to make arrangements about a common policy for clearings with the Romans. Cf. *Lex Vis.*, x, 1, 9 ('De silvis inter Gotum et Romanum indivisis relictis'). But if most of them did, and in their winter-quarters had lived so dispersed among Romans as not to affect place names, one would still expect to find their graves and characteristic grave-goods. It is unclear to me what conclusions as to settlements Courcelle would draw from his comment 'on s'aperçut très vite qu'il s'agissait d'un établissement définitif, car ces fédérés, au lieu de vivre de l'annone, furent cantonnés à la campagne; les chefs nourrirent euxmêmes leurs hommes sur la portion de domaine qui leur avait été attribuée' (*Les Grandes Invasions*, p. 118). See also F. Lot, 'Du régime de l'hospitalité', *Revue belge de philol. et d'hist.*, vol. vii (1928).

[2] It may be noted that the *commonitorium* of the *Lex Romana Visigothorum* is dated 'IIII non. Feb. an. XXII Alarici regis Tolosae' (*M.G.H., Leges*, p. 466).

[3] Cf. E. Delaruelle, 'Toulouse capitale wisigothique et son rempart', *Annales du Midi*, vol. lxvii (1955).

and Lisbon.[1] The requirements of the original *foedus* could have been satisfied in this manner. Hardly a campaigning season in the century can have passed without major Gothic forces being engaged on their proper federate occasions in Spain or Gaul, and, later, as hostile armies pushing forward the Gothic frontiers, or pushing back the Gothic enemies, to the Loire and the Rhône; and it is unnecessary to suppose that warriors would have found winter-quarters in the countryside more congenial than the halls of kings. What I am suggesting is, that, as a people, the Goths in Gaul may never have settled in the sense in which the Franks were to settle; that they may neither have wished to nor been required to. We need not picture every Gallo-Roman *villa* rendered noisome to its inhabitants by the sight and smell of Goths plastering rancid butter on their hair.

This approach to the settlements seems to make sense of what little is known for certain of Gothic and Roman administration in fifth-century Gaul,[2] and casts some light on what Athaulf meant: the Goths were really only fit for a supporting rôle in *Romania*. This is precisely what the *foedus* recognized. It was a political manœuvre of some skill, calling for a large measure of courage in its principal engineer, the patrician Constantius. If it was the last throw of a desperate man whose class was faced with extinction, no member of that class is recorded to have troubled to say as much. The truth is, that the Gallo-Roman landlords did very reasonably for themselves during the troubles of the fifth century. They somehow weathered the storm with their estates more or less intact; they had neither been expelled by the barbarians nor murdered by their slaves.[3] *Potentes* is no idle description

---

[1] Schmidt, *Ostgermanen*, p. 518, asserts that these and other, unnamed, cities were 'mit grosseren Garnisonen belegte Festungen'. This is likely enough, but he cites no evidence.

[2] As summarized by Schmidt, op. cit. pp. 502 ff. ('Innere Geschichte'), who, however, makes the common assumption that any matter adverted to in barbarian legislation must have been of common interest and general application. This is no truer than that what was omitted was negligible (e.g. because Euric omitted the *Novellae* of the Emperor Anthemius from his lawbook, or what we have of it, it by no means follows that he rejected them). Far too little attention is paid to the haphazard nature, diversified purpose and fragmentary survival of the Volkesrechte.

[3] There may be a parallel in the prosperity of certain Roman estates, albeit of humbler folk, in later Vandal Africa, where recent archaeological evidence has shown

of them; their landed wealth and their interest in the cities enabled them to raise private armies at will, and the barbarians had nothing to teach them about personal retainers or about what the Merovingians later called immunities. The same families continue to dominate the countryside and to fill the public offices, lay and spiritual, in the *civitas*. Some of the greatest of these are well-established in the time of Ausonius, are still there when Sidonius came to write, and have not disappeared in the days of Gregory of Tours.[1] Doubtless they were very greedy, but doubtless also the lot of the *colonus* would have been infinitely worse without them. After all, Avitacum was not Oblomovka. The question arises whether some of the senators may not have come to see in the Visigothic *rex* a rallying-point in a Gaul deprived of its emperor. If their *Romanitas*, and still more their religion, was offended by paying court to a barbarian war-lord, their patriotism may not have been, more particularly when they recalled that Gothic troops had made it possible for Aetius to withstand the Huns on the Catalaunian Plain. It has even been thought that some of them, like Arvandus and Seronatus, would have wished to see Euric a Gallic emperor in preference to acknowledging a Rome dominated by Ricimer and Byzantium.[2] This is another piece of conjecture.

Moreover, it is only one side of the picture. We know that the heirs of Roman civilization in Gaul were to be not the kings of Toulouse but the kings of Paris. This was to come about in part through military conquest; but in part also it was the doing of the Gallo-Roman episcopate. It is worth pausing to consider why the bishops ever found themselves in a position to exercise power so decisive.[3] In the first place, it can be said that they were big men, and that they were called to wrestle with great issues quite independent of the consequences of the collapse of

the continuity of Roman legal institutions of the fifth century and the use of legal formulae that echo those of Visigothic Gaul and Spain (*Tablettes Albertini*, ed. C. Courtois, L. Leschi, C. Perrat and C. Saumagne, 1952, esp. pp. 84 and 175).

[1] See the excellent study, and in particular the prosopography, of K. F. Strohcker, *Der senatorische Adel im spätantiken Gallien* (1948).

[2] Schmidt, *Ostgermanen*, p. 487.

[3] General reference may be made to E. Griffe, *La Gaule chrétienne à l'époque romaine*, vol. ii (*L'Église des Gaules au Ve siècle*, pt. 1), 1957.

imperial authority.[1] The problem of how a land of Catholic orthodoxy was to assimilate large groups of Arian *foederati* would naturally seem to be among the greatest of these; but, though they hated Arianism, we do not know that the bishops did much to make assimilation possible; and in the end they found it easier to get rid of their Arian masters. The rule of the bishops, at least by the middle of the fifth century, owes its peculiar power to the fusion of two traditions. The first may be called the missionary tradition that sprang from the impact of St Martin's ministry in the fourth century. It had been apocalyptic and puritanical, and it cut across the lines of the *civitas*. In a word, it was un-Roman. Further, it was perpetuated in a biography of startling merit. The *Vita Martini* of Sulpicius Severus, with its image of the fearless pastor, glorying in *rusticitas* yet not in the least politically inept, is the foundation-stone of the art of ecclesiastical biography in France. It opens the way to the seven huge volumes of the *Scriptores Rerum Merovingicarum* where, however, nothing of the same quality will be found. It is possible to be over-sceptical about the influence of St Martin on the fifth century.[2] I would detect it in more than one funerary inscription that foretells the imminent end of the world in language that is not yet common form.[3] To it, I would add the influence of the rather different missionary fervour of the monks of Lérins and of St Victor's at Marseilles. The outlook of Salvian upon the society he castigated would have been shared by his monastic brethren. The monks that went out to be bishops – Hilary of Arles, Eucher of Lyons, Lupus of Troyes and the like – remained monks, trained to live in obedience to a rule that sorted ill with the pattern of Roman society. Whether they thought Gallic society worth the saving is an open question.[4] Certainly their interests ranged beyond Gaul and ignored the boundaries of peoples. One may recall the reveal-

[1] I mean, theological issues and issues involving social justice. See the important paper of J. N. L. Myres, 'Pelagius and the end of Roman rule in Britain', *Journal of Roman Studies*, 50 (1960), for a possible parallel.

[2] As, for example, is Owen Chadwick, *John Cassian* (1950), pp. 43 ff.

[3] E.g. E. Le Blant, *Inscriptions Chrétiennes de la Gaule*, p. 334.

[4] O. Chadwick, op. cit., is an up-to-date account of the influence of Lérins upon the Gallo-Roman Church, though I agree with Peter Munz, 'John Cassian', *Journal of Ecclesiastical History*, vol. xi (1960), that Chadwick misjudges the revolutionary social implications of fifth and sixth-century monasticism in the West.

ing aside of Avitus: 'peregrinus sacerdos dici non potest, ubi catholica repperiri ecclesia potest'.[1] The influence of such monks transformed the church of Gaul in the fifth century, without, however, transforming Gallic society in the way that they hoped. The newness of this can be sensed in the *Epigramma Paulini* [2] and in the anonymous tractate *De Septem Ordinibus Ecclesiae*.[3] Here was one reason why the civil service lost its best recruits to the service of the church. It lost them also because the church offered the better chance of serving *Romania*; and it is just here that the interesting fusion occurs between the missionary zeal of Tours and Lérins on the one hand, and the old episcopal tradition of service to the *civitas* on the other: it could so easily not have happened. One overlooks the element of the former in the circle of Sidonius Apollinaris, which had its links with the monks. Sidonius clung to a *Romanitas* that was studiously anti-barbarian – Sidonius, whose son was to lead a contingent from the Auvergne to support the Visigoths against Clovis at Vouillé. One ought, in his view, still to look for a career in the imperial civil service, and still pay visits to Rome, 'patriam libertatis, in qua unica totius orbis civitate soli barbari et servi peregrinantur'.[4] This comes as easily and naturally as Claudian's evocation of Rome (just before Alaric's arrival) in his panegyric *de Sexto Consulatu Honorii*. But Rome, as Sidonius well knew, was also the Rome of the popes; and they, too, were concerned to defend and to profit from *Romanitas*. Papal authority is defined in language heavily indebted to imperial precedent. To take one instance: the more one looks at the language of Leo the Great, and the decisions embedded in it, the greater grows the extent of his debt to Roman Law.[5] When the Gaulish bishops received letters of exhortation

[1] *Epist.*, 9.

[2] *Corp. Script. Eccl. Lat.*, xvi, 503-8. There are some corrections to Schenkl's edition by E. Griffe in *Rev. Augustinienne*, ii, 187-94.

[3] Cf. P. Grosjean, 'Notes d'Hagiographie Celtique', *Analecta Bollandiana*, lxx (1957), 159-64.

[4] *Epist.*, 1, 6. The best study of Sidonius and his circle remains C. E. Stevens, *Sidonius Apollinaris and his age* (1933), though A. Loyen, *Recherches historiques sur les Panégyriques de Sidoine Apollinaire* (1942) is useful in a narrower field. L. Duval-Arnould, *Études d'histoire du droit romain au V<sup>e</sup> siècle d'après les lettres et les poèmes de Sidoine Apollinaire* (1888) is less good than Stevens thinks.

[5] The matter goes back beyond Pope Leo. Aspects of it are treated by Peter Classen, 'Kaiserreskript und Königsurkunde', *Archiv für Diplomatik*, i (1955), 82 ff.

or admonishment from the popes (and we have thirty-four of these for the period 404–64), they recognized in them the *auctoritas* not of St Peter only but of the City; and no service is done to our understanding of the fifth-century bishops by trying too hard to disentangle these allegiances. The point was not lost on the Visigoths, who used to distinguish the Gallic Catholics from themselves by calling them Romans: they did not call themselves Romans.[1] But it must have been hard for them to square the progressive withdrawal of Rome's imperial authority with the numerous instances of the exercise of that other Roman authority of the popes, and to have made sense of such an incident as the masterful intervention of Leo the Great over the disputed election to Arles in 445, backed up by a rescript of Valentinian III.

Roman Law has a good deal to do with the strengthening of papal authority in Gaul, as elsewhere, and in determining the attitude of the Visigoths to *Romanitas*. The bishops were aware that they lived under Roman Law and aware, too, that in their *scriptoria* and libraries it was preserved.[2] Because they looked upon the Theodosian Code, and in particular Book XVI, as some guarantee of their position in the state, excerpts from the Code for the use of the Church were not rare in Gaul.[3] But there is another way in which the Church was involved in the survival of Roman Law; in the formulation, namely, of what has come now to be called post-classical Vulgar Law, though Savigny and Brunner called it something different. This was never 'barbarized' law, since the barbarians had almost no effect on its evolution; it was Roman Law,[4] the study and the teaching of which in at least some western cities during and after the invasions can alone

[1] Gregory of Tours, *Liber in gloria martyrum*, 24.

[2] Much has been written on this subject. It is summarized by J. Gaudemet, 'Survivances romaines dans le droit de la monarchie franque', *Revue d'histoire du droit*, vol. xxiii (1955).

[3] Gaudemet, loc. cit. p. 166, n. 52.

[4] See Ernst Levy, 'The vulgarization of Roman Law in the Early Middle Ages, as illustrated by successive versions of Pauli Sententiae', *Medievalia et Humanistica*, vol. I (1943), *A Palingenesia of the opening titles as a specimen of research in West Roman Vulgar Law* (1945), *West Roman Vulgar Law: the Law of Property* (1951) and *Weströmisches Vulgarrecht, das Obligationenrecht* (1956); E. Volterra, 'Western Post-classical Schools', *Cambridge Law Journal*, vol. x (1949); and F. Wieacker, 'Vulgarismus und Klassizismus im Recht der Spätantike', *Sitzungsberichte der Heidelberger Akademie, Phil.-hist. Klasse*, Nr. 3 (1953).

explain why barbarian institutions and laws developed as they did. We do not have to envisage anything systematic or ambitious; but, directly or not, the Theodosian Code, completed in 438, was the source-book and inspiration of the lawyers who found employment under the Visigothic and Burgundian kings. The jurist, Leo, *consiliarius* to the Visigoths and friend of Sidonius, even had some acquaintance with the Law of the Twelve Tables. The compilers of Alaric's Breviary (*Lex Romana Visigothorum*) could master a version of Paul's Sentences that was not the version used by Justinian's lawyers, and the sentences they excerpted show that their interests were their own and not those of Byzantium. Much work is to be done in this field, on the technical accomplishment of the western masters and on the diffusion of their compilations. The names of some of them are known from inscriptions. Why, and for whom, was the text of Gaius copied in southern Gaul in the fifth century, only to have Cassian's *Institutions* written over it a few years later?[1] What legal background, and how much continuity, must we suppose at Lyons for the transcribing of the fine sixth-century Theodosian Code that is now in Paris,[2] or the contemporary copy, also uncial, of Alaric's Breviary that has come to rest in Munich,[3] or the related half-uncial copy of the Breviary in Berlin?[4] Such a group of manuscripts may not prove the existence of a great writing-centre, but it does prove scribal activity[5] and zeal for book-collecting. It does argue a market for legal texts of whatever quality, and a demand from men sufficiently trained to make use of them. *Lex Romana Burgundionum* marks a further stage of that interest.

One use to which these legal texts were put was political. The *Lex Romana* of the Visigoths was compiled in a hurry at King Alaric II's request,[6] and was intended to appease his Gallo-Roman

[1] E. A. Lowe, *Codices Latini Antiquiores*, vi, 726, allows that the primary script of this manuscript (now MS. Autun, Bibl. Mun. 24, S. 28, fos. 97–110) could be Italian or Gallo-Roman, and even goes so far as to think that it might be a local Autun script. Every other consideration seems to me to point to a Gallo-Roman origin.

[2] Bibl. Nat. Lat. 9643 (C.L.A. V, 591).     [3] Clm. 22501 (C.L.A. IX, 1324).

[4] Deutsche Staatsbibl., Phillipps 1761 (C.L.A. VIII, 1064).

[5] This is considered by E. A. Lowe in his *Codices Lugdunenses Antiquissimi* (1924). Some modifications are made in C.L.A. VI and VII.

[6] It may be worth noting the king's name. Was it his father's intention to remind his people of the first Alaric?

and Catholic subjects, and conceivably also the Empire, in not all
of which respects it failed. But we can look further back, to the
vestigial legislation of King Euric, the work of Roman jurists,
succinct and clear, steering a subtle course between Vulgar Law
and Gothic custom, and intended for the use of Goths, not
Romans. There was no political appeasement here, and no need
of it. Perhaps it is not inappropriate that, with the exception of
one manuscript now in the Bibliothèque Nationale[1] and excerpts
in later Visigothic Law, the *Codex Euricianus* is best preserved in
association with the spiritedly barbarian *Lex Baiuvariorum*. We
have no more than fragments of Euric's *Codex* (to be precise,
the last sixty of a possible 336 clauses, though there are gaps, even
here). Their nature is best revealed by the surviving titles: *De
Commendatis vel Commodatis, De Venditionibus, De Donationibus* and
*De Successionibus*. Were I to picture to myself the missing titles,
they would cover the sort of matters that can be found in the
*Pactus Legis Salicae*: namely, *De Manire, De Furtis, De Rapto, De
Vulneribus, De Homicidiis, De Sepibus, De Plagiatoribus, De Migran-
tibus*, and so on; though, were I to find them, I should not
conclude that the Goths were everywhere settled down quietly
on their two-thirds of Roman estates. As Vinogradoff pointed
out, some of this surviving matter is drawn direct from Roman
sources, and by trained civilians: for example, the forbidding of
actions concerning events that had occurred more than thirty
years earlier; the nullification of donations extorted by force or
intimidation, 'a rule which breaks through the purely formalistic
treatment of obligations natural to barbaric law'; and the granting
of equality as to inheritance between men and women.[2] But,
when all has been said, the influence of Roman upon Gothic
practice is not very strong or wide here; and the facts must not
be confused with the forms. No Gothic legislation earlier than
the time of Leuvigild, in the late sixth century, bears any trace
of thinking in terms of a state that is neither Roman nor Gothic
but a fusion of the two; and the process becomes marked only

---

[1] Lat. 12161 (C.L.A. V, 626). This sixth-century uncial manuscript – and highly
illegible it is – was, Lowe thinks, 'written presumably in the Visigothic kingdom,
probably in South France'.

[2] P. Vinogradoff, *Roman Law in Medieval Europe* (2nd ed., 1929), p. 30.

in the reign of Reccasvinth.[1] It would require the survival of a fairly large batch of private *instrumenta* to make me feel sure that even the Eurician regulations we do have were widely applied in his own reign. It seems to me that we are still quite a long way from Athaulf's pipe-dream of a Gothic *respublica* living under law. What we have arrived at is rather a Gallo-Roman *respublica* living under law that makes special provisions in limited matters for a Gothic minority and that otherwise allows that Goths are Goths and Romans, Romans. This in itself is no mean achievement, but it has not the legal interest of *Lex Gundobada*, the Burgundian Law of about the same date, where a more wide-reaching fusion of Roman and Germanic legal elements has taken place. And we can almost look beyond Euric to law-making by his father, King Theodoric I, which he cites, and to some by his brother, Theodoric II, which laws Sidonius termed 'leges', not 'edicta'.[2] Euric required his subjects to stick to the property-boundaries, the 'antiquos terminos', 'sicut et bonae memoriae pater noster in alia lege praecepit'.[3] The Law of Property is not quickly barbarized. Ludwig Schmidt believed that such law-giving, affecting as it did Goths and Romans in their relations with each other, was a conscious step towards royal autonomy.[4] But what autonomy means in such a context, and what Theodoric thought he would gain by it, is not clear to me. Zeumer[5] held that the mere act of codification made Gothic law more Roman. He would have had in mind the kind of comment made by Isidore in the seventh century: 'sub hoc rege Gothi legum instituta scriptis habere coeperunt. Nam antea tantum moribus et consuetudine tenebantur'.[6] But we should not carry this too far. The strong traces of customary Gothic law

[1] Cf. F. S. Lear, 'The public law of the Visigothic Code', *Speculum*, vol. xxvi (1951), and the important remarks of E. A. Thompson, 'The conversion of the Visigoths to Catholicism', *Nottingham Medieval Studies*, iv (1960), esp. pp. 32 ff.

[2] [Of Seronatus] 'leges Theudosianas calcans Theudoricianasque proponens' (*Epist.*, ii, 1). However, it cannot be inferred from this that Theodoric II had even contemplated replacing the Codex with a Gothic equivalent, a systematic barbarian law-book. The reference must surely be to isolated regulations affecting property, if, indeed, it is not in part to be understood as irony. Isidore (see note 6 below) was not necessarily wrong in holding that Euric was the first of his race to produce a body of written law. In this I must disagree with R. Buchner, *Deutschlands Geschichtsquellen* (*Die Rechtsquellen*), p. 7, and with F. Beyerle, *Zeitschrift der Savigny-Stiftung, Germ. Abt.*, lxvii, 4 ff.

[3] *Cod. Eur.*, 277.      [4] *Ostgermanen*, p. 464.
[5] *Neues Archiv*, xxiii, 470.      [6] *Hist. Goth.* (M.G.H., *Auct. Antiq.*, xi, 281).

in medieval Spanish legislation are enough to remind us that, however Roman the disguise, Gothic custom remained Gothic.[1] Now, part at least of this fairly continuous Visigothic involvement in the forms of Roman Law is only conceivable with the assistance of the Church. Alaric's *Lex Romana* shows clear traces of clerical drafting, and the same hand may be detected there as in the canons of the Synod of Agde, summoned in that very year (506) to placate the Roman Church: the hand, namely, of Caesarius of Arles.[2] Behind the group of legal texts from Lyons must lie the resources of the Church of Lyons; and these could not have been less than the resources of the neighbouring Church of Clermont, where in the seventh century Roman Law continued to be taught.[3] Episcopal notaries would have concurred with a pronouncement only slightly later in date, that that Law by which the Church lives *is* Roman Law.[4] It is also part of a threatened heritage, and so to be prized for its very *Romanitas*. It seems doubtful if the secular study of law in Gaul survived at all far into the fifth century;[5] there is no evidence that men like Leo were common. The Church alone could have taken the place of the old public law schools, in so far as anything took their place. Some at least of the Visigoth kings must have come to associate law with the Church, and to have relied to some extent on it in their dealings with their Gallo-Roman subjects. Hence it comes about that, in 462, the pope can write to the Bishop of Arles ordering him to remove his suffragan of Narbonne, about whom 'filius noster', the Arian Frederic, brother of King Theodoric II, had been complaining to him.[6] The Visigoth lords are glad

[1] Cf. E. de Hinojosa, 'Das germanische Element im spanischen Rechte', *Zeitsch. d. Savigny-Stift., Germ. Abt.*, xxxi (1910), 282 ff., and the more recent literature cited by Buchner, op. cit. p. 9, n. 25.

[2] Such is the argument of Eberhard Bruck, *Über Römisches Recht im Rahmen der Kulturgeschichte* (1954). Caesarius was recalled in haste from exile in Bordeaux to prepare the work of the council; an exile to which, like the Bishop of Tours, he had been condemned by Alaric himself. It is not known that Alaric, for all his concessions, ever ceased to be an Arian.

[3] *Vita Boniti*, chap. 2 (*M.G.H., S.R.M.*, vi, 120). But who did the teaching?

[4] *Lex Ribvaria*, 58.

[5] Cf. P. Riché, 'La survivance des écoles publiques en Gaule au Ve siècle', *Le Moyen Âge*, vol. lxiii (1957). But there may have been exceptions, especially in the South.

[6] This extraordinary letter survives in the *Epistolae Arelatenses* (*M.G.H., Epist.*, III, no. 15).

enough to make use of the pope and the bishops and the law by which they live.

But there is another side to the Church's activity, and wider intellectual interests, including some that could not please the Goths in the long run. Lyons had other than legal manuscripts. That is to say, one speaks of 'Lyons manuscripts' when the plain fact is that hardly any manuscripts of the fifth century can be ascribed to places of origin with anything approaching certainty. Most that have been assigned with varying degrees of probability to one place rather than to another have been so assigned on general palaeographical grounds that should not be pressed against evidence of other kinds, that point in other directions. This is not a matter to argue at length here, but it must be mentioned because it affects some fifth-century manuscripts that, I suspect, could as well be Gallo-Roman as Italian in origin; and the way that the issue is some day decided must affect our opinion of the relative state of culture of these two parts of the Empire. Is it good enough to make an *a priori* judgement that Italian cultural standards were the higher and, hence, that any given manuscript that is well-written is more safely assignable to Italy, even though its earliest known provenance was Gallic, or the associations of its contents Gallo-Roman? It is a hard question. Nobody will dispute the scribal primacy of a fifth-century Italy that could produce the *Mediceus* of Virgil. But scribal primacy is not quite what is involved; calligraphy and intellectual appetite do not always go hand in hand; and scribal primacy cannot help anyone to infer much about the original home of, let us say, the fifth-century manuscripts of St Hilary's writings, now scattered over Europe, or about the western legal manuscripts of that century. Both of these groups might as reasonably look to Gaul as to Italy for a home and an origin. There are, too, biblical texts and commentaries, the texts of pagan classical authors, that are assigned to Italy without any argument more weighty than grounds of general probability that in the last resort are scarcely palaeographical at all. Did not the Gallo-Romans for whom the *Querolus* was written make their own copies of Terence, Livy, Virgil, Ovid, Sallust, and Pliny? There are fifth-century manuscripts, or fragments of manuscripts, of all these writers that could, with varying degrees

of likelihood, be Gallo-Roman.[1] There are fragments of a manuscript of Euclid that almost certainly is.[2] When we consider the
range of issues that were being debated by the Gallic clergy,
inside and outside the monasteries, throughout the fifth century,
we can only suppose that the Italian *scriptoria* did an extraordinarily brisk business supplying them with texts, or else that
the Gallic *scriptoria* managed a fair amount of the work on the
spot. I cannot myself believe that Gallic *scriptoria* were innocent
of the short-lived renaissance of interest in Greek writers that
belonged to the 470's, when discussion of patristic and Neo-
Platonic texts was fairly widespread in the southern cities.[3]
The number of reports of pilgrimages to Palestine that origin-
ate from Gaul; the decisions about admitting eastern priests
taken by Gallic and Spanish synods; the kind of material lying
behind such a book as the *De Statu Animae* of Claudianus Mamer-
tus; the activity of the school of Vienne under the *rhetor* Sapaudus;
all these suggest links between Gallic clergy and the Greek-
speaking world, while others point direct to Africa. They are
a warning against making too much of the migration of Gallo-
Roman *rhetorici* to Ireland during the invasions. There were men
left in Gaul able to make use of a wide range of theological texts,
and in the process to hammer out a language adequate to their
special needs. Their doctrinal debates have immediacy. In some
way that has still to be determined, they are the link between the
monastic fanatics of the early fifth century and the episcopal
colleagues of Gregory of Tours in the sixth.

There is a letter from Sidonius to Bishop Basilius of Aix – one
of the negotiators of the peace of 475 – which takes us to one
root of the trouble that wrecked the Roman experiment of a
Visigothic Gaul.[4] He begins by praising the stand taken by

[1] These manuscripts are respectively C.L.A. VII, 974; IV, 499; IV, 498 and VII,
977; IX, 1377; VI and VIII, 809; VI, 725. See the remarks of Paul Lehmann, 'The
Benedictine Order and the transmission of the literature of ancient Rome', reprinted
in *Erforschung des Mittelalters*, III (1960), p. 176.

[2] Verona XL (38) in rustic capitals (C.L.A. IV, 501); overwritten with Gregory's
*Moralia* at Luxeuil in the early eighth century.

[3] P. Courcelle, *Les Lettres grecques en occident* (1948), esp. p. 245, associates this
renaissance with the flourishing Athenian school of Proclus and with the nomination
of a Greek, Anthemius, as Emperor in the West.

[4] *Epist.*, vii, 6.

Basilius against the Arian preaching of the Goth Modahar. He goes on:

> I pour into your ears my grief at the ravages of the great wolf of our times, who ranges about the ecclesiastical fold battening upon lost souls, and biting right and left by stealth and un-detected. The devil begins by threatening the shepherds' throats, knowing it the best way to ensure his triumph over the bleat-ing and abandoned sheep. . . . Neither a saint like you can fitly here discuss, nor a sinner like myself indict, the action of Euric the Gothic king in breaking and bearing down an ancient treaty to defend, or rather extend by armed force, the frontiers of his kingdom. . . . I must confess that formidable as the mighty Goth may be, I dread him less as the assailant of our walls than as the subverter of our Christian laws. They say that the mere mention of the name of Catholic so embitters his countenance and heart that one might take him for the chief priest of his Arian sect rather than for the monarch of his nation. Omnipotent in arms, keen-witted and in the full vigour of life, he yet makes this single mistake – he attributes his success in his designs and enterprises to the orthodoxy of his belief. . . . Do your best, as far as the royal condescension suffers you, to obtain for our bishops the right of ordination in those parts of Gaul now included within the Gothic boun-daries, that if we cannot keep them by treaty for the Roman state, we may at least hold them by religion for the Roman Church (trs. Dalton).

From this letter it could be inferred that Arianism paid; even, that at last, under a strong king, it had been able to make its own contribution to the autonomy that the Goths had always really wanted. Indeed there was no softness about King Euric, and no nonsense about a *foedus* that no longer bore any relation to political facts. We cannot be at all sure that he systematically persecuted the Roman Church, and there is a good deal to be said for the view that such persecution as he did countenance was in the nature of a wartime measure.[1] Modahar is the only

---

[1] The case for persecution rests mainly on Gregory of Tours, *Hist.*, ii, 25, and *De Glor. Conf.*, 47. Cf. G. Yver, 'Euric Roi des Wisigoths' in *Études d'Histoire du*

Gothic preacher who is known ever to have attempted the conversion of the faithful in Gaul. As a rule, the Arian hierarchy
(if we can speak of such) kept remarkably quiet. The fact is, there
never was anything in Arianism that made it a more suitable
religion than orthodox Catholicism for a Germanic nation. Not
in itself nationalistic, it need never have become so.[1] It may not
even have been a particularly long-cherished creed to many of
the Goths.[2] What sharpened Visigothic awareness that Arianism
was not Roman in the way they must once have supposed, was
the hostility of the Catholic bishops among whom they were
settled, and reports of the much fiercer opposition of the African
bishops to the Arian Vandals. In this sense, it was Catholicism
that defined the edges of Arianism and gave it a nationalistic
flavour; but it did not happen at once or quickly. We need not
suppose that the Arian Visigoths were from the first the enemies
of the Gallo-Roman Catholics, much less their persecutors. Sidonius probably exaggerated; for his church seemed to emerge in
fairly good trim from the jaws of the Visigoths; and some had
a feeling that the good old days were on their way back. Yet
his charges are specific. He says that the churches of Bordeaux,
Périgueux, Rodez, Limoges, Javols, Eauze, Bazas, Comminges,
Auch 'and of many other cities' had lost their bishops and been
unable to replace them. Euric may have had special reasons to
distrust the faithful of these cities. Special or general, however,
there is no need to minimize the extent of his hostility to Catholicism. We know from Salvian that there were Visigothic scholars
at the court of Toulouse who were able to revise the Gothic
Bible,[3] and who, in the long run, might have been able to offer
some intellectual opposition to the Catholics. I see no alternative
to supposing that, in the half-century or so that separated the

---

*Moyen Âge dédiées à Gabriel Monod* (1896). Some examples of what churches suffered
during Gothic campaigns by way of pillage will be found in the *Vita* of St Caesarius
of Arles. Cf. E. A. Thompson, 'The conversion of the Visigoths to Catholicism',
*Nottingham Medieval Studies*, iv. (1960), 9.

[1] Cf. A. H. M. Jones, 'Were ancient heresies national or social movements in
disguise?' *Journal of Theological Studies*, vol. x (1959).

[2] Cf. E. A. Thompson, *Journal of Ecclesiastical History*, vii (1956), I – II, who argues
that the Goths were still an essentially pagan people when they entered the Empire in
376.

[3] *De Gub. Dei.* v. §§5 ff.

settlement in *Aquitanica II* from the reign of King Euric, Arian mistrust of Catholics had been fanned by the detestation of Catholics for Arians into something very like the religion of a people, royal in identity of control; and a people, moreover, for the first time jealous for their vernacular liturgy. This growing mistrust coincided with fierce Catholic polemic against heresy of other kinds, and also with increasingly clear statements from the popes about the nature of their supremacy and of the dependence of Catholic bishops upon St Peter's *auctoritas*, defined in Roman juridical terms. Here was a Rome that could dare to act with independence of emperors who lived under barbarian patronage, as well as of those that did not. Its authority, external to Gaul, claimed the allegiance of most of the subjects of the Visigothic kings; and it is not altogether surprising that Euric, 'istius aetatis lupus', took fright. Another Goth, Theodoric the Great in Italy, was to lose his head in just such a manner and with rather less excuse. How hard Euric was pressed the swift collapse of his successor was to show.

Were the Catholic bishops, in their turn, so frightened of Arianism as to risk an open breach with the Goths? It is easy to hear the note of alarm in the letter of Sidonius; but, late in the day though it is, it hardly betrays fear of extinction. To a large extent, the Visigoths had been an irrelevance to the Gallic Church; her big problems had not been created by barbarian movements, and no Gallo-Roman churchman of the fifth century saw with the clarity of Gregory the Great that the barbarians had come to stay and must be wrestled with as whole peoples, ripe for conversion. But indifference to Goths did not lead to compromise over Arian doctrine, even among bishops who worked closely with them. The case of Caesarius of Arles, bishop of the most civilized see in Gaul, is not untypical:

> instruxit itaque et ibi et ubique semper ecclesiam reddere quae sunt Caesaris Caesari et quae sunt Dei Deo, oboedire quidem iuxta Apostolum regibus et potestatibus, quando iusta praecipiunt, nam despectui habere in principe Arriani dogmatis pravitatem.[1]

Caesarius worked long with the Visigoths without ever com-

[1] *Vita*, Book 1, chap. 23 (*M.G.H., S.R.M.*, iii, 464).

promising over their heresy. Much the same position was taken
by his contemporary, Avitus of Vienne, adviser to Burgundian
kings. They do not seem to have feared the outcome. After all,
they were well-entrenched at the level of the *civitas*; they were
rich in property (not in vain did Salvian plead for legacies – 'God
loveth a cheerful giver');[1] and they had ability. Already one can
see in outline the masters of the Franks. So they faced Euric and
failed to be impressed by his successor's concessions. Indeed,
they rather acted on the assumption (correct, as it turned out)
that there was something impermanent about the Visigoths; the
army of occupation was still an army after a century's residence,
and its chieftains had not lost their identity. They had not even
intermarried with their hosts, as Athaulf had when he married
Galla Placidia, though the law that prevented them from doing
so derived from the traditional practice of Rome.

I cannot detect a steady romanization of the Goths over this
time in Gaul; their dip into *Romania* amounts to little in practice.
Still less can I make anything of the theory that, after a bad start,
they made an attempt to create a *Gothia*. This is to make far too
much of a kind of political independence that was wished on
them by the collapse of the Western Empire.[2] I am not at all
sure what one ought to make of Gothic 'expansion' in Gaul.
Jordanes consistently stresses that Euric's advances were neces-
sitated by imperial weakness. In the letter I have already cited,
Sidonius admits that Euric thought he was defending, not extending, his kingdom's frontiers. This is the sort of thing that tyrants
do think, of course; but consider the movements of barbarian
peoples in his vicinity, above all of the Franks and the Alamans.
Within a decade of the Catalaunian Plain, Franks were being used
to put down the Burgundians, to rescue Arles from the Visigoths
and to carry out operations in Armorica and its approaches.
Against such enemies, not against the Empire, the Visigoths
needed to make preparation. It is fatally easy to imagine that the

[1] *Ad Ecclesiam*, i, 8; ii, 14; iv, 2; and elsewhere. In the same sense Sidonius writes
'quicquid ecclesiis spargis, tibi colligis' (*Epist.*, viii, 4); and even St Martin required
the Emperor to restore confiscated church property (*Dialogus*, ii, 7). The very great
social implications of Christian giving are developed by Eberhard Bruck, 'Ethics
versus Law: St Paul, the Fathers of the Church and the "Cheerful Giver" in Roman
Law', *Traditio*, ii, 1944.
[2] In this matter I differ strongly from Schmidt, *Ostgermanen*, 496, and others.

natural enemy of every Germanic king was the Roman emperor, when in fact it was another Germanic king. 'Pushing forward frontiers', 'strengthening independence' and 'establishing autonomy' are phrases of little significance when applied to barbarians; and if one agrees with Gibbon that 'France may ascribe her greatness to the premature death of the Gothic king', it is not because Euric came anywhere near establishing Athaulf's *Gothia*. That the Goths were heretics, and perhaps confused by the changing faces of the power of Rome, made it all the worse. The Gallic setting of these independent *reguli*, not least the setting of their law, makes them look more Roman than they really were. Roman Law never brought about any change in their concept of kingship, at least in Gaul.[1] Later on, in Spain, and within the orbit of Byzantium, it did; but that is another story.

A single campaign was enough to overthrow the Visigothic kingdom of Toulouse; the area originally assigned to them was settled by Franks. Perhaps most of the Goths were already in Spain, where they always seem to have been happier.[2] Some, certainly, retreated upon Narbonne and from that base put up a fight for Septimania against the Franks that Frankish historians managed to gloss over, though Spanish writers did not.[3] As late as the seventh century, the see of Narbonne belonged to the Spanish Church. All this makes it hard to believe the Frankish boast that the Goths were soft. We cannot so easily account for their disappearance from all Gaul but Septimania. The conclusion seems to be that they had failed to ingratiate themselves with *Romania* as decisively as they had failed to create *Gothia* – if either had ever been their intention. They had remained isolated in a Roman province indifferent to their fate; and, in the end, found it easier to pack their bags and go.

[1] I can find no justification for Schmidt's view that 'das westgotische Königtum eine neuere Schöpfung war' (op. cit. p. 512). Under Alaric II as under Athaulf it is still in essentials the war-leadership of a confederation of Germanic tribes; administering law to Gallo-Romans through Gallo-Romans does not much affect the issue.

[2] But it is fair to remember that Hispano-Romans could object to Goths as strongly as did Gallo-Romans: Burdunelus was brought up to Toulouse for execution in 497 (*Chron. Caesaraug.*, s.a., 496–7). Justinian's reconquest of south-eastern Spain still lay in the future.

[3] The seriousness of the Frankish struggle for parts of the Midi is well brought out by E. Ewig, *Die fränkischen Teilungen und Teilreiche* (511–613), (1952).

# CHAPTER THREE

# The Work of Gregory of Tours in the Light of Modern Research[1]

\*

When Wilhelm Levison, one of the great *Monumenta* editors, died in Durham in 1947, he left unfinished two enterprises of major importance to those whose concern is with Frankish studies. The first, a much-needed edition of the *Lex Salica*, he seems to have brought no nearer completion than had his predecessor, Bruno Krusch, or any other of the long line of *Monumenta* scholars who broke their hearts in the attempt to unravel it.[2] The second, the completion of the new *Monumenta* edition of the *Historia Francorum* of Gregory of Tours, to supersede that of Arndt and Krusch, was a good deal further advanced. In fact, the text itself had already appeared in print under the name of Bruno Krusch alone,[3] although it was an open secret that a great part of the burden of editing had fallen on Levison's shoulders. What remained to be published was the critical introduction. This, too, has since appeared in print, having been prepared for the press by Professor W. Holtzmann. We cannot here assess the significance of Levison's views on the manuscript tradition of the *Historia*.[4] The purpose of this paper is rather to look at some of the ways in which historians

[1] *Transactions, Royal Historical Society*, 5th series, vol. I (1951).

[2] See W. Holtzmann's preface to *Aus Rheinischer und Fränkischer Frühzeit* (Düsseldorf, 1948), which is a memorial collection of Levison's papers; and S. Stein, 'Lex Salica I', *Speculum*, xxii (1947), 113–34. Good texts have been provided by K. A. Eckhardt, in the series *Germanenrechte* (*100 Titel-Text*, 1953; *80 Titel-Text*, 1954; *65 Titel-Text*, 1955).

[3] *M(onumenta) G(ermaniae) H(istorica), S(criptores) R(erum) M(erovingicarum)*, fasc. 1 (Books i–vi, 29, 1937); and fasc. 2 (Books vi, 30–x, 1942). Another good text is that of R. Buchner, *Gregor von Tours, Zehn Bücher Geschichten*. This has a German translation.

[4] They have been examined in *English Historical Review*, LXVII (1952). See also Wattenbach-Levison, *Deutschlands Geschichtsquellen*, I (1952), pp. 99–108.

have been using Gregory in the twenty years since the publication of Dill's[1] and Dalton's[2] books; for they were the last English scholars to whom Frankish studies seemed important for themselves.

Gregory of Tours, like Bede after him,[3] ends his *History* with a short passage of autobiography and with a list of his writings.

I have written ten books of History, seven of Miracles, and one on the Lives of the Fathers. I have composed one book of commentaries on the Psalms, I have also written one book on the Offices of the Church. These works may be written in an unpolished style, but I adjure all of you, bishops of the Lord, who after me in this my lowliness shall govern the church of Tours – never to let these books be destroyed or re-written, by choosing out some parts and omitting others, but to leave them all complete and intact in your time just as I myself have left them. But whoever thou art, O priest of God, if our Martianus hath instructed thee in the seven arts . . . if in all these things thou shalt be so skilled as to hold my style inelegant, even so, I pray thee, remove naught of that which I have written. If aught therein please thee, I refuse thee not permission to translate it into verse; but leave my work complete.[4]

Now Gregory's profession of inelegance and incompetence is of course a well-tried device and need not detain us. He shows skill in handling the rhetorical *cursus*, and his powerful use of dialogue is something of his own. His Latin was what he meant it to be; it was realistic.[5] Much more arresting – though again, not wholly new – is his insistence that his writings should be thought of as a whole; they were not to be divided, either by his successors at Tours or by anyone else. Krusch was perfectly correct when he

---

[1] S. Dill, *Roman Society in Gaul in the Merovingian Age* (1926).

[2] O. M. Dalton, *The History of the Franks by Gregory of Tours*, translated with an introduction, 2 vols. (1927).

[3] *Historia Ecclesiastica*, v, 24 (ed. C. Plummer, i, 357).

[4] *Hist.*, x, 31; I have used Dalton's translation. Levison (*S.R.M.*, iv, 781) drew attention to the subscription of Irenaeus of Lyons, in Rufinus, *Hist. Eccl.*, v, 20, 2 (ed. Mommsen), p. 483; 'adiuro te, inquit, qui transcripseris librum hunc . . . ut conferas haec quae scribis et emendes diligenter ad exemplaria'.

[5] See E. Löfstedt, *Syntactica*, II (1933), p. 365. Gregory's conscientious erudition has won the admiration of many scholars, and notably of Kurth and Levillain.

wrote that this passage, Gregory's last testament, should be the basis on which all critical work on the manuscripts of the *Historia* should rest.[1] In any further attempt to decide which was the last version of the *Historia* to leave the author's hands, scholars will have to bear in mind that, if Gregory here meant what he said, this should be the version most closely integrated with his other writings.

The *Historia* is preserved to us in an altogether exceptional number of manuscripts, no less than four belonging to the seventh century. (No Frankish manuscript of a saint's *Life*, perhaps the characteristic form of Merovingian literature, can be dated so early.) But if we wish to form even a rough idea of what the *Historia* meant to the Middle Ages we must, in addition, take account of the number of entries in early medieval library catalogues of *Historiae*, or *Historiae Ecclesiasticae*, which in France at any rate were more likely to mean Gregory than Orosius, Bede, or any of the 'national' historians.[2] Of the surviving manuscripts, some of the earliest contain only the first six books of the *Historia* (that is, to the death of Chilperic in 584), with the remaining four books added later; while others – notably *Casinensis* 275, of the twelfth century – contain the ten books complete. No one questions that, whatever his plan of revision may have been, and whether he added to or subtracted from an original version of the first six books,[3] all ten books – allowing for interpolations[4] – are from the pen of Gregory of Tours.

I return, therefore, to Gregory's injunction that his writings should be regarded as a whole and that, even versified, they should not suffer mutilation. If we wish to make sense of his history we must relate it to the main body of his hagiographical writings,

---

[1] *Historische Vierteljahrschrift*, xxviii (1934), p. 678.

[2] See E. Lesne, *Histoire de la propriété ecclésiastique en France*, iv, *Scriptoria* (1938), pp. 567–8. M. L. W. Laistner points out (*Intellectual Heritage of the Middle Ages*, p. 102) that the oldest manuscript of Bede's *Retractatio* gives Gregory's name as Georgius. His given names were Georgius Florentius, Gregory being adopted in memory of an ancestor.

[3] G. Vinay, *San Gregorio di Tours* (Turin, 1940), pp. 173 and 190, argues that the longer version is older than the shorter.

[4] As, for example, the sermon in *Hist.*, x, 1. See the arguments of O. Chadwick, 'Gregory of Tours and Gregory the Great', *Journal of Theological Studies*, 50 (1949), pp. 38–49, which are not, however, conclusive.

much as we relate Bede's history to his *Lives of St Cuthbert* and *Lives of the Abbots*, and that not merely when Gregory refers us specifically to those writings, as he sometimes does. Even so, we shall not be more than half-way to a full view; for Gregory, unlike Bede, was bishop of one of the greatest sees in Europe, and his writings were only one side of a career of ceaseless activity as administrator, builder, evangelist and (though some will not have it) politician. Gregory was the successor of St Martin; he ruled St Martin's own church, and he was St Martin's biographer and constant champion.[1] The cult of St Martin seems to have coloured all that Gregory ever did, and all that he wrote: 'iste est pro quo Martinus rogat'.[2] It was not simply that Gregory believed, with all his Christian contemporaries, in the miraculous power of the saint's relics and in particular of his sacred *cappa*; he had, in the biographical material available in Tours,[3] an episcopal prototype whom it would have been dangerous to ignore. A tribune's son and a soldier, St Martin had been a monk, a recluse, and a bishop,[4] a great foe of Arianism,[5] and by turns the friend and rebuker of emperors. According to the *Dialogues* of Sulpicius Severus,[6] which Gregory certainly used, St Martin had once, at Trier, forced his way into the presence of the redoubtable Valentinian I, who, grinding his teeth, refused to rise at the bishop's entry until finally induced to do so by a divine application of fire to the seat of his throne. Such was Gregory's hero, the saint to whom he felt himself to stand in the relation of man to lord, the saint who was the very owner of the city and church of Tours. This process of identification whereby Gregory became, in a sense, St Martin, was in no way unusual or unexpected; it happened with other bishops

[1] The *De Virtutibus Sancti Martini* is edited by Krusch in the MGH edition of Gregory's works (1885), pp. 584–661.

[2] Ibid., p. 630.

[3] See R. A. Meunier, *Grégoire de Tours et l'histoire morale du centreouest de la France* (Poitiers, 1946), pp. 27–36, for a summary of Gregory's use of earlier writings on St Martin (Sulpicius Severus, Paulinus of Nola and Paulinus of Périgueux). The book is not otherwise helpful.

[4] É. Griffe, *La Gaule Chrétienne à l'époque romaine*, i (1947), chap. vi, is the best modern account of the career of St Martin.

[5] This point is well made by M. M. Gorce, *Clovis* (1935), p. 168. St Martin was the disciple of St Hilary, the great opponent of Arianism.

[6] *Dialogi*, ii, 5 (Sulpicius has been excellently translated by Paul Monceaux, *Saint Martin. Récits de Sulpice Sévère mis en français*, avec une introduction, 1927).

and other saints all over Europe.[1] Its special significance derives from the prestige of the see of Tours and from Gregory's resolve not merely to rule but to build and to write.

Gregory states that he succeeded as bishop to a cathedral basilica in ruins, destroyed by fire.[2] He rebuilt it on a larger scale and dedicated it in the seventeenth year after his consecration. His friend Venantius Fortunatus described the reconstructed church in a poem entitled *Ad ecclesiam Toronicam quae per Episcopum Gregorium renovata est*,[3] where more attention is paid to the embellishment of the church, and to the mural paintings of scenes from the life and miracles of St Martin, than to architectural features. This is what Gregory himself would have wished: it was the embellishment that counted, exactly as it counted, centuries later, in the enlargement of the church of St Denis by Abbot Suger.[4] Pilgrims, drawn by the fame of St Martin, were a main source of revenue to Gregory's church;[5] and pilgrims needed instruction and entertainment, visual as well as aural. It is just possible, also, that by the close of the sixth century St Martin's reputation no longer went unchallenged in north-western Gaul. Competition may already have been offered at Paris by St Denis, a saint to whom Dagobert was by no means the first Merovingian to feel drawn. The legend of St Denis, the disciple of St Clement and first bishop of Paris, was sufficiently widely known through the *Life of St Geneviève*, and may well, as M. Levillain suggests, have been propagated by the church of Paris since the time of Clovis.[6] But this is conjecture.[7] I merely observe that Gregory's failure to say very much about St Denis and his church is susceptible of two

[1] See A. Marignan, *Le culte des saints sous les mérovingiens* (1899), *passim*, and H. F. Muller, *L'époque mérovingienne* (New York, 1945), p. 82.

[2] *Hist.*, x, 31.

[3] *Carmina*, x, 6 (ed. F. Leo, *M.G.H.*, *Auct. Antiq.*, iv, 234–8).

[4] Cf. the *Libellus alter de consecratione ecclesiae Sancti Dionysii* (E. Panofsky, *Abbot Suger on the Abbey Church of St Denis*, Princeton, 1946).

[5] *Liber in gloria martyrum*, 32, 57 (ed. Arndt and Krusch, pp. 507, 527), on commercial activity in Tours during the feast of St Martin.

[6] L. Levillain, 'La crise des années 507–508 et les rivalités d'influence en Gaule de 508 à 613', *Mélanges Iorga*, pp. 564 ff. On the cult of St Denis in the fifth and sixth centuries, see also S. M. Crosby, *The Abbey of St Denis*, 475–1122, i (Yale, 1942), chaps. 1 and 2.

[7] Margaret Deanesly, 'Canterbury and Paris in the reign of Aethelberht', *History*, xxvi (1941), p. 98, does not consider St Denis a serious rival to St. Martin earlier than the reign of Dagobert.

interpretations, and that in any case the cult of St Martin was a fire that needed regular stoking.

We come, then, to Gregory as a writer. Gregory is the principal hagiographical authority of the sixth century; no other writer approaches him in importance,[1] and this I suspect he would have considered his chief claim to literary distinction. He was, after all, bishop of a city famed for its school and for a fine tradition of letters. Not primarily a classical tradition; Gregory's knowledge of the great Latin authors, whether acquired at Clermont or Tours, was patchy. He wrote a barbarized Latin, such as his *clerici* would understand, the roots of it lying deep in the corpus of Christian Latin literature, and notably, perhaps, in St Jerome.[2] Not the least of a bishop's duties was to teach; and Gregory's hagiographical writings were to serve as a basis for teaching and exposition. In the preface to the *Liber in gloria confessorum* he refutes the charge that a man who cannot distinguish ablative from accusative or masculine from feminine is unfitted to write for the instruction of his church; let those who wish it polish and develop his work to their heart's content; he has done his duty: 'opus vestrum facio'.[3] The *libri miraculorum* were Gregory's extensive contribution to the instruction of a possibly quite small but clearly-envisaged circle in the School of Tours. I cannot accept the view of a recent critic, Signor Vinay, that the *libri* are pedestrian work that in no way distinguish their author from his contemporaries.[4] They are much more than that, though this is not to say that any of them is conceived on the same scale as the *Historia*, or that they are built in the same manner from comparable material. Gregory did distinguish, vaguely, between the functions of an historian and a hagiographer. He knew from experience that the hagiographer, especially when reporting recent events, needed to produce convincing evidence in situations where the historian would be excused the trouble. Even the 'relationem bonorum virorum et

[1] E. W. Kemp, *Canonization and Authority in the Western Church* (Oxford, 1948), p. 31.
[2] His language can no longer be studied, as by Max Bonnet (*Le Latin de Grégoire de Tours*, 1890), without regard to the problems raised by manuscript transmission. Cf. Jeanne Vielliard, *Le Latin des diplômes royaux et chartes privées de l'époque mérovingienne* (1927), p. viii, and Vinay, op. cit. p. 42.
[3] *Liber in gloria confessorum*, pref. (ed. Arndt and Krusch), p. 748.
[4] Op. cit. p. 98.

certae fidei' [1] was insufficient: their very names were required by readers prepared to scoff. Inscriptions had to be reported in detail; and *Passiones*, a form of hagiographical writing inspiring general confidence, had to be drawn upon heavily. [2] Such care for authentication was, after all, a natural corollary for adherents of a faith the attraction of which was partly thaumaturgic. If we wish to watch Gregory at work as an accurate and persuasive reporter of his own doings the place to look is not in the *Historia*. We learn nothing from the *Historia* of his visits to Vienne, [3] or Saintes, [4] or Bordeaux, [5] and if we do learn of them in the *libri miraculorum* it is not because the writer desires to reveal autobiographical detail but because only thus can he vouch for the truth of what he has to tell. The hagiographer's task was to that extent more burdensome than the historian's. He was surrounded by experts in the same *genre* of letters; he wrote for a curious and critical public.

R. L. Poole, a scholar little likely to underestimate the claims of Bede, considered Gregory of Tours the first medieval historian, and indeed the first historian since Ammianus Marcellinus (more than two centuries his senior) who should not more properly be described as epitomizer, biographer, or annalist. [6] This was a far-reaching claim to have staked, and one that may do something less than justice to the great name of Orosius; indeed, it would be right to emphasize Gregory's debt to the Spanish historian. [7] But Gregory himself was none the less an historian; and scholars nowadays are perhaps more concerned than was an older generation to inquire why this should have been so, and why Gregory wrote history and not annals. In his *Historia* Gregory makes two important statements about the nature of the work he had undertaken. The first, in the opening paragraph of Book I, was probably written between 576 and 580. It explains what the author

---

[1] *Glor. conf.*, pref., p. 747.

[2] As in *Glor. mart.*, 34, 35, 37, 47, 56, 85, 103, 104, and *Glor. conf.*, 76; cf. discussion in Vinay, op. cit. p. 147.

[3] *Virt. S. Juliani*, 2, p. 564.      [4] *Virt. S. Martini*, iii, 51, p. 644; iv, 31, p. 657.

[5] *Glor. conf.*, 44, p. 775.

[6] *Chronicles and Annals* (Oxford, 1926), p. 8.

[7] Pierre Courcelle has quite plausibly suggested, thinking along similar lines, that Commodian, hitherto regarded as living in the third century, probably belonged to the fifth, and does this by revealing the poet's reliance upon Orosius. ('Commodien et les invasions du Vᵉ siècle', *Revue des Études Latines*, xxiv, 1946.) See also Dekkers and Gaar, *Clavis Patrum*, 1470-1.

hoped to achieve. He says that he is going to write about the wars of the kings with hostile peoples, of the martyrs with the heathen, and of the churches with the heretics; 'scribturus bella regum cum gentibus adversis, martyrum cum paganis, eclesiarum cum hereticis'; at the same time, to comfort those of his readers who are frightened because the end of the world approaches, he will include extracts from the chroniclers and historians to show how many years have elapsed since the world began; but first, he adds, he must make a detailed statement about the faith he holds, 'ut qui legerit me non dubitet esse catholicum'; this he proceeds to make at some length, holding it to be relevant and interesting.

Now, it has been argued that Gregory's ideas developed considerably while he wrote the *Historia*, and that his original plan, so simply enunciated, was soon left behind and forgotten.[1] I am not convinced that this was so. Gregory could and did get muddled, but he could scarcely have departed in principle from his intention to describe the wars (that is, the Frankish wars – *bella regum*, *bella martyrum*, *bella ecclesiarum*) in a Catholic setting; for times were bad, and were going to get worse. Christians still needed reassurance. Gregory saw himself as a Catholic historian, and I cannot therefore disagree with M. Halphen when he writes that the *Historia* was an 'œuvre d'édification'.[2] Interpreted in a broad sense, all historical writing that depended upon the Augustinian view of history was of this sort: edification or elucidation, even special pleading, was of its very substance and distinguished it sharply from the work of the classical historians. Ammianus' continuation of Tacitus, coming very near to St Augustine in date, is the last considerable historical statement in the tradition of Antiquity. The writer was a tolerant polytheist, his intolerance being reserved almost exclusively for the barbarians (that is, the Germans) whose activities seemed to him to be casting the Roman world into another mould.[3] St Augustine himself was not a writer of history; but he thought deeply about the political implications of Christian, and specifically of Catholic, doctrine, perceived that it could offer no quarter to the antique concept of the *circuitus*

---

[1] Vinay, op. cit. pp. 76 ff.

[2] 'Grégoire de Tours, historien de Clovis', *Mélanges Ferdinand Lot* (1925), p. 240.

[3] Cf. E. A. Thompson, *The historical work of Ammianus Marcellinus* (Cambridge, 1947), p. 5, and M. L. W. Laistner in *The Greater Roman Historians* (Berkeley, 1947).

*temporum* upon which all classical historical technique rested,[1] and outlined a view of the historical process more revolutionary than is commonly allowed. The first Catholic Christian to put St Augustine's historical ideas to practical use was his disciple Orosius; and it is Orosius' way of looking at history that we find in Cassiodorus, Gregory of Tours, Isidore of Seville, Bede, and, through them, in the historians of the Middle Ages.[2]

The nature of the indebtedness of each of these historians to Orosius is a difficult question, and involves much more than the borrowing of phrases or material. If the latter were all that had to be considered, it might well be justifiable to contend, as does Vinay, that Gregory had no more from Orosius than he could find in the early Frankish annals – if such existed.[3] But this is insufficient. How should Gregory have succeeded in writing like Orosius, and not like Ammianus, if he had not first had experience of Orosius? The companion-piece to Gregory's introductory remarks on his duties as an historian is to be found not in Ammianus or in Suetonius but in Orosius' dedication of his seven books to St Augustine: 'you instructed me to answer the vain and perverse chatter of those aliens to the City of God who are called *pagani* because they are country folk, or *gentiles* because they are wise about the things of this world'.[4] Gregory never had to encounter learned pagans, such as Orosius faced; but paganism he knew well, not that of the still unconverted Germanic world but the paganism of his own countryside; and heresy – notably Arianism – was his constant dread. Whether he was right so to dread Arianism is another matter. It may be that the Visigoths had never been very successful, or even keen, proselytizers. But Gregory is difficult to refute. It is not, then, surprising that his historical writing should borrow something of shape and temper from Catholic apologetic. Gregory became an historian because the Catholic communities of Gaul seemed to him to stand in an imminent danger; the times

---

[1] *De Civ. Dei*, xii, 18–20.

[2] Laistner, *Intellectual Heritage*, pp. 13 ff., is altogether too hard on Orosius. A. Momigliano, 'Cassiodorus and Italian culture of his time', *Proc. British Acad.*, xli, 1955, is disposed to consider Cassiodorus the last of the ancients among Roman historians.

[3] Op. cit. 197–200.

[4] Ed. Zangemeister, *Corpus Script. Eccles. Lat.*, v (1882), p. 3.

were bad enough to call forth an explanation: his own church, the church of Tours, required it. In the preface to the completed *Historia*, written at the end of his life, Gregory speaks with an urgent gravity; there is no one but himself left in Gaul to recount and explain what has been happening:

> feretas gentium desaeviret, regum furor acueretur, aeclesiae impugnarentur ab hereticis, a catholicis tegerentur, ferveret Christi fides in plurimis, tepisceret in nonnullis, ipsae quoque aeclesiae vel ditarentur a devotis vel nudarentur a perfidis . . . ingemiscebant saepius plerique, dicentes: vae diebus nostris!

This is plain enough; the preface to the completed work is from the pen of a man a good deal sadder than was the author of the prefatory remarks to Book I. But Gregory's view of his historical duty had not changed.

It is worth giving further consideration to the matter of Arianism. Gregory insists, throughout his writings, that he is a true Catholic and a believer in the Trinitarian doctrine; the God who brings victory to kings in battle and fruitful peace to their peoples, the God whose saints' remains work miracles, is the Catholic God and none other. The Arian God, in whose shape most of the East Germans had first met Christianity, made fewer demands on the intelligence than did the Catholic God and hence – provided he proved a good God – was likely to be the more attractive.[1] The complex doctrine of the Trinity must have seemed strangely unnecessary, not to say impolitic, to men who judged their gods on results and preferred not to confuse them with human beings. Gregory himself tells of the difficulties he had with Chilperic I, a Catholic king of the third generation who insisted on his own interpretation of Trinitarian doctrine, coming thereby dangerously near Arianism,[2] or rather, Sabellianism. The Catholic victory had not been completed with the conversion of Clovis, and in Gregory's day – which was also the day of Pope Gregory the Great – it was still not assured. We ought to take some notice of Gregory's preoccupation with Arianism and special loathing of its most formidable adherents, the Visigoths. Reccared's conversion,

---

[1] See the remarks of R. Latouche, *Les grandes invasions et la crise de l'occident au Vᵉ siècle* (1946), p. 282.
[2] *Hist.*, v, 44.

in Gregory's own lifetime, was only the first step towards the conversion of his people. The Arian theme runs right through the *Historia*. Gregory may have been a mediocre theologian,[1] but he grasped the political implications of Arianism, in which, rightly or not, he saw the hall-mark of the Goths.

Following the only tradition known to him, Gregory saw the past from the standpoint of a Christian moralist. One unhappy result of this has been to induce scholars to adopt the same approach, and modern work on the Franks has thus taken the line either of corroborating Gregory's harsh judgements or of dismissing them. Sir Samuel Dill was a notable instance of a scholar who accepted what he took to be Gregory's verdict, and, assisted by an exaggerated view of the preceding Roman Peace, condemned the Franks outright as unspeakably vile. As he wrote at the end of his chapters on morals:

> It is the most pathetic lesson of history that the labours and happiness of peaceful development are so often wiped out by the upburst of elemental passions which have only slumbered. The long tranquillity of the Roman sway ended in the violence and darkness of the Middle Age. The golden age of Victoria issued in social hysteria, the carnage of a world-wide conflict, the greed of the profiteer, and the destructive fury of anarchism.[2]

M. Prou, on the other hand, saw fit to impugn Gregory's evidence and to argue that the Franks could not possibly have been as bad as he pretended they were.[3] In the opinion of M. Ferdinand Lot, revising in 1940 his part of the fine book originally published in 1934, Prou was wrong and Dill was right: 'l'époque mérovingienne a mauvaise réputation'.[4] Of course the Merovingians have a bad reputation. They were men of blood – more so, perhaps, than some of their detractors realize; let them read M. Hoyoux on Merovingian scalping.[5] But how relevant is this reputation to

---

[1] Vinay, op. cit. p. 22.

[2] *Roman Society*, p. 306. Dill's book was published, posthumously, in 1926.

[3] *La Gaule mérovingienne* (1897), pp. 179 and 235.

[4] Lot, Pfister and Ganshof, *Les destinées de l'Empire en Occident de 395 à 888*, p. 383.

[5] J. Hoyoux, 'Reges criniti: chevelures, tonsures et scalps chez les Mérovingiens', *Rev. belge de philol. et d'hist.*, xxvi, 479–508. Not that he is likely to be right in his main contention, as is shown by E. Kaufmann, Über das Scheren abgesetzter Merowinger', *Zeitschrift der Savigny-Stiftung, Germ. Abt.*, 72 (1955).

our study of the Franks? Why should we bother about their turpitude, when we are so little concerned with that of the Anglo-Saxons? What was the point of Gregory's picture of the immoral Franks?

It is the merit of Signor Vinay to have made a valuable contribution to the answering of these questions, and to have shown that Gregory's attitude towards the Franks was rather more complicated than is generally allowed. In the first place, Gregory made no thoroughgoing distinction between Franks and Gallo-Romans of his own generation. Even in the south, Gallo-Roman gentry and barbarians had mixed; intermarriage had been taking place for generations. Fusion had come about. Gregory's history marks the recognition of this fact; a *vir senatorius*, he wrote for neither strain, but for both. This is the less surprising when one reflects, in the light of modern archaeological and place-name study, on the initial thinness of the Frankish settlement, even in northern Gaul, where administrative centres still retained their Roman names.[1] The Franks had never been a close-knit people, distinct from other Germans and resolved to have nothing to do with the Gallo-Romans. Frankish chieftains, as Professor Koebner points out, were not necessarily accompanied by great followings of Frankish warriors and settlers; and their graves are found in places long favoured by the Gallo-Roman nobility, including the old urban centres.[2] Racial fusion, therefore, was not difficult; and it may perhaps be that, as in contemporary England, a good Roman occasionally lurked behind a Germanic or germanized name.

But if Gregory is not much concerned to disentangle the races in his own day, he emphasizes clearly enough the distinctness of the Franks of the generation of Clovis. Indeed, he may even over-emphasize it, in his anxiety to focus attention on the newcomers as a people of very special characteristics who had something to

[1] Édouard Salin, *La civilisation mérovingienne d'après les sépultures, les textes et le laboratoire*, pt. i (Paris, 1950), discusses the problems involved in attempting to distinguish Frankish from other burials. For the phasing of Frankish colonizing activity, see A. Bergengruen, *Adel und Grundherrschaft im Merowingerreich* (1958).

[2] 'The Settlement and Colonization of Europe', *Camb. Econ. Hist.*, i, (1942), p. 35. Kurt Böhner, 'Die Frage der Kontinuität zwischen Altertum und Mittelalter', *Trierer Zeitschrift*, xix, 1950, shows how, in the Frankish Rhineland, early churches were built over pagan ancestors' graves and cemeteries, and how Christ as protector and conqueror appealed to the Franks of the Rhineland as a motif for gravestones.

bring to Gaul and a mission to perform in it. Their particular gift, for which he never conceals his admiration, was virility. The Goths, by contrast, were cowardly and ignoble[1] as, on the personal plane, was that Arcadius who allowed Theuderic to devastate the Auvergne: 'interea Arcadius sceleris illius auctor, cuius ignavia regio devastata est, Bituricas urbem petiit'.[2] On the other hand, the rebel Munderic, when betrayed and cornered, stood his ground and fought to his last breath against fearful odds, like the hero of a *chanson de geste*; he had virility and Gregory loved it.[3] But to one outlet for Frankish virility Gregory shows a very different reaction, when he exposes the weaknesses of the Merovingians of his own generation. In the preface to Book V, where the history of his own times begins, Gregory castigates the Frankish kings for their *bella civilia*, the dreadful feuds within the same kindred which, as Orosius had shown,[4] could only lead to ruin. Let there be peace between Franks. But that was not to say that there should be peace with their natural enemies: 'would that you, O kings, were practised in such wars as those in which your fathers toiled in the sweat of their brows, so that the peoples, in awe of your unity, might be subjected by your might!'

> Recordamini quid capud victoriarum vestrarum Chlodovechus fecerit, qui adversos reges interficit, noxias gentes elisit, patrias subjugavit, quarum regnum vobis integrum inlaesumque reliquit![5]

And all this Clovis did without silver or gold!

Virility of this nature was not, it may be, very far removed from *feretas* or *saevitas*; but Gregory did not appear to object. *Feretas* was neither good nor bad of itself; it must be borne patiently by those upon whom barbarians fall. There is almost a cleansing quality about it. One thinks of Bede's admiring account of the terrifying Æthelfrith of Northumbria, the ravening wolf, 'rex fortissimus et gloriae cupidissimus . . . qui plus omnibus Anglorum primatibus gentem vastavit Brettonum;[6] or, again, of the four-

---

[1] *Hist.*, ii, 27. Yet Athaulf, according to Orosius, planned to restore Roman prestige *Gothorum viribus* (ed. Zangemeister), vii, 43, p. 300.

[2] Ibid., iii, 12.  [3] Ibid., iii, 14.

[4] *Hist. adversum paganos*, v, 8 (ed. Zangemeister), p. 296.  [5] *Hist.*, v, pref.

[6] *Hist. Eccles.*, i, 34 (ed. Plummer), p. 71.

teenth and fifteenth chapters of Book I of the *Ecclesiastical History*, where Bede, following Gildas, describes the collapse of the luxurious Britons, *corruptae mentis*, before the savage English. Archaeology, too, bears witness to the cult of virility among the Franks, as, for example, in the tuft of hair concealed behind an eighth-century belt-buckle from St Quentin.[1]

Another, and more pleasing, aspect of barbarian virility was *strenuitas*, or vigour, though sometimes it meant no more than plain violence. The dissolute Childeric was redeemed by this quality, for which alone his wife Basina sought him out: 'novi . . . utilitatem tuam, quod sis valde strenuus'.[2] It is a word, once more, of which Bede was fond: he used it of Penda, Cadwalla, Acca, and Tatfrid; and so also was Orosius. It must not be claimed that these martial qualities were the exclusive possession of the barbarian invaders, or that Antiquity had not known how to praise vigour; but it does seem worthy of note that Gregory belongs to that small company of Dark-Age historians, who, recounting the barbarian impact upon one or other province of the empire, noted especially the ferocious vigour of the settlers, and counted it a virtue. Perhaps it is best summed up in Jordanes, another member of the company, in his well-known version of the burial song for Attila, *fortissimarum gentium dominus*, in which song, unlike Professor E. A. Thompson,[3] one may catch no echo of the rhythmical beauty of the original, but yet catch a very strong echo of one barbarian quality that appealed especially to the civilized West.

To Gregory, then, his Merovingian contemporaries seemed little men in comparison with their great predecessor, Clovis. They lacked the redeeming barbarian virtues, though not the vices. One cannot help feeling that Gregory's merciless dealing with them should put us somewhat on our guard. After all, he had reasons for accentuating the vice of the present as against the virtue of the past; and, even if the absence of vendetta may have appeared to him the proper state of affairs, in practice he was involved in a

[1] Cf. Salin, *La civilisation mérovingienne*, iv (1959), pp. 55 ff., and his general discussion of the phylacteries and offerings found among Frankish grave-goods.
[2] *Hist.*, ii, 12. J. P. Bodmer, *Der Krieger der Merowingerzeit und seine Welt* (1957), p. 56, brings together several instances of the use of *strenuitas* and *utilitas*.
[3] *A History of Attila and the Huns* (Oxford, 1948), p. 149.

society where, in Miss Whitelock's phrase, 'vengeance was not so much the gratification of a personal grudge as a duty one owed to the community, for the maintenance of law and order'.[1] Furthermore, the chieftains whom Gregory attacks for their boorishness were among the very men who found pleasure in listening to Venantius Fortunatus and who developed an appetite for some quite intricate Latin versifying.[2] The implications of this striving towards culture have been the subject of research by Professor Reto Bezzola,[3] and will probably stand further investigation, though it is right to add that Bezzola's interpretation of the rôle of Fortunatus revises the traditional picture of Merovingian civilization without destroying it.[4]

But no amount of research will remove the fact that Gregory has a hero, who meant to him something of what Ermanaric meant to Jordanes and Edwin to Bede. Clovis is the *magnus et pugnator egregius*[5] of the whole *History of the Franks*, the founder of a dynasty, the great conqueror. However, there is this difference between Jordanes' hero and Gregory's: Ermanaric, mighty in legend,[6] was not the direct forebear of the Ostrogothic dynasty;[7] but Clovis was the direct forebear of Gregory's Merovingians; and Gregory had, therefore, less occasion than did Jordanes to distort the received traditions of the rise to power of the reigning dynasty. The name of Clovis might well have lived in Frankish tradition without assistance from Gregory; and deliberate distortion is surely not to be imputed to Gregory in his account of the main historical outlines of Clovis' career. The examination to which, in recent years, scholars have subjected Gregory on Clovis, has, on the whole, brought him unexpected credit, even though his chronology needs some serious adjustment. It is now accepted by

[1] 'Anglo-Saxon Poetry and the Historian', *Trans. Roy. Hist. Soc.*, 4th ser., xxxi (1949), p. 84.

[2] The real cultural decline in Gaul started in the seventh century. Cf. W. Levison, *England and the Continent in the Eighth Century* (Oxford, 1946), pp. 150 ff. and Appendix x.

[3] *Les Origines et la formation de la littérature courtoise en Occident*, i (1944), chap. 4.

[4] Curtius, *European Literature*, p. 412, shows how Bezzola, or those he follows, must have misunderstood the Merovingian usage of *dulcedo*.

[5] *Hist.*, ii, 12.

[6] Cf. Caroline Brady, *The Legends of Ermanaric* (Berkeley, 1943).

[7] P. Grierson, 'Election and Inheritance in early Germanic Kingship', *Camb. Hist. Journ.*, vii (1941).

many scholars that Gregory, or his informants, placed Clovis'
conversion, marriage, and campaign against the Alamans ten years
too early, and by so doing made it appear that Clovis had undertaken all his great campaigns as a Catholic.[1] M. Van de Vyver, in a
series of arresting articles, has boldly rearranged Gregory's chronology in a manner which he claims is more than mere juggling with
dates: it is the rearrangement demanded by political sense.[2] Instead of Gregory's remorseless champion of Catholicism, we could
now accept a Clovis who was not concerned with conversion to
Catholicism till 503 – that is, till within eight years of his death. (It
would be another matter to say that he was not concerned with,
or trusted by, Catholics before that date.)

This chronological revision carries with it a reinterpretation of a
whole chapter of Frankish history. The new Clovis and his people
seem to have been dominated, as were also the Ripuarians and
Burgundians, by fear of the Alamans. The victory of Tolbiac re-
leased them from this, and at the same time broke the barrier of
peoples that had been containing the Franks in northern Gaul, in
the old kingdom of Syagrius. Theodoric welcomed the remnant of
the Alamans into his Italian kingdom but also gave Clovis a plain
warning that he must stop. At this point, and not before, Clovis
reached his great decision to be converted, not to Arianism but to
Catholicism, his wife's faith. The effect of this was to place the
Franks and the Eastern Empire in one camp and the Arian world,
led by Theodoric, in another. Again, despite the warnings of
Theodoric, Clovis (now a Catholic) attacked the Visigoths; Theodoric was forced to intervene to save them, while the imperial
fleet attacked the coast of Apulia and Clovis received imperial
recognition on his way north to Paris. M. Van de Vyver concludes
that the unexpected death of Clovis, in 511, was a stroke of good

[1] M. Chaume offers criticism of details in 'Francs et Burgondes au cours du VI<sup>e</sup>
siècle', *Recherches d'histoire chrétienne et médiévale* (Dijon, 1947), pp. 147–62 (reprinted
from *Mém. de L'Acad. de Dijon*, 1940–2).

[2] 'Clovis et la politique méditerranéene', *Études d'histoire dédiées à la mémoire de
Henri Pirenne* (Brussels, 1937); 'La victoire contre les Alamans et la conversion de
Clovis', *Rev. belge de philol. et d'hist.*, xv (1936) and xvi (1937); 'L'unique victoire
contre les Alamans et la conversion de Clovis en 506', ibid., xvii (1938). The last
article is a rebuttal of criticisms advanced by M. Lot (ibid., xvii, 1938). See also the
criticisms of J. Calmette in *Académie des inscriptions* (1946) and *Le Moyen Age*, 53
(1947).

luck for Theodoric, strong though the latter was. Now, although Gregory's picture of the crusading Frank is seriously challenged, the political importance of Clovis' belated conversion gains rather than loses by the dramatic speed of events from 503 onwards. Once the Alaman peril was removed, Clovis was no longer afraid to extend his marauding booty-raids in the obvious direction – towards the rich Mediterranean lands; and he was prepared to do so with the certainty that the Ostrogoths would take the field against him. He may have been heartened by imperial support; indeed, it probably meant more to him than M. Van de Vyver allows. But the risk was great. What drove him on was his endless search for treasure, his fear of the Germanic peoples across the Rhine, and the traditional hatred of Franks for Visigoths. The attack on Alaric could have happened without Clovis' conversion, though possibly the result might have been different. Clovis was not primarily moved by Catholic zeal (though it must not be thought that at any time he was unfriendly to Christians) and the southerners who longed for him to free them from Alaric were not simply escaping the Arian discipline. They were impressed by his reputation as a warrior – 'habere Francos dominos summo desiderio cupiebant' [1] – and so they sought him for their overlord in the place of the timid Visigoth; or some, at least, of them did. Gregory does not mention that Clovis and his successors suffered severe reverses in their Visigothic wars. He has suppressed something but has not falsified his picture. A *dominus* who could win and hold the loyalty of warriors had to show the active virtues of a Clovis; he could never afford to be passive.

On his return from Bordeaux and the south, laden with Gothic treasure, Clovis stopped at Tours, where he returned thanks and made gifts to the saint under whose aegis, if Gregory is right, he had gone to war with Alaric. He there received from the legate of the Emperor Anastasius 'codecillos de consolatu' and clothed himself in a purple tunic and diadem, and rode through the streets distributing gold and silver; and from that day, says Gregory, 'tamquam consul aut augustus est vocitatus'. [2] Gregory has been

---

[1] *Hist.*, ii, 35.
[2] Ibid., ii, 38; cf. editorial note on *codecillos* in the Krusch-Levison ed., fasc. 1, p. 88. Ensslin (*Hist. Jahrb.*, 56, 1936, p. 507) reads *ut* for *aut*.

taken to task for inaccuracy here.[1] Even scholars who think that he knew what he meant believe that the title was of very little significance to Clovis himself, who was, and remained, independent of the Eastern emperor.[2] But it is not difficult to credit Clovis with the wish to be subordinate to Anastasius, though this may not have been the intention of his clerical advisers. The *Augustus* shouts at Tours are more likely to have been the spontaneous acclamations of the people (no doubt led by the clergy) than part of an official imperial proclamation, the effect of which would have been to make Clovis a colleague in the empire. It is just conceivable that Clovis had in mind the imperial pretensions of Athaulf and the imperial titles bestowed by their followers on Thrasamund and Theodoric.[3] To get any nearer Clovis' own intentions is plainly impossible; but one must note the recent suggestion of Professor Courcelle[4] that the intention of the church of Tours was to revive the Western Empire in the person of Clovis, and that this same intention finds its reflection in Gregory of Tours and later in Alcuin. The Constantinian tradition depicted in the famous Lateran mosaic may have been cherished at Tours since the days of Gregory, to whom it had seemed perfectly natural to recognize in Clovis the *novus Constantinus*.[5] This is conjecture, but it has its value to students of the *Historia Francorum*. Whatever tends to relate the author to the circumstances of the church of St Martin deserves to be reflected upon.

Since the publication in 1928 of M. Lot's book on the *impôt foncier*,[6] scholars have considered at leisure its implications for early medieval studies; but they may not have considered it sufficiently in relation to Gregory of Tours, of whom M. Lot made much use. It is claimed that the fiscal reorganization of the Later Empire,

---

[1] Lot, Pfister and Ganshof, op. cit. p. 193.

[2] Cf. Marc Bloch, 'Observations sur la conquête de la Gaule romaine par les rois francs', *Rev. hist.*, cliv (1927), p. 178.

[3] To Ennodius, for example, Theodoric exercised 'imperialis auctoritas' (*Libellus pro synodo*, ed. Hartel, *Corpus Script. Eccles. Lat.*, vi, 1882, p. 298).

[4] *Histoire littéraire des grandes invasions germaniques* (1948), p. 204.

[5] *Hist.*, ii, 31. Van de Vyver, 'La victoire contre les Alamans', p. 79, seems unduly sceptical of the possibility that Eusebius (*Eccl. Hist.*, ix, 9) on the conversion of Constantine could have had some part in shaping events in Gaul.

[6] *L'impôt foncier et la capitation personnelle sous le Bas-Empire et à l'époque franque* (Bibl. de l'école des hautes études, fasc. 253). Lot does not change his position in the complementary volume, *Nouvelles recherches sur l'impôt foncier* (1955).

complicated though it was, worked unchallenged in Gaul as elsewhere until, with the coming of the barbarians, public burdens ceased to be borne by the state and accordingly public contributions, in the form of *capitatio terrena* and *capitatio humana et plebeia*, became anachronistic and indefensible. Direct taxation had, of course, always been resented; M. Lot was within his rights in suggesting a literary tradition of hostility to such taxation at least from Lactantius[1] through Salvian to Gregory himself. The evidence is altogether slighter for the view that Merovingian determination to continue the Roman system of taxation, with increasingly burdensome reassessments, was hated because nothing came of it beyond the personal enrichment of the Merovingians. Gregory hated it because the church, a great landlord, had a vested interest against all taxation. He is proud to relate how he resisted the tax-assessors of Childebert II[2] and tells with relish the story of Chilperic and Fredegundis casting the new tax-lists into the fire.[3] Also, he mentions riots caused by the activities of tax-collectors.[4] But nowhere does he hint that the unproductiveness of taxation was what men hated; they made no comparisons with the past. The true grounds for his attitude are surely that he did not understand why the barbarian kings could not live of their own, and live upon the imperial fisc they inherited, without levies and contributions. Gregory could not be expected to foresee the economic consequences of the alienation of the fisc and of the policy of the granting of immunity pursued by the Merovingians. The Merovingians desperately needed gold,[5] for without it the largesse upon which the loyalty of their followers so greatly depended would be impossible. The hoarding of gold by the barbarian kings is not more remarkable than the liberality with which they distributed it.[6] The need for gold and treasure drove the Frankish kings to venture after venture outside their own territories – notably to Spain and to Italy – and such

[1] *Lib. de mort. persec.*, 23; cf. Lot, op. cit. p. 21.

[2] *Hist.*, ix, 30.     [3] Ibid., v, 34.          [4] Ibid., v, 28.

[5] Cf. S. Hellmann, 'Studien zur mittelalterlichen Geschichtsschreibung: 1, Gregor von Tours', *Hist. Zeitschr*, cvii (1911), p. 5, and the recent article of Madame R. Doehaerd, 'La richesse des Mérovingiens', *Studi in onore di Gino Luzzatto* (Milan, 1949), pp. 30–46. H. Pirenne, *Mahomet et Charlemagne*, pp. 88, 89, considered that customs and dues accounted for a good deal of Merovingian wealth.

[6] Dalton misunderstood the situation when he wrote: 'prodigality was seldom absent, and all the easy chances of a surplus thrown away' (op. cit. i, 219).

seemed to their followers the correct way of replenishing a royal treasure-hoard. To levy contributions upon the lands that were held as a reward for loyal service was to invite trouble.

When, therefore, Gregory disapproves of Merovingian taxation he is voicing the objection of all landlords, Frankish and Roman, lay and ecclesiastical; and, in his simple way, he gives the other side of the story in reporting the famous words of Chilperic: 'pauper remansit fiscus noster'.[1] The bishops, thought the king, were the men with the money. The amount of gold available to the Merovingians would not have been much in relation to what was available, let us say, to East Rome.[2] But Gregory was impressed by the huge quantities involved, as he was impressed by the metal itself. He knew that, besides booty and taxes, the Merovingians filled their treasure chests with Byzantine subsidies[3] and obtained other precious objects from Byzantium.[4] He did not know that the very taxation he detested was in part responsible for the vigour of the Gallo-Frankish coinage. In the words of Dr Sutherland,

> what cannot be doubted is that the necessity for gold coinage was kept at a high level by the taxation system which the Merovingian kings imposed; taxes were probably payable in gold, and one result of Chilperic's 'new and burdensome assessments' must have been an increase in the amount of bullion then coined.[5]

Merovingian gold coinage does not drop seriously in weight before the middle of the seventh century, and up to that time is sustained by adequate, if irregular, supplies of bullion, derived mainly from the sources already referred to but in part also, perhaps, by the release of pagan temple treasures, and by trade.

Gregory is dangerous evidence on the subject of trade. Dr Baynes infers from Gregory's patchy knowledge of southern Italy

---

[1] *Hist.*, vi; and, much to the same effect, the gibe at SS. Martin and Martial, ibid., IV, 16.

[2] Lot, Pfister and Ganshof, op. cit. p. 365.

[3] *Hist.*, vi, 42.     [4] Ibid., vi, 2.

[5] C. H. V. Sutherland, *Anglo-Saxon gold coinage in the light of the Crondall hoard* (Oxford, 1948), p. 21, and chap. 3, *passim*. It should be emphasized, however, that the study of Merovingian coinage has not yet advanced very far and that numismatists, and historians still more, hesitate to draw firm political conclusions from the coin-evidence as at present understood.

and Byzantium that he was only exceptionally able to inform himself on happenings in these parts; he had 'no regular source of information for eastern affairs such as would have been furnished by traders had they been in continued relation with the ports of the eastern empire'.[1] It is, perhaps, unfair to divorce Dr Baynes' view from the wider context of his argument that western Mediterranean trade never recovered from the Vandals; but it is based upon an assumption about Gregory's avidity for any information at any time that is rather hard to make. Probably Gregory selected his information with an eye to his purpose, which was no more to write a history of the Empire than it was to write a history of Anglo-Saxon England. However, Dr Baynes is caution itself as compared with Nils Aberg, who, arguing largely from Gregory's reference to the papyrus trade, contends that the habits of the Franks were Roman and that their need for imports across the Mediterranean was constant.[2] Either way, Gregory is dangerous evidence.

Why, then, was the *Historia* written? Plainly, not to humour the Austrasian court; nor to pander to Merovingian liking for the language of learning. It was meant to be attractive, to sound well, to seem authentic, to impress; and to judge from the manuscripts that remain, it succeeded.[3] Even Bede paid Gregory the compliment of using him, so that, as Levison wrote, 'Gregory thus may have influenced the design of his not unworthy Anglo-Saxon successor in historiography'.[4] (In fact, it seems to me that Bede's debt may be somewhat greater.) To whom, more than to the *clerici* of Tours, would the *Historia* have seemed attractive and useful? To them, and indirectly to the steady stream of visitors and pilgrims to St Martin's shrine, men and women of position and substance coming from all over Gaul and beyond, the *Historia* was surely directed. Here is the historical aspect of the story Gregory had been telling in his hagiographical writings, and it is presented

[1] *Journ. Rom. Studies*, xix (1929), pp. 231–4. Gregory and his circle were rather well informed about Spain. Cf. C. W. Barlow, *Martini Episcopi Bracarensis opera omnia* (1950), chap. I, and Pierre David, *Études historiques sur la Galice et le Portugal du VIe au XIIe siècle* (1947), pp. 117–18.
[2] *The Occident and the Orient in the Art of the Seventh Century*, iii (Stockholm, 1947), p. 19.
[3] Lesne, op. cit., iv, 30–32.
[4] 'Bede as Historian', in *Bede, His Life, Times and Writings* (Oxford, 1935), p. 132. This article is reprinted in *Aus Rheinischer und Fränkischer Frühzeit*.

very nearly in the shape of a prose *geste* – so nearly so, that it was not irrelevant for him to suggest that it might go well into verse. More than that, it belongs to the tradition of Augustinian historical apologetic. It is the story of the barbarian settlement of a Roman province seen, not through Roman, but through Catholic eyes. Armed with this, the church of St Martin might well hope to satisfy the sceptical and to compete successfully for pilgrims with the guardians of St Denis, St Hilary and St Médard. Is it too much to conceive the works of Gregory (in stone and parchment) as an attempt to outbid competitors? Seen in this light, Gregory appears to make sense; see him, as does Dalton, as a writer who failed 'to bring into its due context that antagonism between the landed aristocracy and the Crown which was a cardinal fact of Merovingian history',[1] and he makes nonsense. We ought to obey Gregory's final injunction: 'ita omnia vobiscum integra inlibataque permaneant sicut a nobis relicta sunt'.[2]

[1] Op. cit. i, 30.  [2] *Hist.*, x, 31.

# CHAPTER FOUR

# Fredegar and the History of France[1]

\*

About the year A.D. 660 there died a certain Burgundian known to us, though perhaps not to his friends, as Fredegar or Fredegarius. We have no evidence earlier than the sixteenth century that he was so called, though Fredegar is an authentic Frankish name. He left behind him what, in a word, may be called a chronicle; and it is because of his chronicle, though it is no longer extant in its original form, that posterity is at all bothered with him.

This chronicle was of the nature of a private record that would have been known to very few; and, moreover, it was never finished. Even so, someone (one suspects from a local monastic or cathedral scriptorium, Chalon-sur-Saône perhaps, or Lyons or Luxeuil) got to know of Fredegar's manuscript, and made a copy of it, about a generation later. It was a bad copy, and it was a copy made for a special purpose: bad, because the scribe made heavy weather of the Merovingian cursive before him (his own writing is uncial); and for a special purpose, because he shaped Fredegar, with certain additions and subtractions, into what has been called a clerical *Lesebuch*. His inscription, where he reveals himself as the monk Lucerius, can still be read. Such as it is, this *Lesebuch* survives: it is a Paris manuscript, Bibl. Nat. Latin 10910, the basis of Bruno Krusch's Monumenta edition of Fredegar, and the basis, in my opinion, of any future edition worth the name.[2] Apart from this, we have some thirty other manuscripts of Fredegar (two of

---

[1] *Bulletin of the John Rylands Library*, vol. 40, no. 2 (March 1958). Based on a paper read to the Anglo-American Historical Conference in London on 9 July 1955.
[2] The standard edition is that of Bruno Krusch in *M.G.H., S.R.M.*, vol. ii (1888). My own edition of Book IV and the Continuations of the Chronicle (*Nelson's Medieval Classics*, 1960) contains a fuller discussion of some of the matters raised in this paper and includes a bibliography.

them Harleian manuscripts),[1] descended either, as Krusch held, from the clerical *Lesebuch* or from another copy of the original manuscript made at about the same time. None of those we have is older than the early ninth century, from which it may be inferred that Fredegar came into his own rather suddenly in the Carolingian age. He was copied, in whole or in part, throughout the Rhineland and northern France, from Mehrerau near Lake Constance through Lorsch and Rheims to the monasteries of the Ardennes; and he came to be associated, as one might expect, with copies of the Neustrian *Liber Historiae Francorum*, with Einhard, Bede, and other historians. The St Gallen MS. 547 is a good example of such an association. Fredegar was recognized as history – and as official history, at that. This came about because an early copy of the chronicle (of the late eighth century, it may be) travelled north into Austrasia and came to rest in some Carolingian stronghold, perhaps Metz. The subsequent proliferation of copies is from Austrasia, not from Burgundy. Here Fredegar had the good fortune to fall into the hands of the great family of the Nibelungen, close connections of the Carolingians through Alpaida, mother of Charles Martel; or rather, into the hands of a scribe employed by them to put together a chronicle of Frankish events as seen through Carolingian eyes. This chronicle, the work of several writers, is now known as the continuation of Fredegar; and though its ethos is in important respects unlike his own, it survives only in association with him. We may call the resulting amalgam official because, under the year 751, the continuator writes:

> Up to this point, the illustrious Count Childebrand, uncle of the said King Pippin, took great pains to have this history or 'geste' of the Franks recorded. What follows is by the authority of the illustrious Count Nibelung, Childebrand's son (cont. chap. 35).

Almost all our copies of Fredegar are found in this Austrasian guise, and quite naturally Fredegar reached the Middle Ages in the wake of the historical Nibelungen and under their *auctoritas*,

---

[1] Harley 5251 and 3771. Their contents are described in the *Catalogue of Ancient Manuscripts in the British Museum*, pt. ii (Latin), (1884), pp. 84–85.

carefully copied in great scriptoria that would not otherwise have known him. They made brave but unavailing efforts to 'correct' his highly individual Latin. By this route, too, he first reached the dignity of print, in the pages of Flacius Illyricus (Basel, 1568), Canisius, Scaliger, Freherus and others. Ruinart, in 1699, was the first editor to use a manuscript not of the Austrasian tradition. But the concern of this paper is less with the respectable manu- scripts of that tradition than with the little uncial *Lesebuch*, and what lay behind it. It contains, as it stands, the following items:

The *Liber Generationis*,[1] a Latin translation of the Chronicle of Hippolytus, with additions; the *Supputatio Eusebii-Hieronimi*, a computation from Adam to the first year of the reign of King Sigebert (613); a list of popes to the accession of Pope Theodore (642) later completed to the sixteenth year of Pope Hadrian I (640-1); interpolated extracts from the Chronicle of Eusebius, in St Jerome's version; interpolated extracts from the Chronicle of Hydatius, itself a continuation of St Jerome; a résumé or *Historia Epitomata* of the first six books of the History of Gregory of Tours, stopping at 584; an original chronicle in ninety chapters from the twenty-fourth year of King Guntramn of Burgundy (584, described by the chronicler as the beginning of the end of his reign) to the death of Flaochad, mayor of the Burgundian palace, in 642; extracts from the Chronicle of Isidore, with an *explicit* dated the fortieth year of the reign of King Chlotar (623-4).

A succession of scholars has tackled this intractable list, and though they do not agree about much, they do mostly agree that the order of contents is not quite as Fredegar left it, and in parti- cular that Isidore has become displaced from his rightful position as it is revealed in the important prologue. Some impression of how the chronicle was put together may be given as follows. Early in the seventh century a, to us, anonymous Burgundian de- cided to attach to some local annals a short chronicle of his own. The annals seem to have covered the period 584-604, though they may have gone back further. His chronicle covers the period 604-13. To this collection he added (though it might have

---

[1] M. L. W. Laistner, *Thought and Letters in Western Europe* (2nd ed., 1957), p. 178, has, by inadvertence, confused this with the *Liber Generationum*, the work of an African writer of the fifth century.

happened later) a kind of hand-book of world-chronology: it comprised Jerome, Hydatius, Isidore, and the *Liber Generationis*, though one cannot be sure about their order. He may have found this hand-book, or he may have put it together himself; one cannot tell. In any event, his maximum contribution was a chronological hand-book, some Burgundian annals and a short chronicle covering the decade between the ninth year of King Theuderic and the execution of Queen Brunechildis. He also brought up to date his chronological lists, so far as he was able. His work shows no exceptional knowledge and no indication that he held a privileged position. After a pause of another decade, his work was resumed by a second chronicler of very different calibre; and, to cut a long story short, this is the man with some claim to recognition and respect. Since it is a convenience to preserve the name, let him be Fredegar; let him be so, moreover, without the pedantic prefix 'Pseudo'. He is distinguishable from his predecessor on two grounds; first, his interests and, secondly, his style. A succession of French historians – Lot, Baudot and Levillain[1] – have argued for the unity of the whole chronicle and have emphasized (what is true) that chroniclers took their material where they could get it, so that differences in approach do not necessarily reveal different writers. But when these coincide with differences in style, as here, then surely we must allow multiple, or at least dual authorship. German scholars, starting a century ago with Brosien and ending with Krusch, Hellmann and Levison,[2] have left little or nothing of the case for single authorship, however little they may have agreed among themselves about the number of authors. Indeed, we may well ask how often the phenomenon of single authorship of a medieval chronicle did occur: the more skins of the onion one pulls off, the more one finds beneath. We may

[1] F. Lot, 'Encore la Chronique du Pseudo-Frédégaire', *Revue Historique*, vol. cxv (1914); M. Baudot, 'La question du Pseudo-Frédégaire', *Le Moyen Age*, vol. xxix (1928); L. Levillain, critical review of Krusch in *Bibliothèque de l'École des Chartes*, vol. lxxxix (1928).

[2] B. Krusch, 'Die Chronicae des sogenannten Fredegar', *Neues Archiv*, vol. vii (1882); 'Fredegarius Scholasticus – Oudarius? Neue Beiträge zur Fredegar-Kritik', *Nachr. der Gesellschaft der Wiss. zu Göttingen, philol.-hist. cl.* (1926), pt. 2; S. Hellmann, 'Das Fredegarproblem', *Historische Vierteljahrschrift*, vol. xxix (1934); W. Levison, critical review of Baudot in *Jahresberichte der deutschen Geschichte* (1928); Wattenbach-Levison, *Deutschlands Geschichtsquellen* (Weimar, 1952).

possibly be faced with three authors, as Krusch argued: namely, the Burgundian who took the chronicle to 613, then Fredegar, and finally an Austrasian interpolater; but, at the least, we are faced with two, if, with Hellman, we discard the Austrasian, as we probably should. Fredegar writes a different Latin from that of his predecessor; so different that even his interpolations in the earlier work are sometimes distinguishable. There is nothing subjective about this: we are faced with distinctive linguistic uses – uses of anacoluthon, of adverbs and adjectives, of relative clauses, ablatives absolute, participles in apposition and aorist participles; and with two vocabularies. The first stands nearer to the syntactical usages of Late Antiquity, while the second – a man of vivider and more allusive mind – struggles against a fuller tide of Romance influence on Latin. His language is extremely interesting; and one hesitates to call it barbarous because it is consistent. But Fredegar's history, and not his language, is our present concern. It is necessary only to emphasize that his language would distinguish him from his predecessor if nothing else did.

It is a reasonable guess that Fredegar was a Burgundian, like his predecessor, and quite possibly a native of the *Pagus Ultrajuranus*, from Avenches. We can hazard this because an interpolation in Jerome's Chronicle shows that he knew that Avenches (Roman *Aventicum*) was also locally called Wifflisburg, a name that can only just have been coming into use. It would not be surprising if he were also a layman[1] and a man of some standing in the Burgundian court of the mid-seventh century. He had access to what could reasonably be described as official documents; he was able to interview Frankish envoys and others from the Visigothic and Lombard courts, or from the Slavs; and he had personal knowledge of, and views about, the great men of his world, especially the mayors of the palace. He seems to have had the use of the

---

[1] It will be recalled that Merovingian chancery administration seems largely to have been in the hands of laymen, and that literacy among members of the Gallo-Frankish aristocracy was not then so rare as it was to become. Nor is it surprising that Fredegar, though a layman, should lay stress on the Christian attributes of kingship. See the remarks of E. Ewig in *Das Königtum* (Konstanz, 1956), pp. 21 ff. In my opinion, the case for considering Fredegar a layman must rest mainly on what he does *not* say; a churchman might have evinced a more specialized knowledge and interest at several points in the story which Fredegar allows to pass without comment.

official correspondence of King Sisebut of Spain, to say nothing of the archives of more than one Burgundian church, notably Geneva. Yet his writing is in no sense officially inspired, like that of his far-off continuators, even though it benefits from being put together in informed circles. To identify him more closely than that, and, in particular, to accept Baudot's identification of him with the Count Berthar who makes three appearances in the chronicle, is to indulge fancy too far.

How did Fredegar go to work? He somehow acquired his predecessor's manuscript, and thus had before him a chronicle covering those ten years of Frankish history that closed with the horrible end of Brunechildis – the end, equally, of the most famous vendetta in Frankish history. It left Chlotar II sole master of the *Regnum Francorum*. To the chronicle was already attached a series of Burgundian annals, going back at least to the year 584, and probably also the hand-book of world-chronology, though a case can be made for Fredegar having added this on his own account. We must picture Fredegar consulting this collection, correcting it and adding to it over a period of years. His work was spasmodic, and there were probably gaps of several years in which he did nothing at all. He may have started round about the year 625; and what he probably did first was to construct a bridge between the end of his predecessor's chronicle and the date at which he himself was writing. Thus we have, for the decade 614 to 624, a series of rather scrappy notes that nonetheless serve their purpose. Then he begins to revise the other man's work. Into the *Liber Generationis*, Jerome, Hydatius and Isidore he inserts material of his own – some of it of great interest. He then adds, as a very necessary transition from world-history to the story of his own small world, an epitome of the first six books of Gregory of Tours' History, again with his own interpolations, taking the story to 584. He would at this point have sacrificed any earlier part of the Burgundian annals that there may have been. Thus he had what he probably called five chronicles: the *Liber*, Jerome, Hydatius, Isidore and Gregory; and to them he proceeded to add a sixth, namely the annals and chronicle of his Burgundian predecessor, continued by himself from 614. This is really a notable compilation. But it is only at the year 625 that his own uninhibited writing begins.

From there to 642 we are given a detailed, exciting and chaotic narrative: chaotic in large part because not written on a year-to-year basis. As and when he had the material, and perhaps the leisure, he would add a section covering several years, or would insert a chapter in the earlier material (the famous chapter about Samo and the Wends is an example) or would alter a fact. However, his work bears traces of being unfinished. It ends, abruptly, with a very long description of the vendetta between Willebad and Flaochad, respectively the patrician and the mayor of Burgundy, in 642. In the nature of things, had he had the chance, he would surely have described the settlement of Burgundy that followed. But he was adding material as late as 660. For some reason that cannot now, or yet, be determined, the narrative was never continued beyond 642. He had, it is true, already written his preface or prologue to the whole work; but prologues were not always written last, and there is no apparent reason why his narrative should have stopped where it did, except by chance. Chapter 81 ends with the words: 'How this came about I shall set down under the right year if, God willing, I finish this and other matters as I desire; and so I shall include everything in this book that I know to be true.' It may be that he was getting more interested in turning his collection into a great source-book; and this is what he seems to imply in his prologue. The narrative, consequently, got shelved. He had not divided his six chronicles into four books, as they appear in the earliest extant manuscript, nor had he subdivided his personal chronicle into the chapters that now, in places, make nonsense of them. All that is later work.

Having said this much, by way of introduction, about Fredegar himself, and having briefly described what is in his chronicle and how it got there, it may now be asked why it got there; what, in short, is the standing of Fredegar among the historians of France. The beginning of wisdom in this matter must be Fredegar's own statement in his prologue. It was composed as a prologue to the whole work, and not simply to Book IV (that is, the sixth chronicle), as it will be found in Krusch's edition. This is what Fredegar writes, beginning with an excerpt from St Jerome:

Unless the Almighty helps me, I cannot tell how I can express in a word the labour on which I am embarking and how, in striving to succeed, my long struggle devours days already too short. 'Translator' [1] in our own vernacular gives the wrong sense, for if I feel bound to change somewhat the order of words, I should appear not to abide by a translator's duty.[2] I have most carefully read the chronicles of St Jerome, of Hydatius, of a certain wise man,[3] of Isidore and of Gregory, from the beginning of the world to the decline of Guntramn's reign; and I have reproduced successively in this little book, in suitable language and without many omissions, what these learned men have recounted at length in their five chronicles. Further,[4] I have judged it necessary to be more thorough in my striving for accuracy, and so I have noted in the above-mentioned chronicles, as it were a source of material for a future work, all the reigns of the kings and their chronology. I have brought together and put into order in these pages, as exactly as I can, this chronology and the doings of many peoples, and have inserted them in the chronicles (a Greek word, meaning in Latin the record of the years) compiled by these men – chronicles that copiously gush like a spring most pure.[5] I could have wished that I had the same command of language, or at least approached it; but it is harder to draw from a spring that gushes intermittently. And now the world grows old, which is why the finer points of wisdom are lost to us. Nobody now is equal to the orators of past times, or could even pretend to equality. Thus I am compelled, so far as my rusticity and ignorance permit, to hand on, as briefly as possible, whatever I have learned from the books of which I have spoken; and if any reader doubts me, he has only to turn to the same author to find that I have said nothing but the truth. At the end of Gregory's work I have not fallen silent but have continued on my own account with facts and deeds of later times, finding them wherever they were recorded, and relating of the deeds of kings and of the wars of peoples all that I have read or heard or seen that I can

[1] *Interpretator.*　　　　　　　　　　[2] So far St Jerome.
[3] He means the author of the *Liber*.　　[4] He resumes his citation of Jerome.
[5] *Velut purissimus fons largiter fluenta manantes.* Professor Laistner has suggested to me that he is likely to have built up this phrase from glossaries. There are, however, other possible explanations.

vouch for. Here I have tried to put in all I could discover from the point at which Gregory stopped writing, that is, from the death of King Chilperic.

On the whole, this is as modest, and even as commonplace, a statement of aims as it appears; but not quite. One catches in it a premonition of Bede's insistence on accuracy about sources, echoes of Gregory's profession of *rusticitas*, and of Sidonius' lament on the growing-old of the world, to say nothing of a good foundation of Jerome and thus of Eusebius himself. Yet it is a personal statement. Fredegar wishes it to be understood that he has not just accepted the chronicles of the wise men whose command of language was so far beyond his own; he has collected and inserted into their pages the chronology and the deeds of kings and the doings of many peoples that were not there before; and he has continued with a chronicle of his own times, relating all that he had read or heard or seen that he could vouch for. If he is ignorant, he is careful not to claim for himself an ignorance beyond that of his contemporaries.

What has he inserted into the old chronicles? A foretaste appears in chapter 5 of the first chronicle (the *Liber Generationis*). Into the list of the descendants of Japhet are interpolated two words: *Trociane, Frigiiae*. He wishes it to be understood that the Trojans, and especially such of them as the Frigii, or Franks as he later explains, as made their way west, could trace their descent to a respectable son of Noah. He starts off the second chronicle (Jerome) with the *Regnum Assyriorum*; but it soon becomes clear that the history of Assyria, or of any other of the great empires, is not his real concern; they are introduced as a traditional framework and because the regnal years of their rulers give him a chronology. This is why we find in chapter 10 the founding of Carthage, in chapter 15 the end of the Assyrian empire, in chapter 16 the founding of Rome and in chapter 23 the end of the empire of the Medes; these are used as chronological reckoning-points. His historical interests are two-fold: first, he is intrigued by the history of the Jews in so far as their religion was the fore-runner of Christianity (hence the importance, to him, of Isidore's chronicle); and secondly, he has a particular interest in one corner of Greek history, though whatever is irrelevant to this interest he sets aside. This corner is the Trojan origin of the Franks: Fredegar is the first author to mention it. Briefly, it is accepted that we have here a conceit, invention or misunderstanding, ultimately, though not necessarily directly, based on some literary knowledge; and whether or not we attribute it to Fredegar's imagination, as does Faral in the celebrated appendix to his *Légende Arthurienne*,[1] or to somebody else's, might not seem much to the purpose. One may suspect that Faral was too definite about what was and what was not 'invention', and too quickly dismissed the possibilities of a Gaulish origin of the Frankish legend. We have to remember that, in one form or another, tales of Troy were familiar to educated Gallo-Romans of the Later Empire. The *Excidium Troiae*[2] is one instance of this, and shows us the Troy legend in a tradition distinct from the better-known versions of Dares and Dictys,[3] and in a guise that strongly suggests Gallo-Roman composition. Ammianus (*Rer. Gest. Lib.* XV, 9, 5) tells of fugitive Trojans settling in Gaul, and Ausonius (*Lib.* VI, *Epitaphia Heroum*) sings of the heroes of the Trojan War. On these and other grounds, it is quite reasonable to attribute hellenic tastes to the Gallo-Romans and to see, as does Pierre Courcelle, something like a Greek renaissance in Gaul in the later fifth century.[4] It must, then, be borne in mind that the Gaulish literary atmosphere was already tinged with tales of Troy by the time the Franks arrived, so that we might expect a Frankish-Trojan connection, too, at any time from the fifth century. It surfaces, however, in the literary sense, not before Fredegar; and what we have to face is the undoubted fact that Fredegar, though conceivably also his predecessor, propagated a very powerful fiction. This is contained in a series of interpolations in chapters 4 to 7 of St Jerome. In brief, the story,

[1] E. Faral, *La Légende Arthurienne* (*Bibl. de l'École des Hautes Études*, fasc. 255) (1929), i. App. 1.

[2] Edited by E. B. Atwood and V. K. Whitaker, *Medieval Academy of America* (Cambridge, Mass., 1944).

[3] The reports of Dares and Dictys, alleged eyewitnesses of the Trojan war, add nothing to the story of the ancestry of the Franks. In the free adaptation of Dares that was incorporated in some manuscripts of Fredegar's Chronicle, there is mention of the Trojan princes Francus and Vassus. See Faral, op. cit. i. 287–8, and E. Zöllner, *Die politische Stellung der Völker im Frankreich* (Vienna, 1950), pp. 70–71.

[4] *Les Lettres grecques en Occident* (2nd ed., 1948), pp. 210–53). The conclusions of this study have, however, been attacked by Ferdinand Lot and others.

if we ignore certain contradictions that may be due to dual
authorship, is that the first king of the Franks was Priam. His
people split into two main groups (a third, the Teucri, went off to
become Turks), and of these one made its way into Macedonia
as a mercenary force and became absorbed into the population.
This may have some connection with the legend of the Pannonian
origin of the Franks reported by Gregory of Tours and, as Dill
thought, with the decision of the Emperor Probus to exile a band
of recalcitrant Franks to the Black Sea area in the third century.[1]
The second main group, the Frigii – and here is Fredegar's
novelty – set forth under a king named Francio, whence their subsequent name, Franks (an etymology probably due to Isidore,
who at the same time suggests the right one).[2] Under the valiant
Francio they devastated part of Asia, turned west into Europe,
and finally established themselves between the Rhine, the Danube
and the sea. There Francio died, and his people, reduced in numbers by all their wars, chose thereafter to be governed by dukes.
They did very well against the Romans – notably against Pompey,
whom we find an emperor, busy fighting the German tribes. The
Franks and the Saxons were alone able to resist him: 'post haec
nulla gens usque in presentem diem Francos potuit superare, qui
tamen eos suae dicione potuisset subiugare'. Where, asked Kurth,
will you find a comparable Frankish boast, apart from the longer
prologue of *Lex Salica*?[3] In chapter 8 we then begin to cover
some of the same ground again. Friga, of the house of Priam,
was, we are now told, actually the brother of Aeneas, and thus
the Romans too were the kindred of the Franks. A little later
on, in the fifth chronicle (the epitome of Gregory), Fredegar has
to explain away Gregory's much more cautious statement on
Frankish origins with a careful interpolation or so of his own. In
particular, he now states that when they reached the Rhine, the

---

[1] *Roman Society in Gaul in the Merovingian Age* (1926), p. 6.

[2] *Etymologiarum, Lib.* IX, ii. 101 (ed. W. M. Lindsay, Oxford, 1911), i.

[3] *Histoire poétique des Mérovingiens* (1893), p. 511. He might perhaps have added,
in King Chilperic's account to Gregory of his great golden dish – 'ego haec ad
exornandam atque nobilitandam Francorum gentem feci' (*Hist. M.G.H., S.R.M.,*
1951, VI, 2). Kurth's famous appendix on the Trojan origin of the Franks cham-
pions the view that Fredegar's story was an erudite invention. Camille Jullian, on
the other hand, held that the story went back to the fourth century (*De la Gaule à
la France*, p. 200).

Franks started to build a city named Troy, but the work was never completed. Several explanations have been advanced of this passage. Faral believed that Fredegar is here caught out at an 'invention audacieuse', and that he got his idea from Gregory, who says that when the Franks had crossed the Rhine they passed through Thuringia: 'Thoringiam transmeasse'; and Thoringia becomes Trojia. This may be thought a good deal wilder than the attempts of Mommsen and others to find a suitable Troy among the cities of the Rhineland. Xanten was ancient Colonia Traiana, known in the Middle Ages as Troja Minor. Xanten was re-settled perhaps at about the time when Fredegar was writing, and took its name – Ad Sanctos – from the Martyrs' Church that alone survived of the former Colonia Traiana, destroyed in the mid-fifth century. Archaeologists have recently been busy on the site.[1] There are difficulties about this identification, naturally; but it is quite likely that the Austrasian Franks of the seventh century had made it for themselves, and that Fredegar was here not inventing but reporting; it was one of the things he had heard. Perhaps the most conclusive argument against Fredegar as author of the Frankish-Trojan legend is its presence, in a different guise, in the Neustrian *Liber Historiae Francorum*, put together in the early eighth century.[2] The author of the *Liber* made no use of Fredegar, and had never even heard of him. They are independent witnesses to a tale which they inevitably give in different forms.

One cannot here attempt to disentangle the various strands of the Trojan legend as known to Fredegar. It is enough to draw attention to the part it plays in his story. He has found a distinguished, even an epic, background for his Franks, and has got them to the Rhine, free and independent under their dukes and well able to stand up to the Romans, to whom they are related. This is a far better story than Gregory managed. Taken as a whole, it satisfies racial pride in a new way; it incapsulates the Franks in the history of the great powers of the Mediterranean world, namely the Church of Rome and the Eastern Empire, while at the same time giving them the dignity of historical inde-

[1] See H. von Petrikovits' 'Die Ausgrabungen der Colonia Traiana bei Xanten', *Bonner Jahrbücher*, clii (1952), 41–161. A good plan is provided in Westermann's *Atlas zur Weltgeschichte* (1956), p. 32.

[2] Edited by Krusch in *M.G.H., S.R.M.*, II (1888).

pendence.[1] Chapters 27 and 30 of the second chronicle contain some very interesting interpolations designed to show the completeness and speed of those Roman victories that never included the subjugation of the Franks. In chapter 65 the great Emperor Pompey conquers most of Asia; and it is now safe to call him *genere Francus* merely because he is a Roman, and thus ultimately a Trojan. Fredegar is very skilled at working his interpolations of barbarian history into the fabric of Jerome and Hydatius. He finds room for a brief chapter (46) on the Burgundians, which may, in substance, come from Marius of Avenches; but it is certainly a pointer to what may be called his own domestic interests. He does not think much of the historical Burgundians, and, for all we know, did not consider himself descended from them. On the whole, Fredegar's pride in Frankish blood suggests that he did not carefully distinguish between indigenous and other races in his own Burgundy any more than he did in a wider field. Whatever his blood, whether Frankish or Burgundian in the narrow sense, he would probably have called himself *Romanus*. In chapter 56 he repeats the story of Hydatius, that in the second year of the reign of Anthemius, blood spurted from the ground in the centre of Toulouse and continued so to spurt for a whole day; but he has his own explanation of this: 'significans, Gothorum dominatione sublata, Francorum adveniente regno'. As the barbarian people move increasingly to the forefront of his picture, so it is natural that he should turn from Hydatius to Isidore's chronicle; and as attention becomes increasingly focused on one people, the Franks, so a transition to Gregory becomes equally natural. Gregory's epitome is the bridge between universal history into which Frankish matter is interpolated and Frankish history into which universal matter is interpolated. Fredegar omits Gregory's first book, which was logical, since its latest entry concerns the death of St Martin and its subject-matter is thus Gallo-Roman and not Frankish. He begins with Gregory's account of the collapse of the Vandal kingdom,[2] and so arrives at the Franks, their origin and their history, immediately before their push into northern Gaul.[3]

[1] See the remarks of Helmut Beumann in *Das Königtum* (1956), p. 223.

[2] *Hist.*, II, 9.

[3] It is perhaps worth noting that Fredegar makes no mention of the Franks having participated in the *Adventus* of Germanic tribes into Roman Britain. If the

This is no place for a systematic survey of all the interpolations in the text of Gregory that must be laid at the door of Fredegar. Some are of a purely factual nature, for example in Burgundian affairs, and take the form of a place-name here or a proper name there that Gregory did not know and Fredegar did know. Others look rather like additions made from folk-tale or hearsay or, using the term in the limited sense employed by Dr C. E. Wright, from saga;[1] and this is just as we have been warned to expect. A few examples must suffice. In chapter 9 comes Fredegar's explanation of the birth of Meroveus, the eponymous hero of the Frankish royal house. Clodio was taking a summer bathe in the sea with his wife when she was approached by a sea-beast, 'bistea Neptuni Quinotauri similis. . . . Cumque in continuo aut a bistea aut o viro fuisset concepta, peperit filium nomen Meroveum, per quo regis Francorum post vocantur Merohingii.' There is a note of doubt: the Minotaur *may* not have been the father of Meroveus; it may really have been the lady's husband. But, anyway, that is the story as reported to him. The Franks have not been content with Gregory's more sober account and have used their imagination. There are other stories of the same flavour as, for example, Clovis' wooing of the Burgundian Chrotechildis (chs. 18–19) and Basina's experiences on her wedding night (ch. 12). In the second story Basina thrice roused her husband, Childeric (father of Clovis), and sent him out into the night to report what he should see; and he saw, the first time, lions, unicorns and leopards; and the second time, bears and wolves; and the third time, lesser beasts like dogs, and beasts 'ab invicem detrahentes et volutantes'. She interprets this as the successive stages of degeneration of the Merovingian dynasty: Clovis shall be like a lion, his sons like leopards and unicorns, and their sons like bears and wolves and, finally, the fourth generation shall be like dogs and lesser beasts, and their people shall devastate one another 'sine timore principum'. Let us

---

blood of the Kentish settlers had been predominantly Frankish, one might expect to find some reflection of that migration in Frankish literature, whether or not those settlers had been led by their own chieftains, and whether they hailed from the Middle Rhine, as Mr Jolliffe believed (*Pre-Feudal England, the Jutes*, 1933) or from the Lower Rhine, as Professor Hawkes argues ('The Jutes in Kent', in *Dark-Age Britain*, 1956). Franks were one thing, Frisians another.

[1] *The Cultivation of Saga in Anglo-Saxon England* (1939).

admit that this is hearsay; but is it, as Dill says, 'popular legend'? One may suspect it of being less a countryman's tale than the kind of gloss that an informed public, even an aristocratic circle, might put upon events. It could even have some still undiscovered literary origin. The comment is that of a man quite capable of analysing the political troubles of his own time, who yet wishes to see no alternative to his Merovingians and thinks his compatriots a great deal more impressive than their kindred in Spain and Italy and elsewhere.

There are other long interpolations that equally deserve attention, such, for instance, as the story of Childeric's exile in Byzantium and eventual restoration through the guile of his friend Wiomad the Hun (ch. 11). Although Fredegar gets the name of the then eastern emperor wrong, there seems to lie behind his tale a tradition that Childeric, recently described by Professor Charles Verlinden as 'only the chief of a warrior band',[1] actually owed his rule in Gaul to imperial backing as a rival candidate to the rebel Aegidius. This is worth reflecting upon. Fredegar seems to have had a considerable stock of information about Byzantine affairs, whether or not they directly affected Gaul. The reason may lie in the nearness of Burgundy to Byzantine Italy and to the vital route connecting Italy with Septimania. Thus, he was able to make additions to Gregory's account of the *coup d'état* of Gundoald, which involved Byzantium (ch. 87), and also to interpolate information on Franco-Lombard contacts (chs. 50, 65, 68). The Burgundian court-circle of Fredegar's day, where he certainly had friends, was more than a place where an occasional messenger could be interviewed; it had a long-standing tradition of contact with Byzantium, and must have been a store-house of information about the past. What more likely source for the famous romance of Justinian and Belisarius (II, ch. 61) inserted by Fredegar after Gregory's passage on the end of the Vandalic War? It is a tale of their matrimonial adventures with two Amazon sisters, one of whom – Antonina, wife of Belisarius – holds a command in Africa under her husband. A tissue of nonsense, no doubt; yet Procopius says that Antonina was Belisarius' wife and did accompany her

[1] 'Frankish Colonization: a new approach', *Trans. Royal Hist. Soc.*, fifth ser., iv (1945), 15.

husband on the Vandalic campaign,[1] and elsewhere in the romance is a strange parallel to the life of Pope Vigilius in the *Liber Pontificalis*.[2] It is doubtful if Fredegar ever set eyes on the writings of Procopius or on the *Liber Pontificalis*. In short, he gave literary shape to an already composite story current in the Mediterranean world and repeated in circles where he moved. Gregory of Tours, for all that he was a Gallo-Roman of the Auvergne with many friends in the Midi, was bishop of a see in western Gaul, and had nothing corresponding to the Burgundian court to keep him regularly informed about the eastern Mediterranean world. It would be foolish to over-emphasize this contrast, for Tours was an Austrasian city and the *Epistolæ Austrasicæ* show that the kings of Metz also had their dealings with Byzantium;[3] it is a long way, however, from Tours to Metz.

But Fredegar looks north as well as south. Among his shorter interpolations should be noticed two important references to Rheims. One, well known, is in chapter 21, where he reports that Clovis was baptized by St Rémi *at Rheims*, a detail not given by Gregory and therefore often regarded as a fabrication,[4] particularly since it is followed by Clovis' comment on first hearing of Christ's Passion – that had he been present with his Franks, he would soon have avenged the wrong. And in another place, chapter 16, Fredegar says that the famous vase of the Soissons incident described by Gregory belonged to the church of Rheims. So here we have two allusions to Rheims by a chronicler with no particular interest in the city or the church. This tends to increase the likelihood of their veracity, or at least of Fredegar's acceptance of some local Austrasian source of information, such as a set of annals kept at Rheims or at Metz (at least one interpolation suggests a Metz origin: the story in chapter 72 of how Brunechildis let the little Childebert down in a bag from a window

---

[1] *Vandalic War*, III, xii, 2 ; xiii, 23-24; xix, 11; xx, 1.

[2] Note the remarks of R. Salamon, *Byzantinische Zeitschrift*, xxx (1929-30), 102-10.

[3] A full study of these Frankish-Byzantine contacts has been made by P. Goubert, *Byzance avant l'Islam*, vol. ii, pt. 1 (*Byzance et les Francs*) (1956). His conclusions should however, be treated with caution.

[4] Most recently in Sir Francis Oppenheimer's *Frankish Themes and Problems* (1952). Rheims, however, is preferred by A. H. M. Jones, P. Grierson and J. A. Crook, 'The authenticity of the Testamentum S. Remigii', *Rev. belge de philol. et d'hist.*, xxxv (1957), no. 2, 368.

in Paris, whence he was carried away to safety at Metz. Possibly, too, he used the Metz *Vita Arnulfi*).

This selection of the more characteristic and important of Fredegar's interpolations may serve as a basis for advancing one quite modest claim; namely, that though, in the main, he accepts and understands Gregory's account of Frankish affairs up to the year 584, he is yet able to make significant additions that probably stem from quite reputable sources, oral and written. He was no fool – and no fabricator, having no need to be one.

Lastly, there is Fredegar's own chronicle – his own, that is, apart from a few introductory chapters. Has it any coherence? Is it in any sense controlled by a single view of events? Or is it just an ignorant hotch-potch of whatever came along? The dominant interest of the first forty-two chapters is not in doubt: it is the vendetta of the Visigoth Brunechildis with her Frankish connections, after the murder of her sister Galswintha. It is more than that: it is an indictment and an analysis. Fredegar is perfectly clear that Brunechildis was at the bottom of all the chaos of Frankish politics: his view is put shortly in an interpolation in Gregory (III, ch. 59):

Tanta mala et effusione sanguinum a Brunechildis consilium in Francia factae sunt, ut prophetis Saeville impleretur, dicens 'veniens Bruna de partibus Spaniae, ante cuius conspectum multae gentes peribunt'. Haec vero aequitum calcibus disrumpetur.

This foreshadows the notorious forty-second chapter, where her apprehension, her indictment for the murder of ten Frankish kings and her subsequent execution are described. Equally revealing is the interpolation, as chapter 36 (made after 640), of a long excerpt from Jonas' *Vita Columbani*, which vividly portrays the stormy scenes between the queen and the savage old saint who refused to tolerate Merovingian polygamy.

If we analyse the last forty-two chapters of the chronicle for which no one questions Fredegar's authorship, we find that his subject-matter falls into fairly distinct groups. Six chapters deal predominantly with Burgundian affairs; five with Visigothic Spain and Gascony; six with Lombard Italy; six with Byzantium;

thirteen with the general area of Austrasia and Germany; and the remaining six cover individual themes, such as the death of Dagobert at Saint-Denis, or the eulogies of Aega and Erchinoald, mayors of the palace. Their subject-matter overlaps, and they are of very unequal length; but they give some idea of proportion. Here, Fredegar is not searching wildly for any scrap of intelligence; he must have been in a position to select and to reject. In consequence, what he has left survives because he thought it important. He is able, without moving outside Burgundy, to give a vivid picture of what seventh-century Frankish politics were about, in Burgundy, Neustria, Austrasia and Aquitaine, and also to sketch in, spasmodically, the doings of neighbouring peoples, particularly as they affected the Franks. The picture is in this sense European, and it is a picture by no means entirely derived from hearsay. Fredegar's sources are difficult to distinguish because he was generally successful in recasting his information into his own literary mode. One often has the feeling of his subject-matter jumping all over the place, but jumpiness is not characteristic of his style, which is rather episodic to a degree surpassing even Gregory of Tours. The reader gets a first impression that Fredegar is dealing exclusively with saga-material and with scraps picked up in conversation; but one would not expect this of a man able to manage, however inexpertly, the difficult chronicles that form the bulk of his compilation, and in fact it is not true. To deny that oral sources play their part would be idle; but they are not the whole story, or the part of the story on which he should exclusively be judged.

An example may be found in his chapters dealing with Byzantine affairs. There are six of them, some very long; and five form a block on their own. To them we should add three other chapters interpolated in the chronicle of Fredegar's Burgundian predecessor. They contain long and obviously exaggerated stories, full of dialogue and movement, that somehow do give an authentic impression of such various topics as the Byzantine wars with Persia, Byzantine relations with Italy and Byzantine resistance to the Arabs. Chapter 9 describes how Caesara, the wife of the Persian Emperor Anaulf, fled to Byzantium in disguise and was there baptized; and how, in due course, the conversion of all

Persia followed. Paul the Deacon, who is not known to have used Fredegar, has the same story with less detail and in a different form.[1] There was no Emperor Anaulf, say the commentators. True, but the name sounds like a possible Germanic attempt at Anōsharwān, the Persian name for Chosroes I; and Chosroes did make some remarkable concessions to Christians in his domains; and the name of his Christian and favourite wife, Shīrīn or Sira, could conceivably become Caesara. Look, again, at Heraclius' relations with Dagobert, and at the long description of Heraclius' duel with Chosroes in chapter 64. Heraclius' weapon is an *uxus*, a word used once before by Fredegar (and only by Fredegar) in the sense of a sword or dagger; to Hellmann we owe the suggestion that the word is derived from the Persian ākus, meaning a chisel or a knife; Professor W. B. Henning, on the other hand, has pointed out that Fredegar's account may go back to the source of the Greek historian Theophanes, who writes that Chosroes was killed by arrows, τοξοις; and that *uxus* may reflect a corrupt and subsequently misunderstood (τ)όξον, or rather (τ)όξα.[2] In any event we seem here, too, to be in touch with an eastern Mediterranean tradition. Closely connected with the Byzantine chapters are the Italian; and here it was long ago realized that Fredegar must have made use of traditions that were independently available to Paul the Deacon; and these must, in part, have been literary, for the two writers have too much in common to allow of an oral source when one remembers that they were separated by a century and a half. I am inclined to wonder whether Fredegar may not have had access to a collection of historical material from Bobbio, which would explain not only much of his Lombard and Byzantine chapters but also material concerning Luxeuil and Austrasia that one assumes to have come from Luxeuil itself, if not from some Austrasian centre such as Metz.

To take one early seventh-century sample of his Visigothic chapters, Fredegar tells (IV, 33) of a *dux* named Francio who had conquered Cantabria in the days of the Franks and had long paid tribute to their king; but when the province turned to the Empire

[1] *Historia Langobardorum*, IV, 50 (ed. G. Waitz), p. 173. I am much indebted to Dr J. A. Boyle for advice on Persian matters.

[2] A fuller statement of Professor Henning's views will be found in my edition of Fredegar, p. 53.

the Goths seized it. This rigmarole has never arrested the attention of historians, knowing as they do that the Franks never controlled Cantabria. And yet there was a *dux* Francio, a Byzantine *magister militum* who ruled over the *territorium* of Como until he was forced by the Lombards to flee to Ravenna. This was *circa* 588. Paul the Deacon talks about him.[1] Some confusion between the two is not out of the question.[2]

Fredegar's information about Austrasia and its problems is copious, but lacks clear evidence of direct observation. He is unable, furthermore, to give any reasoned account of Dagobert's great judicial tour of Burgundy (which, incidentally, is the perfect answer to the question 'what were barbarian kings meant to do when they were not fighting'), an account based, one might hazard the guess, on personal knowledge. The tour ends up in Paris, where we learn that his chief advisers, at least on Austrasian affairs, were Arnulf of Metz and Pippin: 'regebatur ut nullus de Francorum regibus precedentibus suae laudis fuisset precellentior'. The Austrasian March against the Slavs and Wends appears to be held without the Austrasians feeling that they were, so to say, merely holding the fort for the rest of the Franks. Then comes a sudden change. Paris seems to have been too much for Dagobert and the result (ch. 60) is a total collapse of morals; he surrounds himself with wives and mistresses, starts robbing churches and forgets the justice that he had loved before. The Austrasians become restive and appear to put the blame on Pippin (ch. 61), though Fredegar here uses obscure language and one cannot be quite certain who is blaming whom. What is certain is that Fredegar himself is in a muddle; and the reason may lie in his use of two distinct sources, the first Burgundian and the second perhaps Austrasian. He goes on to depict Dagobert's increasing difficulties with his eastern March, including the rebellion of Radulf, his duke in Thuringia (ch. 77), and the war against Samo, the extraordinary Frankish adventurer who went on a business trip to the Wends and stayed to be their king (chs. 48 and 68). Fredegar is our first informant on the Western Slavs, the

[1] *Hist. Lang.*, III, 27.
[2] The possibility is discussed by G. P. Bognetti, *Relazioni X Congresso Int. di Sci. Stor.*, iii, 41.

Slavs more particularly of the present area of Czechoslovakia. Without him we should be nowhere, and his information on Slav politics and society is notably reliable.[1] One may, in passing, note that in chapter 48 (a late interpolation) Fredegar remarks that the Wends, before they were liberated by Samo, were subject to the Huns or Avars, who used them as *Befulci*. What were *Befulci*? Fredegar explains: they were mercenaries who were sent into the front line by their masters to bear the brunt of the attack; which is a reasonable gloss on *befulti*. Chaloupecký thinks that the word is a hybrid, *bis + folc*, 'a double regiment'. But, as Theodor Mayer has plausibly shown,[2] Fredegar gives the right explanation of the wrong word. What the Wends actually did was to look after the Avars' herds of buffalo, and hence in their own language would have been known as *Byvolci*, the people who looked after the buffaloes (*byvolů*); and the nearest Latin homophone known to Fredegar was *befulti*, or *befulci*, on which he proceeds to comment. So here again it looks as if he were in touch with a direct source of foreign intelligence and is not just romancing. (There are, in fact, two other instances of his misunderstanding Slav words but doing his best with them.)[3]

In chapter 75 Fredegar recounts how Dagobert gave to the Austrasians his little son Sigebert, as king, and established him in Metz with a suitable treasure and under proper tuition. Why did he make this concession? The answer is 'deinceps Austrasiae eorum studio limetem et regnum Francorum contra Winedus utiliter definsasse nuscuntur': the Austrasians, for all that they hate Dagobert, will now be prepared to stand against the Wendish raiders on their eastern March. So times have changed. This view of Dagobert and, before him, of his father Chlotar deliberately

---

[1] V. Chaloupecký, 'Considérations sur Samon, le premier roi des Slavs', *Byzantinoslavica*, vol. xi (1950), gives a résumé of the important studies of the Polish scholar, G. Labuda. Dr E. B. Fryde has since informed me that he is not entirely persuaded by Labuda's evidence, which is archaeological, that Samo led the Slavs of Moravia.

[2] 'Fredegars Bericht über die Slawen', *Mitteilungen d. Öst. Inst. f. Gesch.*, erg. bd. ii (1929).

[3] *Gagano* in the same chapter, and *Walluc* in chapter 72. Is it possible that the same word *G(k)aganus* (= Khan) has also troubled Eddius, and that we should read *Kagano* for *pagano* when he writes *sub pagano quodam rege Hunnorum degens* (*The Life of Bishop Wilfrid by Eddius Stephanus*, edited by Bertram Colgrave, 1927, chap. 28, p. 56)?

encouraging the autonomy of the Austrasians as their only barrier
against the Slavs, has recently been attacked by Dr Eugen Ewig[1]
and others. Yet it appears to be borne out by *Lex Ribvaria*, a
skilfully-constructed collection of Frankish and other law codified
in the seventh century from one possible motive only: to placate
and bind closer to the Merovingians the people to whom it
would apply – the Franks of the region of Cologne, a particularly
difficult sector of the threatened Rhineland[2] to which the Merovingians had devoted special attention, and from which a Frankish
advance north towards the Lower Rhine was planned and, in part
only, carried out. It shows signs of having been put together by
Burgundian lawyers; and we know that both Chlotar and Dagobert were much influenced by Burgundians. It only suggests
again that Fredegar has tapped an authentic Austrasian source. He
had no great sympathy for Austrasians but he knew where to find
out about them and was always prepared to have a guess at their
motives.

We come finally to Fredegar's two concluding chapters (89 and
90). They are the longest of his own composition, and also the
vividest. The first tells how the Frankish regent, queen Nantechildis, went to Orleans in Burgundy, and summoned to her all
the Burgundian *seniores*, lay and ecclesiastical, and with their
approval appointed Flaochad, *genere Franco*, to be their mayor in
succession to Aega; and the second goes on to tell how Flaochad,
once appointed, looked for an opportunity to destroy an old
enemy, the Burgundian patrician, Willebad. They meet, at last, outside the walls of Autun, and Willebad is killed. The count of the
palace, Berthar, a Transjuran Frank, was, writes Fredegar:

> the first of them all to attack Willebad; and the Burgundian
> Manaulf, gnashing his teeth with fury, left the ranks and came
> forward with his men to fight Berthar. Berthar had once been
> a friend of his, and now said, 'Come under my shield and I will

---

[1] 'Die fränkischen Teilreiche im 7 Jahrhundert', *Trierer Zeitschrift* (22 Jahrgang,
1953), p. 113; 'Die Civitas Ubiorum, die Francia Rinensis und das Land Ribuarien',
*Rheinische Vierteljahrsblätter*, xix (1954), especially pp. 23–27, an admirable survey to
which I am much indebted; K. A. Eckhardt, *Pactus Legis Salicae* (1954), pp. 119–20.
[2] *Lex Ribvaria* has been re-edited by F. Beyerle and R. Buchner, *M.G.H., Leges*,
vol. iii, pt. 2 (1954). I have discussed some of the political implications of the text
and of the editors' views in *English Historical Review*, lxx (1955), 440–43.

protect you from danger', and he lifted his shield to afford cover to Manaulf. But the latter struck at his chest with his lance, and his men surrounded Berthar, who had advanced too far, and gravely wounded him. But when Chaubedo, Berthar's son, saw his father in danger of his life, he rushed to his assistance, threw Manaulf to the ground, transfixed him with his spear, and slew all those who had wounded his father. And thus, by God's help, the good boy saved Berthar, his father, from death. Those dukes who had preferred not to throw their men upon Willebad now pillaged his tents and the tents of the bishops and the rest. The non-fighters took a quantity of gold and silver and horses and other objects.

Pierre le Gentilhomme, the numismatist, plausibly associated Willebad's scattered treasure with coins discovered at Buis (Saône-et-Loire[1]), more plausibly than Baudot associated Berthar with the authorship of the chronicle on the strength of his performance on this occasion. But it is fairly clear that Fredegar had personal knowledge of, and interest in, what happened. He goes on to relate that Flaochad died eleven days after Willebad, 'struck down by divine judgement . . . many believed that since Flaochad and Willebad had sworn mutual friendship in places holy to the saints, and had both greedily oppressed and robbed their people, it was God's judgement that delivered the land from their overweening tyranny: their faithlessness and deceit were the cause of their deaths.' So ends the chronicle. Fredegar does not say that he believed this, though he probably did. What he gives no indication of is a clear-cut fight between the Burgundian aristocracy and the Frankish intruders. The cross-currents were, in fact, more complicated. Both the patrician and the mayor were out to feather their own nests, and both had Franks and Burgundians, laymen and churchmen, in their followings. In fact, this precisely illustrates the point made in the story about Basina; when 'lesser beasts' reign, there will always be a scramble for local influence.

Fredegar had known and understood some of the 'greater beasts'. It is because of him that we know anything of the detail of the reign of Dagobert I. But Fredegar had an equally high opinion of Dagobert's father, Chlotar II, the executioner of

[1] *Mélanges de Numismatique Mérovingienne* (1940), p. 105.

Brunechildis. These two men, Chlotar and Dagobert, were masters of the Frankish scene for twenty-five years between them. After them came a minority and the rule of mayors. Fredegar did not think, or say, that this meant the end of the Merovingians or of Frankish Gaul; but he does show, in the remaining three years of his chronicle, what the clash of uncontrolled local interests meant in practice. In this, as in much else, our whole approach to the central period of the Merovingian age is based on Fredegar's approach; we cannot avoid it.

When all is said, Fredegar is not a Gregory of Tours. He is less learned and more easily muddled, though it is always to be remembered that his work is incomplete. Nor is he the associate of kings. But he is equally vivid with his stories, and the stories do illustrate a consistent approach to events; and further, they do involve personal judgements. He is not perhaps, as he stands, a historian, though, had he ever finished, he might have written that *Historia Francorum* which it is arguable that Gregory never intended to write; but he is a major adapter of other people's chronicles and a major chronicler in his own right. One cannot fail to be struck by the contrast between the political chaos and vendetta of seventh-century France, of which Fredegar himself is in large part our evidence, and the patient skill with which this remote figure builds up his complicated record of events. Surely he deserves serious re-assessment, and higher rank among the writers of the Dark Ages?

CHAPTER FIVE

# Archbishop Hincmar and the Authorship of Lex Salica[1]

\*

In the course of a long career, first as a monk at Saint-Denis and then, from 845 to 882, as Archbishop of Rheims and principal adviser of the West Frankish kings, Hincmar said and wrote much that earned him enemies. One of the charges brought against him in his own lifetime was, in effect, that he was a forger. Pope Nicholas I believed that he had forged documents to deceive the papacy about the metropolitical powers of Rheims, and so wrote to the Synod of Soissons, on 6 December 866: 'Sed adhuc et in alio mira fratris Hincmari rursus accedit astutia, et soli proprio voto favens se inmiscet prudentia;' and, to Hincmar: 'Quamobrem iure fortassis te fraudis aliquid in talibus committere fateri possemus, nisi reverentiae tuae, quod ipse non speras, parcere nostra mode- ratio studuisset'.[2] A century later, the monk Flodoard, who drew heavily on the archbishop's writings for his History of the Church of Rheims, expressed doubts here and there, with *fertur* or *traditur*, about what he read in them.[3] The medieval mind was in general, however, content not to question Hincmar, and his reputation for veracity went without serious critical challenge until the age of Mabillon.[4] Thereafter, the attack developed remorselessly, if slowly. In the mid-nineteenth century first Paul Roth[5] and then Carl von Noorden[6] found grounds for anxiety. But modern

---

[1] *Revue d'histoire du droit*, vol. XX (1952).
[2] *M.G.H., Epist. Karol. Aevi*, IV, pp. 417 and 426.
[3] *Historia Remensis Ecclesiae, M.G.H., SS.*, XIII, Book III, pp. 474–555 *passim.*
[4] *Œuvres posthumes*, II, 343, 344 and 348.
[5] *Geschichte des Beneficialwesens* (Erlangen, 1850), p. 461.
[6] *Hinkmar Erzbischof von Rheims* (Bonn, 1863), p. 395.

criticism of Hincmar really derives from the studies of an altogether more formidable scholar, Bruno Krusch. First in the
Monumenta Germaniae Historica[1] and then in an article entitled
'Reimser Remigius-Fälschungen',[2] Krusch exposed Hincmar to
severe tests in one aspect of his work and took to task, perhaps not
wholly successfully, Godefroid Kurth, who had attempted to defend him.[3] But Hincmar was still not left in peace. The first of the
late Léon Levillain's brilliant *Études sur l'abbaye de Saint-Denis à
l'époque mérovingienne*[4] showed how little reliance could be placed in
yet another of his works. The most recent critic, M. Simon Stein,
has improved on his predecessors. Not content with questioning
the truth of the archbishop's assertions in writings known to be
his, he has attributed to him a fresh field where forgery was
hitherto unsuspected.[5] One purpose of this article is to examine the
premises on which that attribution is made.

It must be said at once that, however cautious we are in our use
of the word forger, Hincmar was a forger. That is to say, he added
to his sources what he never found there, and thus changed their
sense; and he wrote, on occasion, what he wished to be taken for
work of an earlier period. This he did over a wide field, for his
interests embraced history, canon law, theology and hagiography.
Nor is it surprising that such a man should have been capable of
detecting forgery in the work of others. He recognized for what
they were, for example, the Pseudo-Isidorian excerpts from the
Acts of Sylvester and the Nicaean canons contained in the forged
letters of Popes Julius and Felix; and he was very doubtful about

[1] *M.G.H., Auct. Antiq.*, IV, 2 (1885), pp. xxii-xxiv.

[2] *Neues Archiv*, XX (1895), pp. 511-68.

[3] 'Les Sources de l'histoire de Clovis dans Grégoire de Tours', *Revue des Questions
Historiques* (1888), pp. 403-15 (*La Vita Remigii*); reprinted in *Études Franques*
(Paris–Bruxelles, 1919), vol. 2, pp. 232-46. Kurth has recently found a powerful supporter in F. Baix, who has shown in 'Les sources liturgiques de la Vita Remigii de
Hincmar', in *Miscellanea Historica in honorem Alberti de Meyer* (1946), pp. 211-27,
that his surmises about the originality of the oldest extant *Vita Remedii* were right,
and that in MS 1395 of the Bibliothèque de la Ville de Reims and in the eighth
century Rheims Office for St Rémi we have the source of material which Krusch
attributed to Hincmar's imagination.

[4] *Bibliothèque de l'École des Chartes*, 82 (1921).

[5] It is important to follow the development of the author's thought in his three
articles: (1) ' Lex und Capitula' (*Mitteilungen des Österreichischen Instituts für Geschichts-
forschung*, 41, 1926); (2) 'Étude critique des capitulaires francs' (*Le Moyen Age*, LI,
1941); (3) 'Lex Salica' (*Speculum*, XXII, April and July 1947).

the authenticity of the *Capitula Angilramni*.[1] Nevertheless, the present article is no attempt to exonerate Hincmar from all his sins of commission and omission. The first two sections are concerned solely with his historical writings and with the picture he there gives us of an earlier age. Against such a background we may proceed to ask whether he can legitimately be considered, except in the face of compelling evidence, the begetter of *Lex Salica*.

I

Hincmar spent his early life in the monastery of Saint-Denis. It is known that he came to be a person of consequence in the community, for he occupied an office that gave him access to the archives, and was an intimate of the Abbot Hilduin. This intimacy not only introduced him to the elaborate mechanism of forged diplomas and falsified history by which the abbey sustained its territorial claims. It also brought him into touch with the abbey's royal patrons and ultimately saddled him with the delicate task of attempting to reconcile the Emperor Louis the Pious with Hilduin, who had supported Lothar against his father. Léon Levillain argued that one instrument in this act of reconciliation was the compilation known as the *Miracula Sancti Dionysii*. He demonstrated that Hincmar was the author and that the work was completed in haste in the early part of 835.[2] It was soon made the basis of a larger study, the *Gesta Dagoberti Regis*, again from the pen of Hincmar, though perhaps with some assistance from Hilduin.[3] Without going so far as Levillain, who suggested that the

---

[1] Heinrich Schrörs, *Hinkmar, Erzbischof von Reims* (1884), pp. 398 seq. This is still the most useful biography of Hincmar. See also Émile Amann, *L'époque carolingienne* (1937) in *Histoire de l'Église*, edited by A. Fliche and V. Martin, vol. 6, pp. 359–60, for a short summary of recent views on the question of Hincmar's possible connection with the Pseudo-Isidorian circle. The arguments against Hincmar or Rheims having anything to do with the forgery are serious, but are not taken into consideration by Stein, 'Étude critique des capitulaires francs', p. 74. Hincmar, but not Rheims, is exonerated by Karl Weinzierl, 'Erzbischof Hinkmar von Reims, als Verfechter des geltenden Rechts', in *Episcopus, Studien über das Bischofsamt* (Regensburg, 1949), pp. 148 ff.

[2] *B.E.C.*, 82 (1921), p. 111. Doubt as to this ascription is expressed, but not developed, in Wattenbach-Levison, *Deutschlands Geschichtsquellen im Mittelalter, Vorzeit und Karolinger*, I (Weimar, 1952), p. 113, n. 254.

[3] M. Buchner, 'Zur Entstehung und zur Tendenz der Gesta Dagoberti', *Historisches Jahrbuch*, 47 (1927), pp. 252–74.

*Gesta* may have been composed at the request of Louis the Pious himself,[1] nobody could doubt that they were meant as an invitation to the emperor to participate in the reform of the abbey and its restoration to a strict Benedictine observance. The *Gesta* present a well-argued case for the would-be reformers; despite a recent lapse, the abbey had never been anything but a house of monks, and the Frankish kings had always been conscious of their right and duty to intervene in its affairs. The emperor was to understand that this duty – which he swiftly proceeded to fulfil – had been recognized not simply by his own father and grandfather, Charlemagne and Pippin III, but also by Dagobert, next to Clovis the greatest of the Merovingian kings.[2]

Levillain subjects the *Gesta* to a thorough analysis and, in part following Krusch, lists the main sources used. These were, directly or through the *Miracula*: the chronicle of Fredegar (not used for the *Miracula*), the *Liber Historiae Francorum*, the *Vita S. Arnulfi*, Baudemundus' *Vita S. Amandi*, the *Vita Audoini*[3] and (Levillain's own discovery) Gregory of Tours' *Historia*. The author also had knowledge of the *Vita S. Genovefae*, the *Vita S. Eligii* and various documents, genuine and fabricated, stored in the abbey's *chartrier*. The list is not exhaustive, but it reveals the range of historical material available to a Saint-Denis monk in the mid-ninth century, and it leads Levillain to the conclusion that 'les *Gesta* sont donc plus qu'on ne le croyait encore une marqueterie de textes, et leur valeur historique ne trouve pas dans la présente étude un regain de confiance'.[4] It might be prudent to modify this judgement,[5] but in the main it must stand. The historical value of the *Gesta* is the value of their several sources and little else. They add hardly anything to our knowledge of the reign of Dagobert.

The *Gesta* do, however, afford us some idea of Hincmar's own views on a narrow field of Merovingian history. The total sources at his disposal must have been considerable. Yet his picture is a

[1] *B.E.C.*, 82 (1921), p. 114.

[2] *Études*, II, *B.E.C.*, 86 (1925), pp. 42–43.

[3] W. Levison, 'Kleine Beiträge zu Quellen der fränkischen Geschichte', *N.A.* (1902), p. 354, first demonstrated this connection.

[4] *B.E.C.*, 82 (1921), p. 87.

[5] S. M. Crosby, *The Abbey of St Denis*, I (Yale, 1942), p. 43, attaches more importance than did Levillain and Krusch to the legends reported by Hincmar.

restricted one. His subject is the abbey of Saint-Denis, not the Merovingians. Thus, we find that he rejects a golden opportunity to give a full-length portrait of Dagobert as a king, because he thinks that it might bore his readers:

Longum est enarrare, quam providus idem rex Dagobertus in consilio fuerit, cautus iudicio, strenuus militari disciplina, quam largus elemosinis quamque studiosus in componenda pace ecclesiarum, praecipueque, quam devotus extiterit in ditandis sanctorum coenobiis, praesenti opere declarare, minusque necessarium et maxime ob fastidientium lectorum vitandum tedium, praesertim cum nullis abolenda temporibus luce clariora earum rerum extent indicia.[1]

In the *Miracula* he had also declined to go into any details about Dagobert because they would have been out of place.[2] This betrayed no lack of respect for, or of interest in, the great king whose singular concessions to the abbey were not only the first of their kind but also the real foundation of its incomparable prosperity.[3] Rather, it showed Hincmar's determination to remain relevant. Only when Dagobert's activity affected Saint-Denis was he prepared to enlarge at length on what he had read, and to fabricate details that suited his plan. An instance of this is believed to be provided by chapters 6 to 11, where the author relates how the young Dagobert took refuge from Chlotar's wrath at the shrine of St Denis. The story demonstrated the powerful protection that the patron saint and his two companions, Rusticus and Eleutherius, could extend, even to kings. But the chroniclers make no mention of a Duke Sadregisil or of any such incident. The story might be considered traditional or the invention of Hincmar. The extraordinary parallel, drawn attention to by Levillain,[4] that it affords to the incident of the young Lothar's rebellion against Bernard of Septimania, his father's friend, hints at the latter, though it does not prove it. Dagobert, through St Denis' protection, had been pardoned by Chlotar. Louis the Pious was being asked to pardon Lothar for a similar crime, and, with Lothar, his supporter Hilduin of Saint-Denis. Do these details justify Levillain's view that

[1] *M.G.H., S.R.M.*, II, chap. 42, p. 419 (ed. Krusch).
[2] *B.E.C.*, 82 (1921), p. 81.    [3] *Études*, IV, *B.E.C.*, 91 (1930), pp. 5–14.
[4] *B.E.C.*, 82 (1921), p. 106.

Hincmar drew not upon tradition but upon his own fancy for the account of Sadregisil? It adds, in any event, a fresh incident to the life of Dagobert; but it is to the greater glory of St Denis. 'On doit toujours supposer chez un forgeur de documents un interêt quelconque'.[1] The purpose of the *Gesta Dagoberti* is sufficiently plain; it draws closer the links binding the Frankish kings to the abbey under the roof of which many of them had been brought up and buried, and does so at a critical moment in the abbey's fortunes. Hincmar's employment of sources and his subtractions from as well as additions to them, meet precisely this need.

It is likely enough that Hincmar's readiness to use information acquired in his youth at Saint-Denis is also revealed in his conciliar letter of 858 to Louis the German, which refers to the opening, years earlier, of the tomb of Charles Martel at Saint-Denis.[2] He may himself have heard an account of the incident from an older monk and have written down what, in essentials, is the story of the *Visio Eucherii*. At least he had heard tell of it, and of the sinister conjectures then circulating about Charles' eternal fate. Years later, he is not afraid to use this knowledge to frighten an aggressive king.[3]

II

Hincmar moved from Saint-Denis to Rheims in 845 without losing his deep sense of loyalty to the former. The two communities were already held together by an act of association as a *societas precum*,[4] and to this he referred in an affectionate letter addressed to old friends in the abbey: 'petensque ut apud communem patronum beatissimum Dionysium in sacris orationibus sui memoriam jugiter haberent.[5]

There can be no question that he took with him to Rheims not only the historical technique learned and practised in the Saint-Denis *scriptorium* but also copies of some of the writings for which

---

[1] *B.E.C.*, 91 (1930), p. 14.
[2] *M.G.H., Capit.* II, pp. 432 ff.
[3] See the comments of B. de Gaiffier, 'La légende de Charlemagne, le péché de l'empereur et son pardon', *Recueil de travaux offert à M. Clovis Brunel* (1955), p. 493.
[4] d'Achery, *Spicilegium*, IV, 229. On such associations, see Wilhelm Levison, *England and the Continent in the Eighth Century* (1946), 101 ff., 165.
[5] Flodoard, *Hist. Eccl. Rem.*, III, 25. (*M.G.H., SS.*, XIII, p. 538).

he had there been responsible. The two oldest extant manuscripts of the *Gesta Dagoberti* belong to Rheims and Saint-Bertin (the latter almost certainly copied at Rheims)[1]. Years later, at Rheims, he added a third book to the *Gesta*, which must have been close at hand when he settled down to compose his *Vita Remigii*. The same sense of construction, the same preferences for material and the same tricks of style characterize both works, and leave no room for doubt that they are from the same pen.[2]

The *Gesta* purport to be what they are not: the deception is wholesale. In the *Vita*, however, Hincmar in plain words confesses that he is editing an older Life of St Rémi. What he does not admit to is the handsome contribution of his own fancy to the scattered pages of that Life which he states he used:

Sicque prefatus liber cum aliis partim stillicidio putrefactus, partim soricibus conrosus, partim foliorum abscisione divisus in tantum deperiit, ut pauca et dispersa inde folia reperta fuerint.[3]

The occasion of the *Vita*, like that of the *Gesta*, was purely practical. It was designed to further the interests of the Church of Rheims,[4] and its background was Charles the Bald's seizure of Lorraine on Lothar's death in 869, and his coronation by Hincmar at Metz.[5] The St Rémi of Hincmar's *Vita* is not the St Rémi of the earliest extant *Vita Remedii* nor of Gregory of Tours. He has become God's instrument in the anointing with heaven-sent oil of the Merovingian dynasty in the person of Clovis. Further, he is papal vicar with precisely those judicial powers over his suffragans that Hincmar, perhaps developing the tradition of St Boniface,

---

[1] *B.E.C.*, 82 (1921), p. 92.   [2] Ibid., pp. 93–100.

[3] *M.G.H., S.R.M.*, III, p. 252. See Krusch's comments, *N.A.*, XX (1895), p. 512. Levison (*Aus rheinischer und fränkischer Frühzeit*, p. 22) draws attention to a similar allegation at the end of the *Vita* of Bishop Eucharius of Trier (*Acta Sanctorum*, June, I).

[4] An earlier stage in the growth of the territorial importance of Rheims is conveniently studied in L. Dupraz, *Le Royaume des Francs* (Fribourg, 1948), subject to the reservations of L. Levillain in *B.E.C.* (1948), pp. 269–70, and of the present writer in *Bull. Inst. Hist. Research* (November 1949). See also P. E. Martin in *Zeitschrift f. Schweizerische Geschichte*, 29 (1949), pp. 278–82.

[5] E. H. Kantorowicz, *Laudes Regiae* (Berkeley, Univ. of California Press, 1946), *passim*.

was himself seeking to establish. In brief, the new *Vita Remigii* laid a firm foundation for the advancing of claims by the Church of Rheims over its own suffragans and over the crown; and upon it Hincmar's successors built.[1] It might be possible to defend the archbishop against some of the charges of outright forgery brought against his *Vita*. For example, Krusch has not convincingly established that the testament of St Rémi contained in it is witnessed by several names that Hincmar must have invented.[2] Nor has he established that Hincmar invented place-names.[3] Neither language nor content are against the testament, nor on technical legal grounds can it be condemned as a forgery. Not once is there any slip to betray the forger's hand, although the text is elaborate. On the contrary, what more likely than that the magnificent archives of the Church of Rheims should have preserved the testament of its greatest bishop?[4] Apart from the testament, an instance of where it is possible to take a more favourable view of Hincmar's part in the *Vita* is his evidence for the history and cult of St Montanus, prophet of St Rémi's birth.[5] But in general the *Vita* contains a high proportion of fabrications: 'diese ist keine Geschichtsdarstellung sondern eine kirchenpolitische Schrift'[6]. Its present interest lies neither in the fabrications nor in the truthful historical writing as such, but in the picture each gives us of the writer's view of early Merovingian history; for the *Vita*, written near the close of Hincmar's life, is, as it were, an historical counterpart to the earlier *Gesta*. The first covered the brief period of the resuscitation of the Merovingian house, as seen from the viewpoint of its greatest abbey. The second was concerned with the foundation of that house, this time seen through the eyes of a great Frankish archbishop.

In chapter 11 of the *Vita*, Hincmar gives a résumé of Frankish history in the migration period as he found it in the first ten chap-

---

[1] Cf. P. E. Schramm, *Der König von Frankreich*, I (1960 ed.), pp. 113, 146. St Rémi did, however, baptize Clovis, and probably at Rheims. See also E. Lesne, *La Hiérarchie épiscopale* (1905), pp. 175, 183.

[2] *N.A.* (1895), p. 549.

[3] Ibid., p. 556.

[4] A. H. M. Jones, P. Grierson and J. A. Crook, 'The authenticity of the *Testamentum S. Remigii*', *Rev. belge de philol. et d'hist.*, XXXV (1957), n. 2.

[5] J. van der Straeten, *Analecta Bollandiana*, LXXIV (1956).

[6] *N.A.* (1895), p. 537.

ters of the *Liber Historiae Francorum*.[1] He adds nothing to the picture beyond a word or explanatory phrase here or there. But when the story reaches Clovis in Gaul, serious additions are made. The author of the *Liber*, following Gregory of Tours, writes: 'Eo tempore multae ecclesiae a Chlodovecho exercitu depredatae sunt. Eratque ipse tunc fanaticus et paganus.'[2] He then goes on to the famous incident of the vase of Soissons. But Hincmar here inserts a passage on St Rémi, the news of whose miracles, he says, at once won the hearts of the Franks: 'et rex illorum libenter illum audiebat, et audito eo, multa faciebat et a multis nequitiis se cohibebat'.[3] Clovis set out for Rheims, 'per viam quae usque hodie propter barbarorum per eam iter Barbarica nuncupatur', and waited outside with his army, not wishing to damage the city. Then follows the vase incident.

It is surely a misuse of terms to brand as forgery what is in fact a reasonable glossing of a text. Given the *Liber* and Gregory's History, Hincmar has drawn some plausible conclusions and added some information of a local nature. The information about the name of the road is likely to be accurate. So, too, is an addition to the vase story, where Hincmar explains that the Frankish *Campus Martius* was named after the God of Battle, not after the month of March.[4] Should a different view be taken of Hincmar's treatment of the baptism of Clovis, which rests on no known historical foundation and is intended to be the key to the claim, advanced by the Church of Rheims in the ninth century, that it alone had the right to anoint the Frankish kings? The long passage begins at chapter 14 with the request of Clovis' queen that St Rémi should preach salvation to her husband. The *Liber* covers the matter in a few lines; but Hincmar gives a detailed account of how Clovis, Chrotechildis and St Rémi prepared themselves for the ceremony of baptism. When, with the help of miracles, he had sufficiently instructed the pious barbarian in the way of salvation, St Rémi was filled with the spirit of prophecy and foretold the fate of Clovis' seed:

Qualiter scilicet successura eorum posteritas regnum esset

[1] Ed. Krusch, *M.G.H.*, *S.R.M.*, II, pp. 215–328.
[2] Ibid., chap. 10, pp. 251–2.      [3] *Vita Remigii*, chap. 11, p. 292.
[4] Cf. Levillain, 'Campus Martius', *B.E.C.* (1948), pp. 62–68.

nobilissime propagatura atque gubernatura et sanctam aecclesiam sublimatura omnique Romana dignitate regnoque potitura et victorias contra aliarum gentium incursus adeptura, nisi forte a bono degenerantes, viam veritatis reliquerint et diversos vitiorum fuerint secuti anfractus, quibus neglegi aecclesiastica solet disciplina, et quibus Deus offenditur, ac per hoc regna solent subverti atque de gente in gentem transferri.

The words are those of Hincmar, not St Rémi, but the picture they afford of the Merovingian dynasty, at first safe under ecclesiastical favour but later declining and finally losing the crown for neglect of *aecclesiastica disciplina*, may be called commonplace in the ninth century. Hincmar is not fabricating the picture or even adding to it except in narrowing the ecclesiastical patronage to the Church of Rheims. Certainly it was not the Merovingians he wished to magnify.

The passage continues:

Quod de Moyse scriptum legimus, quia splendida facta est facies ejus, dum respiceret in eum Dominus, hoc et in beatum Remigium luce splendida illustratum factum fuisse audimus: quoniam, sicut Moyses legislator populo veteri erat a Domino constitutus, ita et beatus Remigius euvangelicae gratie lator populo in proximo per fontem baptismatis innovando extitit munere Christi electus.[1]

So St Rémi was the Moses of the new people and his heirs the guardians of their tabernacle. 'Patrone,' asks Clovis, 'est hoc regnum Dei quod michi promittis?' This simple admission, put into the mouth of the greatest of the Franks in the form of a question, is more significant than the account of his baptism, which follows, for without it the sort of baptism which Hincmar envisaged would have been inconceivable. As is well known, the startling innovation is the descent of a white dove bearing an ampulla of chrism;[2] but she descends 'obsequente beato Remigio', and it is St Rémi who confirms the king with this chrism after raising him from the baptismal font. It is 'per beatum Remigium',

[1] *Vita Remigii*, chap. 14, p. 296.
[2] F. Baix, loc. cit. p. 219, shows that even here Hincmar had his source in the Rheims Liturgy.

further, that all the Franks are stated to have been converted and baptized after the defeat by Clovis of his northern kinsman, Ragnachar. Hincmar thought it worth while to insert this detail while omitting the dramatic story of Farro, which he found at this point in the text of the *Liber* as well as of Gregory's History. His practice was to use sufficient of the general narrative to give his *Vita* a firm historical setting. The Gothic campaign, for example, is shortened, and a passage is inserted to make St Rémi the patron, if not the instigator, of this notable attack on 'Alaric the Arian'.[1] The bestowal of consular rank on Clovis by the Emperor Anastasius is the occasion of a long letter allegedly from Pope Hormisdas to St Rémi bestowing on the latter vice-papal powers.[2] But Gregory's attractive picture of the new Augustus riding from St Martin's church into the city of Tours, distributing gold and silver to the crowds along the route, is omitted.[3] Hincmar's inspiration lasts even to the death of Clovis:

> et eodem momento, quo mortuus est Hludowicus Parisius, revelante spiritu, sanctus Remigius, cum esset Remi, defunctum fuisse cognovit et sibi assistentibus indicavit.[4]

Enough has perhaps been said about the *Vita Remigii* and the *Gesta Dagoberti* to give a reasonable idea of how Hincmar looked at Merovingian history and what use he made of it. However we react to his historical technique,[5] the last thing that could be said of him is that his object was the glorification of the Merovingians for themselves. We may now turn to a very different work and consider whether it can possibly be attributed to the same pen. In short, can *Lex Salica* be counted among those writings referred to by Flodoard: 'scripsit praeterea plura, ad quae nos enumeranda sufficere non putamus'?[6]

---

[1] *Vita*, chap. 19, p. 311.  [2] Ibid., chap. 20, p. 312.

[3] *L.H.F.*, chap. 17, p. 271; *Historia*, Bk. II, chap. 38 (*M.G.H., S.R.M.*, I, 1, 2nd ed. by Krusch and Levison, pp. 88–89).

[4] *Vita Remigii*, chap. 20, p. 313.

[5] Krusch is unjust: 'der wahre Zweck der Geschichte ist nach ihm die Sammlung unverbürgter Gerüchte, und das hat er durch Verdrehung eines Anspruchs Beda's herausgebracht'. (*N.A.*, XX, 1895, p. 515.) The author of the best section of the *Annales Bertiniani* busied himself with much more than the collecting of unfounded rumours.

[6] *Hist. Rem. Eccl.*, III, chap. 29. (*M.G.H., SS.*, XIII, p. 554).

### III

Despite the vast amount of learning lavished on them, there was until very recently no definitive text of any of the continental barbarian laws except the *Leges Visigothorum Antiquiores*.[1] Inability to decide what precisely the barbarian laws were, and thus what principles should underlie the establishing of critical texts, lay at the root of the notorious difficulties with which the *Monumenta* editors of the *Leges* section found themselves faced;[2] and their greatest difficulty was with *Lex Salica*.[3] It is true that representative manuscripts of the important texts of *Lex Salica* had been edited in parallel columns by Hessels;[4] but this was no substitute for the critical text towards which scholars have been striving, and which has now been realized by K. A. Eckhardt's critical edition of the principal recensions.[5] The basic difficulty is that the *Lex* survives only in manuscripts that are centuries later than the period to which much of the matter seems to refer. The earliest of these manuscripts belong, most scholars hold, to the late eighth and early ninth centuries, though in the circumstances there is no *a priori* reason why the earliest extant manuscript should have special authority or significance. What matters more is the relationship of the manuscripts to each other. Examination of a large number of them convinced Stein that none could with certainty be dated before the middle of the ninth century and this led him 'to the rather simple fact that *Lex Salica* has been transmitted to us only by the Carolingian Church and through no other sources'.[6] He went further, and saw *Lex Salica*, as we now have it, as a forgery of the Rheims school, put together under the supervision of Archbishop Hincmar.[7]

[1] Ed. K. Zeumer, in M.G.H., *Fontes Iuris Germanici Antiqui, in usum schol.* (1894) and *Leges Nationum Germanicarum*, I (1902).

[2] These difficulties are described, perhaps too graphically, by S. Stein, 'Lex Salica I' (*Speculum*, XXII, April 1947).

[3] 'Die Leges sind von Anfang an das grösste Schmerzenskind der Monumenta gewesen'. (P. Kehr in his obituary of Emil Seckel, *N.A.*, 46, 1926, p. 160.)

[4] J. H. Hessels, *Lex Salica: the ten texts with the glosses and the Lex Emendata* (London, 1880). To this is appended H. Kern's valuable study of the Frankish words in *Lex Salica*.

[5] *Germanenrechte, Neue Folge, Westgermanisches Recht: Lex Salica, 100 Titel-Text* (1953); *Pactus Legis Salicae, introduction and 80 Titel-Text* (1954); *65 Titel-Text* (1955).

[6] 'Lex Salica I', p. 125.

[7] 'I do not want to affirm that Hincmar was the author of the forgery known under

Stein's polemical views on the dates of manuscripts must surely fail to carry conviction. If one manuscript of *Lex Salica* can be proved to have been written before about 840 the whole of his theory must collapse. It may be observed, for example, that although Munich 4115 is one of the manuscripts for which 'scholars with authority and experience beyond doubt have advanced more recent dates',[1] it is dated by W. M. Lindsay as 'saec. VIII–IX';[2] by Rudolf Buchner as '8/9. Jahr.';[3] by Levison as 'about 800';[4] by Bernhard Bischoff as 'wohl um 800 oder bald danach';[5] and by Eckhardt as 'gegen 800'.[6] No scholar of authority and experience has implied, let alone stated, that this manuscript could belong to the late ninth century. '8th–9th century' implies that it belongs to the late eighth or early ninth century. Of course, no absolute proof is afforded by the opinion advanced by these scholars; but it is enough to remind us that in deciding so narrow an issue of dating we must not expect agreement among palaeographers and should not attempt to advance historical propositions on the strength of what some of them say. However, Munich 4115 is but one example: Paris Bibl. Nat. Lat. 4404 is probably as early in date, and Wolfenbüttel, Weissenburg 97 earlier still. In any case, those who are disposed to think that *Lex Salica* is what it purports to be would not be unduly disturbed if the oldest extant manuscript were proved to date from the mid-ninth rather than from the late eighth century. Stein might have used palaeographical evidence as a supporting argument, if first he had established that there was a sound historical case for holding that *Lex Salica*

---

the name of *Lex Salica*. Not because of lack of clues, but solely because I do not want to spend my time on questions of secondary importance' (ibid., II, p. 409). In brief, Stein does believe that Hincmar was the author of *Lex Salica*.

[1] Ibid., II, pp. 399 seq.

[2] *Early Irish Minuscule Script* (Oxford, 1910), p. 46, n. Lindsay does, however, incorrectly give the provenance of the manuscript as Fulda.

[3] *Textkritische Untersuchungen zur Lex Ribuaria* (Leipzig, 1940), pp. 56–57. See also Buchner 'spalaeographical arguments in the first section of his *Kleine Untersuchungen zu den fränkischen Stammesrechten, 1 (Deutsches Archiv,* 1951, pp. 59–102). He adds the important point that *Lex Salica* is recorded in library catalogues – in particular in the 821/2 catalogue of Reichenau – earlier than the mid-ninth century.

[4] *England and the Continent in the Eighth Century* (Oxford, 1946), p. 139, n. 1.

[5] *Die südostdeutschen Schreibschulen und Bibliotheken in der Karolingerzeit,* I (2nd ed., 1960), p. 16.

[6] *Pactus Legis Salicae, 80 Titel-Text,* p. 25.

was a ninth-century forgery. But he established nothing of the sort.

'Sur la date de rédaction de la Lex Salica, il a été écrit beaucoup de folies... La période qui va de 508 à 511 est la seule admissible.' Such is the judgement of M. Ferdinand Lot,[1] based, like that of most modern writers, upon the work of Heinrich Brunner,[2] 'dont l'opinion . . . nous paraît avoir victorieusement résisté à tous les assauts'.[3] Without feeling quite so confident that *Lex Salica* was actually committed to writing so early, we must still ask how this famous code, promulgated in the reign of Clovis himself, could have failed to obtain even a passing reference in any extant source of the early Frankish period. There is no satisfactory answer. One could wish that Gregory of Tours, who knew about the Law of the Burgundians,[4] had troubled also to mention the Law of the Franks. But neither does he mention the Laws of the Visigoths, the fame of which, in Gregory's own day, no scholar has ever questioned. In England, Bede's reference in his *Historia Ecclesiastica* to Aethelberht's Laws[5] prevents the making of a case that the Kentish Laws are no older than their oldest manuscript, the *Textus Roffensis*, written when Aethelberht had been five centuries in his grave; and no scholar ever seriously contended that the Kentish Laws are not what they purport to be, however corrupt and garbled the text may have become over the centuries,[6] or that by Aethelberht's Laws is to be understood anything but just those tariffs of fines that are preserved to us in the *Textus Roffensis*. In the comparable case of *Lex Salica*, Stein attempts an unhappy compromise. He argues at length that the *Lex* as it survives is in for-

[1] In Lot, Pfister and Ganshof, *Les Destinées de l'Empire en Occident de 395 à 888* (2nd ed., 1940), p. 194, n. 75. Krusch, late in life, was even more definite, and opted for the year 507, in his article 'Die Lex Salica: Textkritik, Entstehung und Münzsystem' (*Historische Vierteljahrschrift*, 31, pp. 417–37).

[2] *Deutsche Rechtsgeschichte*, 1 (2nd ed., Leipzig, 1906), pp. 434–40.

[3] F. L. Ganshof, 'Note sur le sens de "Ligeris" au titre XLVII de la Loi Salique et dans le "Querolus" ', in *Historical Essays in Honour of James Tait* (1933), p. 111. Eckhardt, loc. cit. p. 31, agrees.

[4] (Of Gundobad) Burgundionibus leges mitiores instituit ne Romanis obpraemerent (*Hist.* II, chap. 33).

[5] *Venerabilis Baedae Opera Historica* (ed. C. Plummer, 1896), vol. 1, p. 90. Strictly, Bede provides evidence that Kentish Laws attributed to former kings were known and observed by his Canterbury friends at the close of the seventh century.

[6] A. S. Diamond, *Primitive Law* (2nd ed., 1950) has indeed advanced some opinions of this kind, but they are not sufficiently developed to be taken seriously.

mat, and to a large extent in content, a forgery of the ninth century, but then concedes that it must contain an unspecified number of Salic 'norms' that were genuine.[1] It is inconceivable how these genuine 'norms' could have survived to the ninth century except in the form in which we now have them. No compromise is possible. Nor is it possible to compromise over nomenclature. *Lex Salica* means a particular code, and Stein has produced no conclusive reason why the term should have had the wider and more general meaning of *Lex Dominica* in earlier writings than Hincmar's, e.g. in Capitulary 142.[2] Perhaps it would not be going too far to add that, if *Lex Salica* did not survive in its present form, it would be necessary, having regard to the common historical situation that produced all the Germanic Laws, to posit the existence of something very like it.

Stein insists – and this is no small service – on the importance of studying manuscripts in their entirety and on the danger of isolating one text from its neighbours in the same manuscript. Thus, in the case of Bibl. Nat. MS Lat. 10758, formerly of the monastery of St Rémi at Rheims, he has no difficulty in showing that, taken as a whole, it casts much light on the historical interests of the *scriptorium* where it was written.[3] He maintains that it was written at Rheims during the reign of Hincmar, that it reflects his own personal interests, and that its text of *Lex Salica* has thus a special significance. If we allow (what is uncertain) that MS 10758 was written in the time of Hincmar, neither its orthography nor the fact that it includes an important series of Carolingian capitularies on which Stein casts unmerited doubt, can assist us to the

---

[1] 'Lex Salica II', p. 415.

[2] *Capitula Legi Salicae Addita*, of 819 or shortly afterwards, and not, as Stein believes, of the reign of Charles the Bald (ed. Boretius, *M.G.H., Capitularia Regum Francorum*, I, pp. 292–3). Stein ineffectively attacks the evidence of this, and other, capitularies in 'Lex und Capitula', *M.I.Ö.G.*, XVI. I note the criticism of this article (which, however, is misquoted) by J. Pétrau-Gay: 'il ne suffit pas de constater qu'à l'époque carolingienne la *lex* aussi bien que le *capitulum* émanent du roi. L'organe d'émission, le roi, est en effet le même, mais la nature juridique des décisions royales peut être différente suivant qu'il s'agit de la *lex* ou du *capitulum*'. ('La Laghsaga Salienne et l'intérêt de ses survivances historiques en vue d'une classification juridique des capitulaires des rois francs', *Rev. hist. de droit français et étranger*, 1935, p. 285.) In general, however, Pétrau-Gay's work has not met with approval. Cf. U. Stutz, *Zeit der Savigny Stift., Germ. Abt.* (1920), and Emil Goldmann, ibid. (1936).

[3] 'Étude critique des capitulaires francs', *MA* (1941) (LI), pp. 34 seq.

conclusion that its *Lex Salica* is also 'forged'. Such a conclusion can only proceed from historical premises. Stein further believes – and this also is a service – that philology in the narrow sense is no infallible guide in helping us to date such a text. Krusch, the learned editor of so many Merovingian texts, firmly held that the distinction between Merovingian and Carolingian Latin was that the former was corrupter than the latter and thus the original corruptions of Merovingian texts were perpetuated in transmission by Carolingian scribes who would never have dreamed of committing such monstrosities in compositions of their own.[1] It is true that the line between Merovingian and Carolingian Latin (by which we mean, more simply, Early and Late Frankish Latin) is more blurred than some have thought; that corrupt Latin was written even at the height of the Carolingian renaissance; and that no 'standard' Merovingian Latin ever existed. The Latin the Franks used was always developing. Can we, however, follow Stein when he asserts that the corrupt language of *Lex Salica* in MS 10758 cannot be proved to be Merovingian but is, on the contrary, a deliberate Carolingian attempt to give an impression of simple-mindedness?[2] 'Merovingian Latin in a Carolingian manuscript can only be ascertained if this Latin stands out against a background of correct Latin.'[3] This may be so; but the onus of proof rests with the critic who holds that a Merovingian text is not a Merovingian text but a Carolingian text; and nothing is proved by the suggestions that MS 10758 may be in Hincmar's hand; that it is odd that so cultivated a hand should have copied, or committed, so many blunders; and that in Rheims no attempt should

---

[1] This judgement on Krusch, 'Lex Salica I', p. 126, finds some support from R. Buchner, op. cit. pp. 8 seq., and in Carl C. Rice, *The phonology of Gallic clerical Latin after the sixth century* (Harvard, 1902), pp. 5, 6; but it can be carried too far.

[2] 'Lex Salica I', p. 132. Stein also points out that other parts of the same manuscript (e.g. excerpts from Isidore) are equally full of blunders, designed to prove the scribe's simplicity and thus his inability to forge. But he does not show whether the blunders in the various parts of the manuscript are predominantly of the same nature, nor, if they are, can such a charge be sustained without very full evidence. Mistakes in other manuscripts he seems rather inclined to attribute to deliberate archaism. It might be helpful to collate the verbal forms of *Lex Salica* with those found in the most important repository of Merovingian spelling, the Bobbio Missal. This was edited by E. A. Lowe for the Henry Bradshaw Society in 1920, and commented upon by A. Wilmart, E. A. Lowe and H. A. Wilson in vol. LXI (1923) of the same Society's publications.     [3] Ibid., p. 128.

have been made to correct these blunders. All this is very interesting and difficult enough to explain. But wherein lies the proof that MS 10758 and all the texts allegedly derived from it, whether 'emended' or not, are not in fact copies of Merovingian texts in Merovingian manuscripts?[1]

If, however, we grant that Stein has said enough to cast suspicion upon *Lex Salica*, what evidence does the text itself afford of non-Merovingian origin? Two points in particular that rouse his suspicions are, first, its equation of 40 denarii with one solidus, and secondly, the apparent belief of the compilers that penalties for murder and theft consisted of fines only. Merovingian numismatics are obscurer than most branches of that science, and not all numismatists would at present care to assert that at no time prior to the coinage reforms of the seventh and later centuries could 40 denarii have been equated with one solidus.[2] A defence of such an equation has indeed been advanced.[3] However, the only witnesses that can at present be cited in support of *Lex Salica* are clause 41 of the Council of Rheims[4] (813) and chapter 32 of the *Vita Remigii*, where Hincmar introduces the testament of St Rémi with the warning:

Exemplar testamenti a beato Remigio conditi, in quo lector

[1] Not the least fanciful of Stein's adventures is his attempt to explain the orthographical differences between more or less contemporary manuscripts of *Lex Salica* as intentional efforts to give the impression of several texts derived from different traditions.

[2] See P. Le Gentilhomme, *Mélanges de numismatique mérovingienne* (Paris, 1940), p. 139, where two possible solutions are suggested: (1) that the text refers to a time when the Frankish gold solidus was fixed as equivalent to 40 old Roman silver denarii; or (2) that the Salic denarius is the real denarius struck in the late seventh and early eighth centuries, when, because of the collapse of the gold coinage, the silver denarius acquired a 'valeur libératoire'. In the second case (preferred by Le Gentilhomme) the evaluations of fines would thus be later glosses.

[3] By A. Dopsch, *The Economic and Social Foundations of European Civilization* (London, 1937), pp. 364, 5; (*Wirtschaftliche und Soziale Grundlagen der europäischen Kulturentwicklung*, 2nd ed., Vienna, 1924, part II, pp. 493, 4) and by Eckhardt, loc. cit. pp. 17-31, though not very convincingly.

[4] Ut domnus imperator secundum statutum bonae memoriae domni Pippini misericordiam faciat, ne solidi, qui in lege habentur, per quadragenos denarios discurrant, quoniam propter eos multa periuria multaque falsa testimonia repperiuntur (*M.G.H., Conc.*, II, i. p. 257). Professor Ganshof suggests to me that there could be a reference to the *Lex Salica* ratio in Capitulary 39 of the year 803, of which chap. 9 reads: omnia debita quae ad partem regis solvere debent, solidis duodecim denariorum solvant, excepto freda quae in lege Saliga scripta est; illa eodem solido quo caeterae compositiones solvi debent componatur (*M.G.H., Capit.*, I, p. 114).

attendat, quia solidorum quantitas numero XL denariorum computatur, sicut tunc solidi agebantur, et in Francorum lege Salica continetur et generaliter in solutione usque ad tempora magni Karoli perduravit, velut in eius capitulis invenitur.[1]

Now, Hincmar may have been mistaken, or his source may have been mistaken. But what possible purpose could have been served by his inventing a new coinage-ratio for the Merovingians? It is plain that if it already existed in *Lex Salica*, the testament in the *Vita Remigii* would, by referring to that coinage-ratio, increase its chances of being taken seriously. But what would *Lex Salica* itself have gained by perpetrating the initial falsehood?

Secondly, Stein pleads that *Lex Salica* nowhere reveals that the Merovingians punished murder and theft with death and were not content to consider these crimes emendable. But why should *Lex Salica* be expected to reveal this? The early barbarian law codes provide, how fully we cannot guess, current tariffs of crimes that were commonly emendable. Their compilers would have seen no necessity to add that there was such a thing as political expediency (as exemplified in the *Pactus pro tenore pacis*) and that kings did in practice interfere to impose severer or lighter sentences than custom allowed, especially when their private interests were directly involved; nor would the writers of narrative have seen cause to explain to readers and hearers familiar with the compositions for everyday crime that the terrible punishments of their stories were exceptional. Appropriate penalties in these and other cases must often have been difficult to arrive at. In the Burgundian Law (LII, 5) the king thinks it well to issue a warning that the moderate penalty of composition that he has allowed in a particular case may not be repeated in future, when total forfeiture of property and also the death penalty may be incurred. We may instance, too, the statement, in chapter 26 of the laws of Wihtred, King of Kent in the late seventh century: 'if anyone catches a freeman in the act of stealing, the King shall decide which of the following three courses shall be adopted –

---

[1] *Vita Remigii*, chap. 32, p. 336. Mr Philip Grierson, in a letter to the present writer, expressed the opinion that the Frankish penalties were first formulated in terms of silver deniers (*siliquae*), and were later given rough solidus equivalents under Clovis, when silver deniers no longer existed.

whether he shall be put to death, or sold beyond the sea, or held to ransom for his wergild'. Are we to suppose that Wihtred's predecessors did not, on occasion, exercise a like equity, even though they do not say as much in their codes? Similarly, is it not clear that *Lex Salica* does not, and need not, tell the whole story about murder and theft? Yet even so, it would be hazardous to contend that the hanging criminals whose bodies it was a serious offence to cut down (titles 67 and 68) had not met their fate for murder or theft. However that may be, Hincmar and his friends had read Gregory's *Historia* and knew well the range of royal vengeance under Clovis and his sons. What purpose, then, would he have served by pretending otherwise? It is surely rather too subtle as a corroboration of the view he later expressed in chapter 21 of the *De Ordine Palatii*, that barbarian laws sometimes needed softening.[1]

There is yet one further obstacle that any protagonist of Stein's theory must surmount, and that is the intricacy of the forgery itself. It presupposes intimate knowledge of other barbarian codes, and ready access to them. That knowledge would certainly not seem out of place at, for example, such a house as St Gall, which had a remarkable legal collection, including a late seventh-century copy of Rothari's Edict[2] and at least five manuscripts of *Lex Salica*. Nor might it seem out of place at Reichenau or Niederaltaich, both closely concerned with the recording of Bavarian and Alamannic Law, and directly linked with the learning of Visigothic Spain.[3] Rheims, too, had some such background,[4] and

[1] (On cases being referred to the palace): si quid vero tale esset quod leges mundane hoc in suis diffinitionibus statutum non haberent, aut secundum gentilium consuetudinem crudelius, sancitum esset, quam Christianitatis rectitudo vel sancta auctoritas merito non consentiret, hoc ad regis moderationem perduceretur, ut ipse cum his qui utramque legem nossent, et Dei magis quam humanarum legum statuta metuerent, ita decerneret, ita statueret ut, ubi utrumque servari posset, utrumque servaretur; sin autem, lex saeculi merito comprimeretur justitia Dei conservaretur (c. 21, ed. M. Prou, Paris, 1885, *Bibl. Éc. H. Ét.*, fasc. 58, pp. 54–56 and ed. V. Krause, *M.G.H., Capit.*, II, p. 524–25). I doubt if *'gentilium consuetudo'* is exclusively unwritten custom, as Prou believed. Theodulf of Orleans, whom not even Stein could connect with the authorship of *Lex Salica*, also commented on the severity of contemporary laws and compared them unfavourably with the Pentateuchal Laws (*M.G.H., Poet. Car. Aevi*, I, 517 ff.).

[2] See P. A. Dold, 'Zum Langobardengesetz' (*Deutsches Archiv*, 4, 1940). J. M. Clark, *The Abbey of St Gall as a centre of Literature and Art* (1926) is not helpful here.

[3] See Konrad Beyerle, *Lex Baiuwariorum* (Munich, 1926), introduction.

[4] See F. M. Carey, 'The Scriptorium of Reims during the Archbishopric of Hincmar' (*Classical and Medieval Studies in Honour of Edward Kennard Rand*, New

Stein would have done a great service had he assembled and evaluated the evidence and considered the possibility of continuous interest in barbarian law at Rheims from Merovingian times onwards. Was Hincmar heir to a Rheims tradition in which *Lex Salica* played a part? If so, he was well equipped to appreciate it, for he already had outstanding skill as a canon lawyer. The Pentateuchal Law was at his finger-tips; and its influence upon later barbarian laws may not have been slight.[1] He was also familiar with Roman Civil Law, as he shows in his references to the 'sextus decimus liber legum' (Book XVI of the Theodosian Code), and had access, if not to the *Breviarium*, then certainly to some such collection as Paris Bibl. Nat. Lat. 12445 or Berlin Phillipps 1741 (a Rheims manuscript, though of the tenth century).[2]

However, there is a greater difficulty. We are to suppose that, employing some fragments of genuine legal tradition, Hincmar set down in writing the archaic text now known as *Lex Salica*; and that, having done so, he saw to it that the text was rapidly disseminated in a variety of versions that simulated a complex manuscript tradition. He even furnished his text with a refinement which, in the event, proved unnecessary. He glossed it in a bogus archaic language.[3]

This is no place to examine at length the complicated issues raised by the Malberg glosses. To dismiss the labours of Grimm and Kern as 'vague and arbitrary' is childish.[4] They have made a serious case for the obvious explanation of the glosses – that they are the corrupt shreds of the Frankish tongue, of which no other example survives. How remote this tongue was from ninth-century Old High German – the language Hincmar would surely have turned to as a basis for such a forgery – may be seen by comparing them with the surviving fragment of an Old High German translation of *Lex Salica*.[5] It is true that 'modern scholarship long

York, 1938). Rheims had in the ninth century a copy of the fundamental barbarian code, the Visigothic. It is now Paris Bibl. Nat. lat. 4668 (R. 2 in Zeumer).

[1] Cf. Levison, *Aus rheinischer und fränkischer Frühzeit*, p. 253.

[2] Cf. J. Gaudemet, 'Survivances romaines dans le droit de la monarchie franque', *Revue d'histoire du droit*, XXIII (1955), pp. 168, 176.

[3] A comparable case of the possible later insertion in a text of archaic words and phrases is that of the Three Fragments (Irish), which are discussed by F. T. Wainwright, *English Historical Review*, vol. LXIII (April 1948), p. 157.

[4] 'Lex Salica II', p. 410.          [5] Text in Hessels, p. xliv.

ago abandoned the hypothesis of the existence of a Germanic text of *Lex Salica*' (if by that we mean a Germanic text of which our present *Lex Salica* is a translation), and that 'surmising a Germanic text, we rob the Latin text of its reason of being.'[1] It seems possible that the Frankish tongue survived in Gaul, at least in isolated pockets, side by side with the Latin, to a later date than was once supposed,[2] but the existence of the glosses as Frankish technical terms do not imply the existence of a written Frankish text, and Calmette was only partially right when he postulated a mixture of genuine glosses and references to, or *explicits* of, an earlier Frankish text.[3] But this is beside the point. There was very little interest in the vernacular among educated men in the eighth and ninth centuries. The immense missionary undertaking of St Boniface and his English colleagues (to say nothing of Frankish successors) leaves no evidence of wide diffusion of vernacular gospels, or near-gospels: virtually all we have is the *Heliand* and Otfrid's *Liber Evangeliorum*. Why should Hincmar have had any interest in written vernacular? What reason could Hincmar have had for thinking that vernacular glosses added to his text would increase the chances of its being accepted at its face-value? What reason had he for supposing that barbaric laws had ever been written, or glossed, in any other language than Latin? The only laws certainly written in the vernacular (the Anglo-Saxon) were not, so far as can be ascertained, known to him, though, at any rate partially, he had read Bede's *Historia Ecclesiastica*, with its famous passage on the laws of Aethelberht.[4] To conclude that we can no longer translate or understand the purpose of the Malberg glosses is to find ourselves in no worse case than the scribes who slavishly copied them in the ninth century, and is surely a more judicious position than is that of the man who believes they were fabricated.

[1] 'Lex Salica II', p. 410. See Wattenbach-Levison, *Deutschlands Geschichtsquellen im Mittelalter, Vorzeit und Karolinger*, 1 (1952), p. 95.

[2] See W. von Wartburg, *Umfang und Bedeutung der Germanischen Siedlung in Nordgallien* (1950), *passim*.

[3] 'Observations sur les gloses malbergiques de la Lex Salica' (*B.E.C.*, 1899).

[4] When Hincmar refers to Bede's *Chronica* (as in Sirmond, *Hincmari Archiepiscopi Remensis Opera*, vol. 1, pp. 23, 215, 695) he means the *De Temporum Ratione*, which closes with a chronicle. But his preface to the *Vita Remigii* quotes Bede's preface to his History, addressed to King Ceolwulf.

To have forged *Lex Salica* would, therefore, have demanded of Hincmar a subtlety somewhat beyond anything we have a right to credit him with. But even if he had had that subtlety, what reason can be advanced for the forgery? Its object 'was to extol the splendors of *temporis acti* and to furnish accessory norms supplementing those in force'.[1] But does it do either of these things? Are we to suppose that the famous *Lex Salica* passage in the *Liber Historiae Francorum* in fact inspired Hincmar to compose both the prologue and the Law?[2] We have already seen the kind of historical interests Hincmar indulged himself with, and the kind of historical fabrication he was prepared to risk. Neither the *Vita Remigii* nor the *Gesta Dagoberti* can seriously be taken for efforts to extol the splendours of *temporis acti*; their intention was quite other; but they positively resound with Merovingian praises as compared with the text, if not with the prologues, of *Lex Salica*.

*Lex Salica* is a literary as well as a legal text,[3] a text conserved by, and in, ecclesiastical circles. During the centuries that separated its first commital to writing from the earliest extant manuscript, it was added to and suffered both emendation and corruption. Like St Benedict's Rule, also written in the *lingua vulgaris*, its grammar and vocabulary must have been a constant challenge to emendators. That no manuscripts earlier than the late eighth century survive is no cause for wonder, for this is only a special instance of a more general phenomenon.[4] It is not surprising that in an antiquarian age, like the ninth century, it should have enjoyed a sudden vogue, and been disseminated in a variety of texts rich in

[1] 'Lex Salica II', p. 415.

[2] Tunc habere et leges coeperunt, quae eorum priores gentiles tractaverunt his nominibus: Wisowastus, Wisogastus, Arogastus, Salegastus, in villabus quae ultra Renum sunt, in Bithagm, Salechagm et Widechagm. (*M.G.H.*, *S.R.M.*, II, p. 244). A non-extant (?) manuscript of this chronicle is ascribed to St Rémi's monastery, Rheims. The editor, Krusch, reprints Bouquet's description (*Recueil*, II, p. xiii): 'Gestorum stilus in codice Remigiano limatior est quam in aliis: voces barbarae ac minus Latinae puriori Latinitati redduntur. Qui Gesta recognovit, floruisse videtur post Hincmarum, a quo sanctae Ampullae historiam mutuatus fuerit'. But how long after Hincmar?

[3] The point was well made by Beyerle, op. cit. p. xxxix, with reference to the *Lex Baiuvariorum*, and is correctly, if too strongly, applied by Stein to *Lex Salica* ('Lex Salica II', p. 417). It applies to all the barbarian laws.

[4] Hardly anything, for example, survives of the *Lex Euriciana*, for Reccasvinth ordered all the old law books to be destroyed. (*Lex Vis. Recc.* II, i, IX. Zeumer, p. 44).

sometimes meaningless emendations. The apparently sudden dissemination of manuscripts of *Lex Salica* in the ninth century may in part have been due to the great dispersal of Franks entailed by Charlemagne's policy of using them in the government and settlement of his Empire. *Vassi dominici* settled in Bavaria or Italy would still be entitled to judgement by *Lex Salica*, and might well desire to produce evidence of what this was, particularly at a time when traditional law was wearing thin and men wished to consult something written before giving judgement. The Italian capitularies contain several references to the Salian Franks, i.e. those acknowledging *Lex Salica*.[1] The *Lex* was even embellished with a new or re-written prologue.[2] It is, of course, a poor argument that a prologue full of the glory of the past cannot have been added in the reign of Pippin III because he was 'anti-Merovingian', when of such sentiments Stein produces no earlier witness than Einhard, who wrote some sixty years after Pippin's death. As it happened, Pippin and his contemporaries echoed, in their barbarian fashion, the very sentiment of the *Prooemium* to Justinian's Institutes: 'inperatoriam maiestatem non solum armis decoratam sed etiam legibus oportet esse armatam'. However, Stein does make effective use of Einhard to show that Charlemagne's emendation of *Lex Salica* is not as simple a matter as at first it looks. Einhard does not state that Charlemagne emended the barbarian written codes, but 'cum adverteret multa legibus populi sui deesse – nam Franci duas habent leges, in plurimis locis valde diversas – cogitavit quae deerant addere et discrepantia unire, prava quoque ac perperam prolata corrigere. Sed de his nihil aliud ab eo factum est nisi quod pauca capitula, et ea inperfecta, legibus addidit'.[3]

He meant therefore to emend *Lex Salica* and its sister, *Lex Ribvaria*, but never succeeded in doing so. It may, perhaps, be necessary for us to modify the accepted picture of the *Lex Salica Emendata*, according as to whether we accept Stein's interpretation of

[1] I owe this point to Mr Grierson.
[2] Kantorowicz, op cit. p. 58, observes how the longer prologue is a blend of acclamation and litany peculiar to the Carolingian age. On the dating of the prologues and their political significance see Elisabeth Pfeil, *Die fränkische und deutsche Romidee des frühen Mittelalters* (1929), pp. 80–96.
[3] *Vita Karoli Magni*, c. 29 (ed. L. Halphen, '*Les Classiques de l'Histoire de France au Moyen Age*', 3rd ed., 1947), p. 82.

the title in MS 10758;[1] though, whichever view finally prevails, Charlemagne's reputation as legislator will not be much affected by arguing that, for a short time, his grandson was also *Carolus Magnus*.[2]

The value of *Lex Salica* to the historian is in urgent need of reconsideration. Stein has raised many points of importance, not least among them the rôle of Rheims and of Hincmar himself in the history of the transmission of the text; and there is a real danger that scholars, angered alike by his inaccuracy and his assertiveness, may dismiss the good with the bad. But nothing is gained – and in these early stages, something may be lost – by attributing to Hincmar and his circle a forgery at once difficult and pointless. His mind was at home with legal texts. He knew that 'populus sine lege populus sine Christo est.[3] He certainly knew *Lex Salica*; perhaps the very manuscript he handled has been preserved, as Stein urges. It would have been impossible for a man of his tastes not to have been interested in such a text. Indeed, he expressly refers to it on more than one occasion, as when, in a letter to the king on behalf of the bishops, he writes:

> defendant se quantum volunt qui huiusmodi sunt, sive per leges, si ullae sunt, mundanas, sive per consuetudines humanas, tamen si Christiani sunt, sciant se in die iudicii nec Romanis, nec Salis, nec Gundobadis, sed divinis et Apostolicis legibus iudicandos.[4]

But this is a direct equation of *Lex Salica* with the Visigothic

[1] 'Lex Salica II', p. 395. My own examination of Vatican MS Reg. Christina Lat. 991, of the tenth century (or earlier?) leads me to agree with R. Buchner (op. cit. p. 88) that it may be an official text of the emended barbarian laws then current, and accordingly may have a special importance in the history of *Lex Salica Emendata*.

[2] Confusion between the two emperors can, of course, occur, as in the ninth-century liturgical acclamation in Metz MS 351. (See Kantorowicz, op. cit. p. 73, n. 30).

[3] *De duodecim abusivis saeculi* (ed. by S. Hellmann in A. Harnack and C. Schmidt, *Texte und Untersuchungen zur Geschichte der altchristlichen Literatur*, series III, vol. 4, Leipzig, 1909, p. 59). The influence of this seventh-century Irish tract on political thought in the ninth century is rightly emphasized by M. L. W. Laistner, *Thought and Letters in Western Europe* (2nd ed., 1957), pp. 144–46.

[4] *De raptu viduarum*, Sirmond, op. cit. vol. 2, p. 234. Dated by Schrörs '860?–882' (op. cit. p. 559). The letter does not, so far as I can tell, appear in the first part of the new *Monumenta* edition of Hincmar's correspondence (1939). Did Hincmar draw upon Merovingian historical material for purposes of illustration in his extensive political correspondence? A preliminary survey leads me to suspect that he did not.

and Burgundian Codes. *Lex Salica* was to the writer a particular and a comparable code. Are we really to suppose that the whole Frankish episcopate for which he speaks had had time to assimilate so recent a 'forgery' as the new Frankish code from Rheims? A definitive study of *Lex Salica*, Stein rightly concludes, 'can be accomplished only in connection with other Volksrechte.'[1] It seems that our chances of selecting, let alone of reconstructing, the 'original' *Lex Salica* are remote indeed. Probably there never was an 'original' in the diplomatic sense. All we can do is to choose between the various sets of historical circumstances that might have produced a law committed to writing. And the traditional choice is not yet much affected by Stein's suggestive comments about the interest of Rheims in the text.

## IV

In his old age, Hincmar devoted himself to the writing of contemporary history. Twenty-one years (861–882) of the *Annales Bertiniani* are his work.[2] Here he was continuing, and knew that he was continuing, the great Carolingian tradition of the Royal Annals; and, for all his prejudices, his range of knowledge and interest make this section of the *Annales* the most remarkable, by far, of the sources for the reign of his master, Charles the Bald, 'ex progenie Hludowici regis Francorum incliti, per beati Remigii Francorum apostoli catholicam praedicationem cum integra gente conversi'.[3] But it is in a second piece, the *Ad proceres regis et de ordine palatii*,[4] that Hincmar speaks most clearly – and for the last time – about the past. His assurance that his views are in the main the reflection of those of Adalhard of Corbie, 'domni Caroli magni imperatoris propinquum', has met with scepticism, for Adalhard's *libellus* had gone, leaving no trace.[5] It is inherently

[1] 'Lex Salica II', p. 418.
[2] Ed. G. Waitz, *M.G.H., SS, in usum schol.* (1883). This edition is, in general, excellent; however, a new edition by the late L. Levillain and the late F. Grat, was announced. cf. F. L. Ganshof, 'Notes critiques sur les Annales Bertiniani' (*Mélanges Felix Grat*, vol. 2, Paris, 1949).
[3] Ed. Waitz, p. 104.
[4] His shorter treatise, *De regis persona et regio ministerio*, is made up of excerpts from earlier writers, and contains little or nothing of his own views.
[5] A notable sceptic is L. Halphen, 'Le De ordine Palatii d'Hincmar' (*Rev. Hist.*, clxxxii, 1938, and reprinted in *A travers l'Histoire du Moyen Age*, 1950).

possible, even probable, that Adalhard might have written such a book. But whether or not he did so, Hincmar's interpretation of the material is his own. With the Merovingians he is hardly at all concerned. As always, there is room for Clovis, the faithful convert of St Rémi,[1] but little enough for the Merovingian palace and none at all for *Lex Salica*. The author hurries on to the true burden of his tale, the unfolding of the felicities of Charlemagne's court-procedure, all skilfully arranged to give the sovereign the minimum of administration and as much time as possible for contemplation of his spiritual duties. Charlemagne might not have recognized all of this picture of his daily life; but that was how the heir of St Rémi saw the heir of Clovis. We may deny, if we wish, the truth of much of Hincmar's history, from Clovis to Charlemagne included. We may wonder why its scholarly author should have had an historical conscience so different from Bede's. But what we cannot deny is its relevance and effect.[2]

[1] Chap. xiv (ed. Prou), pp. 36 seq.; (ed. Krause), pp. 522-3.

[2] Several friends, notably Professor F. L. Ganshof and Mr Philip Grierson who read this article in typescript, gave me valuable advice, for which I thank them.

CHAPTER SIX

# The Bloodfeud of the Franks [1]

*

Among the debts owed by the Germanic tribes to the Romans must be reckoned, with certain reservations, the debt of law. The earliest *Volksrechte* bear traces of the complex legacy of Roman Vulgar Law.[2] Few scholars nowadays, students of Frankish history and law, could agree with Waitz that 'von Recht kann wenig die Rede sein',[3] or would deny that the barbarian successor-states do in fact become the more intelligible as the wanderings of the *Codex Theodosianus* and its western derivatives are kept in mind.[4] And yet a danger lurks here, too; the danger of overlooking the simple truth that the core of all Germanic customary practice was German. This is why it is worth spending a little time upon the most undoubtedly Germanic of all barbarian institutions, the bloodfeud, and to invite consideration of it, moreover, not as an incoherent interlude between Gaius and Glanvil, but as a sociological experiment instructive in itself. We see, as the barbarians did not, the whole panorama of forces, procedural and moral, arrayed against feud, and to some of them this paper will presently draw attention. We note the development from the private feud-settlements of the Germans to public and royal arbitration and intervention, even if we do not always see the corollary, that the legal processes of the *Volksrechte* succeeded just

---

[1] *Bulletin of the John Rylands Library*, vol. 41, no. 2 (March 1959): a lecture delivered in the John Rylands Library, Manchester. I wish to thank Mr Philip Grierson and my wife for reading the lecture in draft and for making several valuable suggestions.

[2] See, for example, Ernst Levy, *West Roman Vulgar Law, The Law of Property* (1951) and *Weströmisches Vulgarrecht, das Obligationenrecht* (1956); J. F. Lemarignier, 'Les actes de droit privé de Saint-Bertin au haut moyen âge. Survivances et déclin du droit romain dans la pratique franque', *Rev. Internat. des Droits de l'Antiquité*, vol. 5 (1950); J. Gaudemet, 'Survivances romaines dans le droit de la monarchie franque du Ve au Xe siècle', *Revue d'histoire du droit*, vol. xxiii (1955).

[3] *Deutsche Verfassungsgeschichte*, i (1880), 200.

[4] The point is developed in chapter I.

because they derived from feud-processes and closely followed them. We note, too, the continuing pressure of the Church and of Late Roman legal tradition in favour of the abandonment of feud. None of this can be gainsaid. But the death of feud and the better things that replaced it are one thing: the fact of its life, another. Allowing for all these pressures upon it, feud yet lived for centuries in western Europe without frontal attack and without stigma. What, then, was its indispensable strength? What actually happened when feud threatened and broke out?

These few pages are limited to the evidence of those who witnessed and described feuds that we can still read about; but before turning to them, there are certain preliminary matters that require clarification.

In the first place, it is not difficult to arrive at what, for these purposes, is a working definition of feud. We may call it, first, the threat of hostility between kins; then, the state of hostility between them; and finally, the satisfaction of their differences and a settlement on terms acceptable to both. The threat, the state and the settlement of that hostility constitute feud but do not necessarily mean bloodshed. Indeed, it is not certain that a legal right to blood, however we understand it, should ever be assumed among the Franks without proof. There is no mention of such right in *Lex Salica*, and the famous rebuke of the *iudex loci* to the man who avenged his brother's death without leave points in another direction.[1] But of moral right there is no question. Feud is never a crime until it is made so, and cannot till then be studied within the context of criminal law. In brief, it is a way for the settlement of differences, whether through violence or negotiation or both,[2] even though it would be vain to look for any such definition in the sources of the early Middle Ages. We must search for our feuds, incipient or flourishing, in a maze of terms that can mislead: the Frankish *faithu*, latinized as *faidus*,[3] may mean what we are after,

[1] Gregory of Tours, *Vitae Patrum*, 8, 7 (*M.G.H., S.R.M.*, i, 697).

[2] Professor D. Whitelock, *The Beginnings of English Society* (1952), p. 43, makes clear this intimate connection. She further thinks that in England the heavy expense of homicide-payment had much to do with the continuance of feud by fighting.

[3] It may, significantly, mean the injured party's share in composition. Cf. H. Brunner, *Deutsche Rechtsgeschichte*, i (1906), 231; *Lex Salica*, 35 (ed. K. A. Eckhardt, *Pactus Legis Salicae, 65 Titel-Text*, 1955); and J. M. Pardessus, *Diplomata*, ii (1849), no. 431, p. 229.

or it may mean something different; feud may lurk behind *inimicus*, *hostis*, *vindicta*, *intentio*, *altercatio*, *bella civilia*, or it may not. As an institution, feud remains undefined by those who have resort to it. If they help us to distinguish feud from any and every sporadic outbreak of violence, they do so unwittingly. All vengeance is not feud, and all bloodshed is not bloodfeud. If we really wish to see bloodshed practised as a fine art, we cannot do better than turn to Byzantium, mistress of the West in this as in so much else.

Vendetta may be studied, even today, in almost any quarter of the globe, in Arabia or Africa, for instance, or nearer home among patriarchal societies in the mountains of Albania, Sicily, Sardinia and Corsica; and it is so studied by the sociologist.[1] We can learn from him and afterwards look with a new eye to the more particular study of feuding in medieval Europe, and paradoxically may find it easier not to use events of the tenth century to illustrate situations in the fifth, and not to think that Anglo-Saxon laws or Scandinavian sagas are applicable to the Frankish or the Gothic scene.[2] Just here, the great German legal historians came to grief, though it is easy to see why they did so. The concern of this paper is with the Franks of Gaul in the Merovingian age, and it does not take as evidence the feuding practices of the barbarian contemporaries of the Franks, apart from such as were intimately connected with them, like the Burgundians or the Visigoths; neither does it call upon the practices of Carolingian Europe, where feud of a very different sort may be studied. The evidence is Frankish, and specifically literary; the evidence of the historians and the chroniclers and the writers of saints' *Lives*. Why should they have included their tales of feud? Was it as a warning to the furious, or

---

[1] I owe much to Max Gluckman's *Custom and Conflict in Africa* (1955). Margaret Hasluck, *The Unwritten Law in Albania* (1954) and I. Shapiro, 'The Sin of Cain', *J.R. Anthropological Inst.*, 85 (1955) are suggestive.

[2] The point is forcibly made by F. L. Ganshof, 'L'Étranger dans la monarchie franque', *Recueils de la Société Jean Bodin*, vol. x, pt. 2 (1958), 8. This is not to say that the student of Frankish feuding can neglect the important general ideas contained, for example, in English writings on Anglo-Saxon feuds – e.g. in F. M. Stenton, *Anglo-Saxon England* (2nd ed., 1947); F. Pollock and F. W. Maitland, *The History of English Law*, vol. ii (1895) and Maitland's *Collected Papers*, vol. i (1911); R. W. Chambers, *Beowulf, an Introduction* (1921); H. M. Chadwick, *The Heroic Age* (1926); F. Seebohm, *Tribal Custom in Anglo-Saxon Law* (1911); and B. S. Phillpotts, *Kindred and Clan* (1913). Nor can he overlook the excellent evidence of the feuds of the Lombards.

could they not resist a good story? Did they report the exceptional or the commonplace? Why is their evidence sometimes at variance with what the Frankish laws bid us believe?

To the Hun, Attila, there was nothing like a good feud: 'quid viro forti suavius quam vindicta manu querere?' [1] He spoke thus for warriors far beyond, and more civilized far than, his own Hunnic warbands. All the barbarian invaders of the Empire loved a feud. Not even the learned Cassiodorus could suppose otherwise. [2] We may term it the classical feud of the migrating period, though, of course, it lasted longer; it was that kind of kin-hostility where there was killing in hot blood and with all publicity for the sake of honour, most particularly in avenging an act of treachery. [3] This was the true vengeance, girt about with a magical symbolism that may have remained potent for much longer than we know. Hot blood was never to be overlooked; while in it, a man and his kin might be excused almost anything, and no amount of teaching ever quite persuaded the medieval mind that it was wrong. It will crop up, in various forms, in the evidence. [4] But it is only one kind of feud, and there were many others (at least in the Merovingian era) that arose out of theft, cattle-rustling, accidental injury or mere misunderstanding. The tariffs of the *Volksrechte* warn us at a glance that homicide was but one among many injuries from which feud might spring. The facts hardly suggest that the Franks spent more than a small portion of their time

---

[1] Jordanes, *Getica*, ch. 39 (ed. Th. Mommsen, *M.G.H., Auct. Antiq.*, V, pt. 1, 1882, 110).

[2] *Variae*, I, 38; *M.G.H., Auct. Antiq.*, xii (1894), 36.

[3] R. W. Chambers pointed out that an act of treachery made the acceptance of composition particularly difficult (op. cit. p. 278).

[4] Cf. F. Dahn, 'Fehdegang und Rechtsgang der Germanen', *Bausteine*, ii (1879), 80, 83, 106, 108; Brunner, DRG. i. 120, 222; and Julius Goebel, *Felony and Misdemeanor*, i (1937), 85. Goebel's misleading sub-title, 'A study in the history of English criminal procedure', has caused this volume, which is largely concerned with Frankish procedure, to be somewhat overlooked on the continent. It attacks Brunner's theory of the Germanic 'peace' and hence of outlawry, while still regarding feud as 'an interminable antiphony of violence'. There is, however, an important review by Heinrich Mitteis, reprinted in his *Die Rechtsidee in der Geschichte* (1957). As concerns the study of feud, Goebel's special merit is to have summarized the conclusions of a very important study by Franz Beyerle, *Das Entwicklungsproblem im germanischen Rechtsgang*, I, *Sühne, Rache und Preisgabe in ihrer Beziehung zum Strafprozess der Volksrechte* (Heidelberg, 1915), published as vol. x, pt. 2, of *Deutschrechtliche Beiträge*.

defending their honour. Blood tends to cool. The interesting cases
of feud are seldom clear-cut affairs of honour and betray, even
then, the natural pulls inherent in feud-society towards settlement and composition. Fighting may be fun, but only a grievous
injury or a series of misunderstandings will lead to the destruction
of the man-power of a family, let alone of a kin. Composition,
offering a natural escape, stretches back far beyond the tariffs of
Lex Salica to composition in kind in the early Germanic period.
The world, private and official, stood ready to arbitrate.

Of the pressures working against whatever traditional forms of
feud the Franks brought to Gaul, one was the extreme complexity
of Gallo-Frankish society. Already far advanced from the com-
parative simplicities of Tacitus's *Germania*, the Franks of the fifth
and sixth centuries settled in a variety of ways upon the Gaulish
countryside. We find them at home in abandoned Roman *villae*, in
Gallic *vici*, at work in small or large groups upon upland ranches,
mixing in varying proportions and over a long period in Gaulish
and barbarian settlements other than Frankish.[1] How, in these
circumstances, could the kin remain a coherent social force?
Kindred must rapidly have become scattered over wide areas and
the ties of blood within a single settlement become hopelessly
intermixed. You could leave your kin and presumably join another;[2] and the claims of lordship (already active in Tacitus's time)
might well pull against the claims of kin.[3] How could the kin
charged with responsibility for feud, whether the agnatic kin or
the wider circle of blood-relations,[4] be mobilized for war except
as a small *ad hoc* vengeance-group? So we arrive somewhere near
the situation envisaged in another context by Professor Gluckman, where the mere elaboration and interdependence of kin-
groups may ensure a kind of immobility. Common blood and

[1] R. Latouche, *Les origines de l'économie occidentale* (1956), pp. 41 ff. summarizes recent work.

[2] *Lex Salica*, 60 (*De eum qui se de parentilla tollere vult*) and 46 (*De acfatmire*). See the remarks of Max Pappenheim, 'Über künstliche Verwandtschaft im germanischen Rechte', *Zeitschrift der Savigny-Stiftung, Germ. Abt.* xxix (1908), 313, 320.

[3] I agree with T. H. Aston that 'relatives and followers were never mutually exclusive categories' (*Trans Roy. Hist. Soc.*, 5th series, viii, 1958, 79). Nor must we overlook the added complexity of the godparental relationship; cf. Pappenheim, op. cit. 307, and J. P. Bodmer, *Der Krieger der Merowingerzeit und seine Welt* (1957), p. 40.

[4] Brunner, *DRG.*, i 112, 120.

propinquity will always make for settlement. This is not to imply
that feud-war will not break out on a minor scale nor that the idea
of fighting is abandoned. Far from it. The sanction of feud-war is
the reality that lies behind every feud-settlement and agreement to
pay and receive composition; but it is difficult to implement and
not lightly to be entered upon, even when a man has a lord to
uphold his quarrel or is himself a lord strong in dependants,
whether or not of his blood. (One may suspect that in practice the
assistance of kindred and of such dependants was often not clearly
distinguishable.) The kin, especially such members as lived within
easy reach, must often have been called upon to meet and act as
judges and arbiters in family disputes that were none the less feud-
disputes because unlikely to lead to bloodshed. They it was who
agreed to pay, or to accept, the heavy price of blood, or to disown
the offending kinsman; and other duties too were thrust upon
them, beyond what the *Volksrechte* reveal.[1] The Frankish kin was
probably less often involved as a fighting force than as a compos-
ing one. From the mere nature of their settlement, it must be
wide of the mark to conceive of the Franks being at all often
engaged in major kin-warfare.

Against feud also stood the Church, with its teaching and its
practice opposed to bloodshed.[2] There can be no doubt that the
Frankish Church was for arbitration and composition; Gregory of
Tours himself describes for us an occasion when he acted in per-
son as arbitrator.[3] Such is the sense of the well-known words of
Avitus on the subject,[4] the plea of St Bonitus for *concordia*,[5] St
Germanus on *inhonesta victoria*,[6] the whole tenor of the fascinating
*Liber Scintillarum* of Defensor of Ligugé,[7] to say nothing of the
Church's intimate connection with our earliest manuscripts of the
*Volksrechte*. (We can associate some of these manuscripts with a

---

[1] See *Lex Salica*, 58 (*De chrenecruda*) and 62 (*De compositione homicidii*); *Formulae Salicae Bignonianae* 8, *Noticia de homicidio* (M.G.H., *Formulae*, 1886, p. 230); *Pactus pro tenore pacis* 2 (*M.G.H., Capit.* i, 1883, 4).

[2] This is well expressed in Lot, Pfister and Ganshof, *Les destinées de l'empire en occident* (1940), p. 310. See also A. Michel, 'Vengeance', *Dict. de Théol. Cath.*, xv, 2 (1950), cols 2613-23.

[3] *Hist.*, VII, 47.    [4] ibid., III, 6.    [5] *M.G.H., S.R.M.*, vi, 121.

[6] *M.G.H., Epist.*, iii (*Epist. Mero. et Karo. Aevi*, i), p. 123.

[7] Edited by Dom Henri Rochais in *Corpus Christianorum, Series Latina*, cxvii, pt. i (1957).

known church or churchman, as for instance one fine collection with St Gallen, or the ninth-century copy of the *Lex Baiuvariorum*, now in Munich,[1] with Bishop Hitto of Freising.) But how will you get arbitration without the sanction of bloodshed? How, if a cleric, can you be sure of putting from your mind the claims of your own blood? One Frankish bishop at least, Badigisil of Le Mans, made no bones about this: 'non ideo, quia clericus factus sum, et ultur iniuriarum mearum non ero?'[2] He might, had he known it, have cited in his favour a letter from a pope to an Italian *Magister Militum*, instructing him to avenge the bearer for his brother's murder.[3] More interesting, however, are the difficulties in which less bellicose clerics found themselves. How could they reconcile their views with that *ultio divina* that was their own main prop in a wicked world? Look through his writings for the view of Gregory of Tours on divine vengeance and it will be found that he visualizes it as nothing less than God's own feud in support of his servants, who can have no other kin. God will avenge crimes specially heinous in the Church's eyes – parricide for example, crimes within the family generally and crimes involving all who lack natural protectors. The agent of vengeance may be God himself directly intervening to strike down the culprit (for instance, with sickness) or it may be a human agent, as the king. At all events, God's vengeance is of the same nature as that of any head of a family or warband. He strikes to kill, to avenge insult – to himself, to his children or to his property. The Frankish churchmen cannot in any other way see *ultio divina* in a society dominated by the bloodfeud.[4] We may know that Romans xii, 19 – 'mihi vindicta, ego retribuam dicit Dominus' – has nothing to do with bloodfeud, but to the Franks and Gallo-Romans it was not so clear.[5] We must not, then, expect to find Gregory of Tours, brought up to bloodshed, protected by an avenging God and on at least one occasion more than indulgent towards the ferocious

[1] Clm. 19415.
[2] Gregory, *Hist.*, VIII, 39.　　　[3] *M.G.H., Epist.*, iii, 696.
[4] Examples of the attitude of the Frankish Church to divine vengeance are: Gregory, *Hist.*, I, 2, 41; II, 10; III, 5, 28; IV, 20; V, 5; VII, 3, 29; X, 13; also *M.G.H., S.R.M.*, iv, 710, 715, 731; ibid., vi, 281, 377; *Vita Columbani*, ed. Krusch, p. 213.
[5] Romans xii, 19 is in fact cited at the close of the account of how God protected St Willibrord from the custodian of the idol on Walcheren (*Vita Willibrordi*, 14; *M.G.H., S.R.M.*, vii, 128).

treachery of his hero Clovis,[1] opposed to all bloodfeuds merely because they were bloody. His attitude and that of his contemporaries, constituting the attitude of his Church, is, in general, opposed to the sanction of bloodfeud but tends in practice, and for no shameful reason, to be equivocal. He is often opposed to bloodfeuds without seeing the need to state and maintain a case against bloodfeud.

Roman Law, on the other hand, had no need to be equivocal. It had had no truck with feud since the far-off days of the XII Tables.[2] The Theodosian Code and its Visigothic derivatives take their stand on the personal responsibility of the criminal, the *auctor sceleris*;[3] his kin should not suffer for him: 'ille solus culpavilis erit qui culpanda conmiserit'.[4] The Burgundian and Merovingian kings were in varying degrees influenced by their legal advisers in this direction.[5] Burgundian Law in particular tends towards compromise; it admits, for example, occasions when a kin might pursue a killer without, however, pursuing the killer's kin.[6] But even in Visigothic Spain, a stronghold of Vulgar Roman Law, King Wamba was quite clear that any killer was in the *potestas* of the injured kin.[7] If the Visigoths and the Burgundians found difficulties in applying Roman practice among peoples otherwise inclined, we might well look for trouble with the Merovingians.

One question, therefore, on which we must search for light in the Frankish evidence, is the extent to which the Merovingian kings succumbed to these pressures and turned against feud.

---

[1] *Hist.*, II, 42.
[2] On the situation before the XII Tables, see David Daube, *The Defence of Superior Orders in Roman Law* (1956), pp. 19 ff. See footnote 1, p. 144. For a comparable Old Testament situation, cf. Shapiro, loc. cit. p. 36, where it is emphasized that Deuteronomy xxiv, 16 ('every man shall be put to death for his own sin') belongs to one of the later legal codes.
[3] Apart altogether from Roman Law, the Germanic kindred shows some tendency to make the wrongdoer personally responsible, especially when faced with finding a heavy wergild.
[4] *Lex Visig Reccessvind.*, VII, *Antiqua* (ed. K. Zeumer, *Leges Visigothorum Antiquiores*, 1894, p. 180, who also cites 11 *Dig.* xlviii, 4 – *extinguitur crimen mortalitate*).
[5] Cf. F. Olivier-Martin, *Histoire du droit français* (1948), p. 56.
[6] *Lex Burg.* ii. 7, *M.G.H.*, *Leges Sect.* 1, ii, pt. 1 (1892), 43; cf. *Lex Burg.* xviii, ibid., p. 56; and see the sensible interpretation of E. Levy, *Das Obligationenrecht*, p. 347.
[7] Cf. Brunner, *Forschungen* (1894), p. 492. *Hist. Wambae*, ch. 9, *M.G.H.*, *S.R.M.*, v, 508.

Some distinguished scholars have had no doubt that they succumbed very largely;[1] but a different case could be argued. What,
it might be asked, could the Frankish kings do with a disintegrating kin-system in which the individual more and more
escaped from kin-responsibility and kin-protection? What active,
legislative support could they lend to a situation where in practice,
as Maitland saw in an English context, every new feud demanded
an entirely fresh kin-grouping?[2] The Merovingians thus remained
independent of, if not unaffected by, the teaching of Church and
civilians; it was, as we shall see, still right in Merovingian eyes to
enter upon the process of feud, whether it was to lead through
bloodshed or composition to ultimate satisfaction. Without the
sanction of blood, composition would have stood a poor chance
in a world lacking not simply a police-force but the requisite
concept of public order.[3] It is easy to imagine that, with the recording of the *Volksrechte* and the publication of instruments like
the *Decretio* of Childebert II, the *Pactus pro tenore pacis* and the
documents of the formularies of Marculf and others, we have
moved into a new world of royal authority. Useless to deny that
the earlier Merovingians were extraordinarily powerful and much
feared. But yet, when we come to inquire what it was that made
the composition-tariffs of *Lex Salica* work and why wergilds and
lesser compositions were in fact paid, the answer is, not fear of
local royal officials but fear of feud; or rather, it is both. To be
sure, the Merovingians have an interest in intervening in the
course of feuds when possible and where they can see profit ac-
cruing to the fisc through fine or confiscation; the *fredus* was
worth having; this is expressed procedurally;[4] but at what time in
barbarian history would chieftains not have intervened in the
feuds of their followers for similar reasons?[5] The Romans did
much the same. No new principle was at stake. One can detect no
blow at the principle of feuding in the famous titles of King

[1] e.g. Olivier-Martin, *Histoire*, p. 127; Goebel, *Felony and Misdemeanor*, pp. 21, 27.
[2] *History of English Law*, ii, 239.          [3] Goebel, op. cit. pp. 39–43.
[4] Goebel, op. cit. pp. 103 ff., 114.
[5] Cf. *Form. Marculfi*, i, 32 (*M.G.H., Formulae*, p. 62) insists, naturally enough,
that no feud should follow when royal officials have intervened to exact penalties.
But this does not seem to have helped Chrodin in the story in Fredegar's chronicle,
III, 58 (*M.G.H., S.R.M.,* ii). See also Goebel, op. cit. p. 90.

Chilperic's *Edictum*:[1] namely (*tit.* 8) that the *malus homo* (that is, professional malefactor), who cannot make composition and whom his kin will not redeem, may be turned over to his accusers, and (*tit.* 10) that the *malus homo* who cannot redeem himself and is beyond the control of his kin may be slain by anyone without incurring risk of feud.[2] Is King Childebert deliberately narrowing the function of feud when he forbids killing *sine causa* and decrees that such a killer shall neither make composition nor have it made for him, and that his *parentes* and *amici* shall suffer for it if they try to do so? Brunner thought he was;[3] but it cannot be proved. At least it gave the king a chance to finish his title with a little Roman flourish: 'iustum est ut qui novit occidere discat morire'. On the other hand, there are passages that reveal the Merovingians actively defining and approving occasions of feud; for instance, by attempting to sort out the degrees of responsibility for taking vengeance within the kin.[4] As Goebel puts it, the Merovingians were concerned with harsh answers to instant questions: 'What is to be done about professional crime? May offenders be executed? Can the fisc take their property?'[5] Groping for answers and grappling with problems that lay outside the kin (a case in point is murder as distinct from homicide), they now and again struck a glancing blow at feud; traces of such will be found scattered in their laws. But this hardly amounts to a deliberate attack upon the principle of feud.

It may be well to state that Gregory of Tours, from whose History much of our evidence of feud is drawn, was not interested in feud as such, and he might have been surprised to hear that some historians have seen in his writings the picture of a society disintegrating through feud. Of one special, because unnatural, kind of feud he particularly disapproved: the civil wars between members of one kin, the Merovingians themselves; and in the prologue to his Fifth Book he exhorts them to slay their enemies,

[1] *M.G.H., Capit.*, i, 8–10.

[2] See Goebel, op. cit. p. 53.

[3] *DRG.*, i, 329; also A. Halban-Blumenstock, 'Königsschutz und Fehde', *Zeitsch. der Sav.-Stiftung, Germ. Abt.* xvii (1896), 74. Miss Phillpotts, *Kindred and Clan*, p. 195, seems to be seriously astray.

[4] *Lex Salica*, 41, add. 2; *Lex Ribvaria*, 77 (ed. F. Beyerle and R. Buchner, p. 129); also Brunner, *DRG.* i, 226 and Beyerle, *Das Entwicklungsproblem*, p. 500.

[5] Op. cit. p. 62.

not each other. 'Cavete bella civilia' he cries, meaning by this that specially heinous type of feud – heinous because self-destroying – the rising of *proximus in propinquum*;[1] yet his own evidence shows that this very propinquity of blood was one of the factors that led his warring Merovingians towards settlement. They did not enjoy fighting one another. It is worth looking at some of Gregory's examples of feud within the royal kin or involving the royal kin.

We may take first a feud between the Merovingians and the royal Burgundian house, a feud brought about by a woman. Gregory gives it some prominence.[2] The Merovingian queen Chrotechildis, by birth a Burgundian, urges her sons to avenge the deaths of her parents, not on the murderer, her uncle Gundobad, but on his sons, Sigismund and Godomar. In other words, the Merovingian princes were being required by their mother to attack their second cousins. This they proceeded to do and, defeating the Burgundian princes, imprisoned one of them, perhaps with the intention of obtaining a heavy composition. It is only on a later occasion, after a second attack had become necessary, that the Merovingian Chlodomer decides to kill the imprisoned Sigismund and his family: they are all thrown down a well. There is more to the feud than this; but its features are clear: two royal kins, related by marriage but distinct and separated by a considerable distance, show no hesitation in attacking one another, the one taking vengeance for blood on the second generation of the other. There is something to suggest that complete and early submission by the Burgundians might have induced the Merovingian princes to accept a settlement on terms. But the Burgundians would not submit. Gregory himself has no adverse comment to make on the reason for the feud.[3] We must suppose that he thought it justifiable. What he disapproves of is the slaying in cold blood of the captive prince and family as an act rather of military prudence (to prevent attack in the rear) than of vengeance intended from the first. Chlodomer himself deserved to die by a ruse in the subsequent battle: his head was raised on a spear,

[1] *Hist.*, V, prol. Exile and confiscation were a characteristic Frankish reaction to the killing of near relatives (cf. Goebel, op. cit. p. 109).
[2] *Hist.*, III, 6.
[3] Some historians look upon the story as essentially a myth. I do not know why.

so publicly demonstrating the Burgundian viewpoint in the feud.

Gregory has other cases of Merovingian feuds with princes outside the Frankish orbit. One, that between the Ripuarian Franks and the Thuringians, follows directly on the Burgundian feud.[1] The *iniuria* of which the Frankish king here complained was a breach of trust: it did not prevent his killing his Thuringian rival by a trick. Trickery, indeed, was a commonplace of Frankish feuding; it might happen at any stage of a feud short of the final agreement, and particularly in the penultimate stages of arbitration or armistice; and nobody thought any the worse of it.[2] An entire group of Merovingian feuds was waged with their southern neighbours and connections by marriage, the Visigoth kings.[3] We find King Childebert marching to Spain to avenge his sister, wife of the Arian Amalaric. She had sent him a bloodstained handkerchief in proof of the treatment she had suffered for her faith.[4] His motive in marching to kill Amalaric was not brotherly affection; it was duty; and duty normally did dictate such kin-action.[5] But duty could be satisfied short of bloodshed; for, a little later, Gregory tells of the Merovingians sending to the Goth Theodohat for proper composition for the killing of their cousin, a lady who deserved her fate if anyone did; and in fear he paid them 50,000 *aurei*.[6] Inevitably he had been threatened with destruction if he failed to pay; that was the sanction of the composition. Dalton long ago showed how inaccurate the story was in detail;[7] and yet the point remained for Gregory's readers: the death of Theodohat's victim was shameful, feud was the only answer – and composition was perfectly in order.

[1] *Hist.*, III, 7 and 8.

[2] Goebel, op. cit. p. 29: Beyerle, op. cit. pp. 117 ff.

[3] I leave out of account a presumably apocryphal tale related in bk. II, ch. 58 of Fredegar's chronicle (*M.G.H., S.R.M.*, ii, 82–3) of the feud between Clovis and the Visigoths, who came armed to parley with the Franks and were adjudged by Theodoric the Great, acting as arbiter, to owe as composition that amount of gold that would cover a mounted warrior with spear erect. Beyerle, op. cit. pp. 269, 313 ff., 328, 349, has emphasized the importance of the description for arbitration procedure for the feuds of Fredegar's own day. See also *Form. Marc.*, II, 16, 18 (*M.G.H., Form.*, pp. 85, 88) and *Form. Andecavenses*, 6, 42 (ibid., pp. 6, 19).

[4] *Hist.*, III, 10.    [5] The point is made by J. P. Bodmer, *Der Krieger*, p. 20.

[6] *Hist.*, III, 31.

[7] *The History of the Franks by Gregory of Tours*, ii (1927), 513–14.

An independent group of Merovingian-Visigoth feuds involve Guntramn, Merovingian king of Burgundy. Guntramn is a rich gift to the historian of feud. A prudent, calculating man, and ruler of the most romanized part of Frankish Gaul, one might well expect to find his face, if anybody's, set against feuding. Yet it is not. Guntramn is all for feud and keenly aware of his duties as senior representative of his kin. Enraged at the death of his niece Ingundis and of her Visigoth husband, Hermenegild, he arranges to attack Spain, which leads his adversary to plan elaborate distractions for him in Gaul.[1] But Guntramn's implacable hatred, it must be emphasized, had to do with avenging the death of Ingundis. He will not, he says, receive an embassy from the Visigoth Reccared 'donec me Deus ulcisci iubeat de his inimicis',[2] neither should his other niece, Chlodosind, go as bride to the land where her sister was slain – 'I cannot tolerate it that my niece Ingundis should go unavenged'.[3] This he declares, although the Visigoths were ready to close the feud by giving the most solemn oath to make amends.[4] The ramifications of this feud were substantial and indirectly involved the eastern emperors, in whose hands was the little son of the princess Ingundis. Letters were exchanged[5] and there was some coming and going of ambassadors by way of imperial Africa. It was in Carthage that the ambassadors of King Childebert were slain in a brawl. The Emperor Maurice offered twelve men as compensation: the Franks might do as they liked with them, or alternatively the Emperor would redeem them at 300 *aurei* each. The offer was rejected: how did Childebert know that these men were the guilty men, or, come to that, even free men?[6]

Another, and more complicated, group of royal feuds are within the Merovingian dynasty. About some of them hangs that air of tragic necessity that in general was a theme of Germanic literature,[7] as when a man cannot take vengeance in his own family; though

---

[1] *Hist.*, VIII, 28.  [2] *Hist.*, IX, 16.
[3] *Hist.*, IX, 20.  [4] Cf. Beyerle, op. cit. pp. 349, 421.
[5] *M.G.H.*, *Epist.*, iii. 149 ff. I treat with reservation the comments of P. Goubert, *Byzance avant l'Islam*, II, pt. 1 (1956), 95 ff. without however entirely accepting the reconstruction attempted by his critic, Walter Goffart, 'Byzantine Policy in the West under Tiberius II and Maurice' (*Traditio*, xiii, 1957).
[6] *Hist.*, X, 4.
[7] Cf. D. Whitelock, *Beginnings*, p. 39.

more than once a Merovingian finds that he must pursue and kill a treacherous son.[1] The most famous of them, involving the entire Merovingian house, sprang from the murder of the Visigothic princess Galswintha by her Merovingian husband, King Chilperic, allegedly at the instigation of his mistress Fredegundis. Traditions of polygamy died hard among the Merovingians, and the mistresses of Chilperic saw no reason to grant to the Visigothic princess the position of unique influence she demanded; so she died – quietly, and with the evident intention that her great dowry should remain intact in her husband's hands.[2] But Chilperic's royal brothers would have none of this and planned to seize Galswintha's dowry and to avenge her murder by deposing him. One of them, Sigebert, was the husband of Brunechildis, sister of the murdered woman; and but for this, and the undying hatred of Brunechildis for Fredegundis, it may be doubted whether the brothers would ever have taken much notice. What we have, then, is a fraternal feud contrived by wives and stretching over three generations. Of necessity it also involved the royal Visigoth house. King Childebert, requiring Guntramn to surrender Fredegundis to his vengeance, demands: 'Give up to me this murderer, who killed my aunt (Galswintha) and then my father (Sigebert) and my uncle (Chilperic) and cut down my cousins (Merovech and Clovis).'[3] Later, the demand is repeated; Guntramn must surrender this sorceress, this killer of kings, to vengeance.[4] But he will not, because he is not convinced of the charges; further, she is the mother of a king – and that, to the Merovingians, meant rather more than being the wife of one.[5] Uncommitted, yet drawn towards it, Guntramn saw the hopeless tragedy of this feud; he speaks feelingly of the iniquitous custom of killing kings and declares his intention not merely of killing one of the murderers employed, but of pursuing the man's kindred 'in nonam genera-

---

[1] *Hist.*, IV, 20; V, 14, 18. On the technical sense of *hostis* and *inimicus* see Beyerle, op. cit. p. 223. The situation is rather different in *Beowulf*, lines 2435-2443, where a father laments his inability to avenge the death of one son, accidentally slain, upon another.

[2] *Hist.*, IV, 28. Fredegar, III, 60, says that she was suffocated. Venantius Fortunatus, *Carm.*, vi, 5, does not mention murder.

[3] *Hist.*, VII, 7.      [4] *Hist.*, VII, 14.

[5] I agree with Bodmer, *Der Krieger*, p. 18.

tionem' [1] – that is, to the ninth degree of relationship.[2] He was determined to catch the murderer of his brother Chilperic. How, he asks Gregory of Tours, can he be counted a man if he fails to avenge that death within a year?[3] The bishop retorts that Chilperic had thoroughly deserved his end and this Guntramn certainly knew without its affecting his view of his own duty. All this and much else springs from the murder of Galswintha. Who shall say that composition might not soon have been reached among the brothers had not their family in practice lived as three distinct families in three distinct realms? However that may be, one of the grimmest features of this Merovingian feud is the employment of hired assassins.[4] If it be argued that such should play no part in feud, it can be asked how otherwise two women were to prosecute a feud in which their menfolk (and above all Guntramn, head of the family) were by no means always clear where duty lay, particularly when the matter of the dowry was not uppermost. The point is surely plain: it was the wrong kind of feud; not feuding but feuding within the kin was what led to pointless bloodshed that stopped nothing and offered few of the normal opportunities for compromise and settlement, even if it did offer some abnormal ones. The end of the story is related by Gregory's continuator, Fredegar. To him we owe the unforgettable account[5] of the arrest of the old queen Brunechildis by Chlotar, her arraignment and condemnation for the deaths of ten Merovingian kings, and finally her horrible death under the hooves of an unbroken horse. Those present at this scene, and Fredegar himself, saw this as the final expiation of a long feud. Is it, perhaps, this expiation rather than 'unitary rule' that lends an air of auspicious anticlimax to the subsequent reigns of Chlotar II and Dagobert?

Perhaps enough has been said of royal feud to make the point that, excepting the feud of Brunechildis with Fredegundis and others consequent upon it, there seemed, as a rule, nothing wrong about it to the participants, and often not to Gregory. It would be profitable to pursue the course of later Merovingian feuds in the pages of Fredegar and to interpret the relations of Pippin III, first

---

[1] *Hist.*, VII, 21, 29.
[2] Cf. Brunner, *DRG.*, i, 325.
[3] *Hist.*, VIII, 5.
[4] Cf. Beyerle, op. cit. p. 246.
[5] *Chron.*, IV, 42.

Carolingian king, with Ghislemar[1] and with Waiofar of Aquitaine[2] in terms of family feuding. But in this matter we may leave the last word with Gregory. Towards the close of his History he describes the scene at Poitiers when a riotous princess, another Chrote-childis, was brought to account. She stood at bay, begging that no violence be done her: 'I am a queen', she says, 'and a king's daughter, cousin of another king; take care, for the day may come when I shall take my revenge.'[3] The blood-vengeance of a Merovingian, in a word, was to be feared; it could be pursued with great resources; composition might not seem attractive, as it did with humbler folk (provided that they were not asked to pay it). The royal kin, moreover, had a way of sticking together and up-holding the feuds of its members against other kins, notably outside Frankish Gaul. Yet the forces making for settlement exist all the time, and are on occasion successful. The conscience that is shocked at feuding within the royal kin is not simply ecclesiastical: it is the conscience of a feuding society that rests, even while it disintegrates, on the idea of the unity of the kin.

A second and no less significant group of feuds we may classify as non-royal; in other words, they do not involve the Merovingians as principals, though they often do involve them as kings. In this group, if anywhere, evidence should be forthcoming of royal intention to suppress feud as an institution. We may start, as before, with Gregory's contribution.

Two courtiers – *retoricis inbutus litteris*, moreover[4] – fall out because of the arrogance of one of them, named Secundinus, towards the other, Asteriolus.[5] The king reconciles them, but a fresh *intentio* breaks out. This time the king makes a judgement, which strips Asteriolus of his honours and places him within the power of Secundinus. However, he is protected by the queen, and not till after her death is Secundinus able to claim his rights and kill him. But Asteriolus left a son who, growing up, made pre-parations to avenge his father – 'coepit patris sui velle iniuriam vindecare'. Secundinus thereupon fled in panic from one *villa* to another, and finally, seeing no escape, took his own life 'ne in

---

[1] *Chron. contin.*, 4.     [2] *Chron. contin.*, 41 ff.     [3] *Hist.*, X, 15.
[4] Père Grosjean has pointed out to me that this does not entitle them to be called *rhetorici*.
[5] *Hist.*, III, 33.

manus inimici conruerit'. Gregory, relating this, makes no comment; he thought the story worth the telling but had no strong
feelings about it. Yet to us it reveals an interesting fact: two
families of courtiers, living their lives under the very nose of the
king their lord, are able to pursue their differences in feud without
the king being able to stop them. First, they ignore the reconciliation he makes, and later, in the second generation, they flout his
subsequent judgement by renewing the feud. Nor can Secundinus
see any hope of royal protection against the vengeance of his
victim's son. Hence he takes his own life. The king can do nothing
to stop the feud; indeed, he does something to ensure its continuance. Did he really suppose that the son of the murdered man
would hold his peace? It does not look as if the king's part in the
matter was at all different from that of any other lord called upon
to arbitrate between feuding dependants; he did what he could,
but the issue was one of blood and, in the end, passed beyond his
power to control. Perhaps he let it pass without regret.

Another feud, having certain features in common with the feud
of Secundinus, concerns two well-born families who fall out over
a wife's repute.[1] The husband's kin go, as was customary, to her
father, requiring him either to prove her innocence or to kill her.
He decides to take an oath to her innocence, and this is made in the
presence of both kins in the church of Saint-Denis in Paris.[2] But
the husband's kin declare this to be a perjury, whereupon swords
are drawn and there is bloodshed before the altar, although, as
Gregory remarks, both kins were 'primi apud Chilpericum regem'.
The matter was referred at once to the king, to whom both parties
hastened; but he would have nothing to do with them and sent
them back to the bishop. They then made composition with the
bishop and were forgiven. That is, they were forgiven their riotous
behaviour in church; but the feud remained. A few days later, the
woman was summoned *ad iudicium*, but strangled herself, so clos-
ing the matter. It may well be that she took her life on instructions
from her father's kin, who by now knew her to be guilty. Whatever the *iudicium* to which she was summoned, one cannot but be

[1] *Hist.*, V. 32.
[2] Beyerle, op. cit. pp. 417, 420, 470, discusses the place of the solemn oath in the
settlements of feuds and the pronouncements of the *Volksrechte* on adultery. A good
example of how a well-supported oath would carry conviction is *Hist.*, VIII, 9.

struck by the limited nature of the king's intervention; there is no question, as Dahn points out,[1] of his punishing breach of the law or of the peace or the shedding of blood among those closely attached to his court. His mind is taken up with the act of sacrilege. The right and the duty of kin to clear or punish a member, man or woman, who has impugned its honour is not called in question by the king – nor, for the matter of that, by the church.

Other feuds involving women make the point with equal clarity, as, for example, when a well-born woman goes off with a priest, darkening the insult to her kin by dressing as a man to escape detection.[2] Her kin catches her and, 'ad ulciscendam humilitatem generis sui', burns her. Then, surprisingly, they accept composition of 20 *aurei* from the Bishop of Lisieux for the priest, who subsequently runs off with another woman, whose husband's kin catch him and torture him, and would have killed him if he had not again been rescued by the Bishop. But the startling feature of the case is the reaction of Gregory of Tours. Does he think the Bishop was right to offer composition for the priest, and the kin to accept it? He does not: to his mind, it was the accursed thirst for gold that caused the first woman's kin to hold the priest to ransom till someone could be found to pay the composition. By implication we are to understand that the priest should have shared the fate of the woman he seduced. All the same, was it no more than the accursed thirst for gold? May it not have been that honour was satisfied with the woman's death and that her kin had no strong feelings about the priest? Wherever feelings are not strong, or are divided, there tends to emerge an inclination towards composition, if only it can be got; and this, it cannot be too strongly insisted, is by Merovingian times felt as part of the feuding process. It crops up in quite unexpected situations, as here, or when Childeric the Saxon paid composition to the sons of the criminal Avius, whom his men had killed in a brawl.[3] Gregory is obviously surprised that he should have paid: 'composuit tamen'; compose he did – and the sons accepted it.

There were times, however, when a king would decisively in-

---

[1] *Fehdegang*, pp. 99 ff. See also Brunner, *DRG.*, i, 127.
[2] *Hist.*, VI, 36.    [3] *Hist.*, VII, 3.

tervene to break an incipient feud. Gregory recounts how a free-born girl, carried off to the bed of the drunken duke Amalo, struck him with his own sword; and he died, though not before he had had time to admonish his retainers that she had done nothing worthy of death.[1] The admonition did not foreclose feud: that was a matter for the dead man's kin to decide; but it did give her a chance. The girl then fled to the king (not to her own kin, of whom nothing is said). Gregory says that the king was moved by pity to grant her her life and, further, to take her under his written protection against the dead man's kin. This did indeed foreclose feud; and Gregory makes it clear that the *verbum regis* and his *praeceptio* were, in this case, adequate protection. But why did the girl go straight to the king? And why did he protect her, instead of leaving her to the protection of her kin? It sounds like a good case for composition; yet of this the king deliberately deprived the dead man's kin. Halban has argued[2] that the king simply felt that feud would be wrong and that, in acting as he did, he overstepped normal practice – and this even if she had no kin and thus a special claim to his protection. Goebel, too, has seen here an extraordinary and early instance of the power of the *verbum regis*.[3] What neither has noticed is that her victim was a duke who would have come under the royal protection. Is not this why she flees straight to the duke's master and why his first act is to grant her what is forfeit, her life? Thereafter he can excuse her the consequences of feud, too. In fact, the girl had a very good case, with the victim's own evidence in her favour. Why should the injured kin have received compensation where the king was prepared to overlook his servant's murder? The king indeed fore-closed a feud; but it is hard to see that he acted in a way that could be interpreted as a blow at the principle of feud.

One last example may be taken from Gregory. He devotes a long chapter[4] to the feud between Sichar and Austregisil; a feud as instructive as it is intricate. Its outline is as follows: the time is Christmas, and the setting is in the vicinity of Tours, Bishop Gregory's own see. It is entirely local to Tours, yet Gregory calls it *gravia bella civilia*, for all the world as if two kings were locked

---

[1] *Hist.*, IX, 27.      [2] *Königsschutz*, p. 71.
[3] Op. cit. p. 50.      [4] *Hist.*, VII, 47.

in mortal strife. Sichar, Austregisil and their friends (local land-owners, it seems) were giving a party in the village of Manthelan, when the local priest sent a servant to invite them to his house. One of them (presumably Austregisil or a connection) kills the servant, the party clearly having reached an advanced stage. Now Sichar was bound by ties of *amicitia* to the priest and went off to the church, of all places, to lie in wait for Austregisil. A fight ensued, Sichar finally bolting for home and leaving money, cloth-ing and four wounded servants at the priest's house. Austregisil now burst into the house, killed the servants and carried off the goods. We next meet both parties appearing before a *iudicium civium*: it finds Austregisil guilty of homicide and theft. A few days later, *inito placito* (that is, after an arrangement had been reached whereby Sichar was to receive composition and forgo further vengeance),[1] Sichar heard that the stolen goods were still in the hands of Austregisil's kinsman Auno, and others of his following; so Sichar renewed the feud by a night attack, when Austregisil and others were slain and much property taken. At this point, Bishop Gregory himself intervened by summoning both parties and, in conjunction with the local *iudex*, he advised them to come to an agreement. He says that he feared that the trouble might spread; sons of the Church were being lost; let the party that was in the wrong make composition; and, most remarkable of all, if he could not afford the composition (which by this time would have been ruinously heavy),[2] the Church would pay it. But the party of Austregisil, at this stage represented by Chramnesind, son of Auno, refused composition. Sichar now thought that he had better see the king; but on the way he had trouble with one of his slaves, who wounded him. The news got about that he was dead. This was the signal for Chramnesind, 'commonitis parentibus et

---

[1] See the comment of R. Buchner, *Gregor von Tours, Zehn Bücher Geschichten*, vol. ii, 154.

[2] G. Monod stresses this in his account of the feud, 'Les aventures de Sichaire', *Revue Historique*, xxxi (1886). See also Beyerle, op. cit. p. 523, who cites the gloss on *Lex Salica*, 58: 'Lege, quae paganorum tempore observabant, deinceps numquam valeat quia per ipsam cecidit multorum potestas.' G. F. Jones, 'Was Germanic Blutrache a sacred duty?' *Studia Neophilologica*, xxxii (1960), cites this feud in sup-port of the argument that what really motivated men to pursue a feud was per-sonal to each man (e.g. shame, or hope of fame). This indeed is something; but it is not all.

amicis', to lay waste Sichar's property and to drive off all his cattle. At this point, the count of the city intervened. The judgement was that Chramnesind, having refused composition and then renewed hostilities, should forfeit half the sum originally awarded him, and that Sichar should pay him the other half. The Church then paid the half-composition, as it had promised to do, and both parties swore the solemn oaths of the final settlement and gave *cartae securitatis*.[1] 'Et sic', says Gregory with a sigh of relief, 'altercatio terminum fecit.' But he was wrong; the most interesting part was yet to come. Years later[2] – and students of Anglo-Saxon history will at once think of a parallel in the feud of Uhtred and Thurbrand[3] – we find Sichar and Chramnesind fast friends. They are at dinner together. It crosses Sichar's mind to remark jovially that Chramnesind ought to be very grateful to him for killing off his relatives, so endowing him with a fine composition, without which he would be penniless. Naturally the feud comes flooding back into Chramnesind's mind and he thinks 'nisi ulciscor interitum parentum meorum amittere nomen viri debeo et mulier infirma vocare'. So he dowses the lights, smashes in Sichar's head, and flees to King Childebert; but not before he has hung his victim's body on a fence and thus fulfilled the requirements of feud that the outcome of vengeance should be publicly displayed and not hidden.[4] Sichar unfortunately had been a protégé of the queen, the formidable Brunechildis, and Chramnesind had reason to fear the worst. Eventually he was able to prove that he had slain his victim *super se*, which has been understood to mean 'for his honour'[5] or 'of necessity'.[6] It was a classic case of *homicidium se defendendo* and he got off.[7] That was indeed the end of the feud. Much has been written about it. Gál insists that the court proceedings have the air of a feud tribunal;[8] Halban sees it as an irruption of royal

---

[1] An example of such a *carta*, whereby a man, *intervenientes sacerdotes* and others, accepts a composition on behalf of his kin for the killing of his brother, is *Form. Marc.*, II, 18. Cf. Beyerle, op. cit. p. 332.
[2] *Hist.*, IX, 19.
[3] Symeon of Durham, *Opera* (Rolls Series), i, 218–19.
[4] Cf. *Lex Salica*, 41 add. 2; *Lex Ribvaria*, 77.
[5] Dalton, op. cit. ii, 388.    [6] Buchner, *Gregor von Tours*, ii, 259.
[7] Beyerle, op. cit. 497–8, 256, 353.
[8] *Die Prozessbeilegung nach den fränkischen Urkunden des VII–X Jahrhunderts* (Gierke's *Untersuchungen zur deutschen Staats-und Rechtsgeschichte*, vol. 102, 1910), p. 18.

authority into a feud beyond what the formularies state was customary;[1] Brunner detects a clash between *Volksrecht* and *Königsrecht*;[2] Dahn, on the other hand, thinks that church and king intervene surprisingly little;[3] and Goebel equally stresses the feebleness of the intervention of public authority.[4]

Is not this, put another way, the point? Outraged kinship proves too strong for any pacification; and that this was felt to be morally right is evidenced by the king's final award. We may observe, too, the number of checks to bloodshed that are met with on the way. There stands the local court of arbitration, to say nothing of the count, the bishop and the king, ready to throw their weight into the scales on the side of composition and settlement. There is nothing clear-cut about it from start to finish; the case drifts from blood to arbitration, and back again, without ever becoming what we would call legally clear. Royal intervention and court procedure are fluid; the transition from one type of procedure to another is bewilderingly easy; and this the *Volksrechte* and the formularies would hardly suggest. But they settled it in the end.

Without question, Gregory best records the feuds of the Franks; but we must turn, leaving him still far from exhausted, to Fredegar. First, the feud of Ermenfred with Chainulf.[5] It is over in a few words. Ermenfred, son-in-law of the great Aega, kills Count Chainulf at a court held at Augers. In consequence, his landed possessions are savagely attacked by Chainulf's kin and many others, all with the express approval of Queen Nantechildis. Ermenfred seeks refuge in church at Rheims and thus escapes the royal wrath. That is all. It is a stray gleam that reveals a powerful and level-headed queen urging on an injured kin to feud. But Fredegar has a much better feud, that between Flaochad and Willebad.[6] Nantechildis again, acting as regent, appoints the Frank Flaochad to be mayor of the palace in Burgundy – a strongminded if imprudent decision. On his first progress through Burgundy, the new mayor came upon the patrician Willebad; and he discovered, says Fredegar, an old hatred that had long lain hidden in his heart. He planned to kill him. For his part, Willebad lost no chance of belittling Flaochad. We next move to a Burgundian

[1] *Königsschutz*, p. 73.   [2] *DRG.*, i, 281.   [3] *Fehdegang*, pp. 90, 99.
[4] Op. cit. p. 22.   [5] *Chron.*, IV, 83.   [6] *Chron.*, IV, 89, 90.

court held at Chalon. Willebad arrives with a great following. Flaochad plans an attempt on his life, which is foiled; instead, he marches out of his *palatium* to fight him. Amalbert, Flaochad's brother, interposes to pacify them. Flaochad now calls on the new king, Clovis II, to help him. Willebad is summoned to appear before the king at Autun and arrives with a big following, well knowing that Flaochad, Amalbert and others intend to set upon him. The king tries in vain to entice the victim within the city walls; instead, his enemies again have to march out against him. The fight is described vividly. It seems to have been something of a family engagement, with most people sitting round as spectators. Berthar, a supporter of Flaochad, is narrowly saved from death by his son Chaubedo. Willebad is killed. Eleven days later, apparently before the feud had entered a further phase, Flaochad died of a fever. Fredegar here sees divine judgement. Both Flaochad and Willebad were robbers and tyrants; what is more, they had repeatedly sworn friendship on holy relics – that is, had solemnly agreed to terminate feud. It is an interesting scene described, one might think, by an eye-witness: the opponents, typical barbarian warriors quarrelling about we know not what, backed by their kins and their retainers, are each quite ready to make an end of the other by trickery. We are given, too, a straight hint that they had patched up the feud more than once. It ends in a skirmish under the walls of Autun, a skirmish that has something of the flavour of a duel, by which feuds were on occasion terminated.[1] Or rather, it ends in God's judgement on the survivor. Nothing is said of the course of law as it affects the quarrel of such important men; and the king, whether or not present at the final scene, made it possible, even if, a boy, he was the mouthpiece of others.

To work through the seven volumes of the *Scriptores Rerum Merovingicarum* is to be made aware that feuds are like volcanoes. A few are in eruption, others are extinct, but most are content to rumble now and again and leave us guessing. Every so often we pass across the edge of a quarrel that, if only the writer had followed it up, would have turned out to be feud. The language of feud and its assumptions lie in the minds of the Frankish chroniclers and hagiographers, as witness the curious account in the

[1] e.g. Fredegar, *Chron.*, IV, 51, 71. Beyerle, op. cit. pp. 413 ff.

mid-ninth-century *Gesta Dagoberti* of how the sons of Sadregisil failed to obtain their heritage through not having avenged their father's murder;[1] or how the author of the *Vita Anstrudis* preferred not to identify the family that murdered the only brother of Anstrudis, since she sought no vengeance, although they attacked her too: 'quorum nomina et stirpem dicere iniuriam esse putamus';[2] or again, how Ulfus, tortured as he thought through the agency of St Germanus of Paris, flung his sword-belt at the bishop's feet with the cry 'my life will be required of you by the king – and by my kin!'[3] It is the same in the story of St Léger[4] and of many another Frankish figure whom it would be pointless to enumerate. None of these writers saw feud steadily giving ground to other and less bloodthirsty processes of law sponsored by enlightened kings.

We have come to the brink of the Carolingian age, the age of Charles Martel and St Boniface. If a new day dawned in the history of feuding, it was concealed from the continuators of Fredegar and the compiler of the *Liber Historiae Francorum*; and concealed too, from Archbishop Hincmar, as he looked back from the vantage point of the next century.[5] Why did St Boniface become doubtful about the propriety of regarding Gregory of Utrecht as a likely successor?[6] Because, it seemed, Gregory might have become involved in feud, his brother apparently having killed the uncle of the *Dux Francorum*; and nobody knew how the *discordia* would end. The *Dux* might decide to avenge his uncle's death fairly widely on Gregory's family. We may assume that this did not, in fact, happen; but the career of Gregory of Utrecht might have been very different had it not been for the threat over-

---

[1] *M.G.H., S.R.M.*, ii, 413–14. Krusch here cites *Lex Romana Visigoth. Paul.* iii. 7, 1 (ed. Haenel, p. 384): 'quicunque a familia sua occisus fuerit, hereditas illius ab herede adiri non potest nisi prius de familia quaestio fuerit ventilata et mors occisi fuerit vindicata', where, as my former colleague, Dr Arnold Ehrhardt, assured me, the Roman sense of *familia* should preclude any idea of feud. In Mr Grierson's view, the Roman state would first have intervened where a family-killing was concerned precisely because feud could not operate effectively; outraged public opinion may have demanded it. Later, a legal action was provided. Finally, the State took over cognizance of homicide itself.

[2] *M.G.H., S.R.M.*, vi, 69–70.      [3] *M.G.H., S.R.M.*, vii, 385.

[4] *M.G.H., S.R.M.*, v.

[5] *Vita Remigii, praef., M.G.H., S.R.M.*, iii, 251.

[6] *S. Bonifatii et Lullii Epistolae* (ed. M. Tangl, 2nd ed., 1955), no. 50, p. 83.

hanging his kin at a critical moment. The Mainz version of the *Life* of St Boniface[1] affords a sudden insight into the view of feud held by one of the most powerful Frankish dynasties of the Rhineland. Bishop Gerold of Mainz was killed in a skirmish with the Saxons. His son and successor, Gewilib, did not consider this an unavoidable accident of battle. Instead, he made careful inquiries to discover who actually killed his father, and he succeeded. In due course, while on an expedition against the Saxons with either Charles Martel or Carloman, he sought out his victim and invited him to meet him in the River Weser to discuss terms.[2] And there Gewilib killed him, with the words 'accipe quo patrem vindico ferrum!' The writer goes on to say that neither the king nor the nobles considered that Gewilib had done anything blameworthy in avenging his father thus, though he (the writer) clearly did. 'Rudi populo rudis adhuc presul' is his epitaph for Gewilib, and it sounds well enough; but the great dynasts of the Rhineland would not have thought so, and Gewilib's Carolingian overlord did not think so.

We are not now concerned to consider how far, if at all, the Frankish outlook on feud was modified by Charlemagne. No historian believes that he was particularly successful; the question is simply what his intentions were.[3] Nor, again, must we be misled by developments in court procedure (for example, in the *jurati* being summoned by a judge instead of by the parties to a feud) that tended to strengthen royal resistance to private feud-procedures without necessarily betraying a change of heart.[4] Charlemagne's position, as revealed in his capitularies, may be variously interpreted.[5] If the *Admonitio Generalis*[6] be taken as an

---

[1] Ed. W. Levison, *Vitae S. Bonifatii* (*Script. Rer. Germ. in usum schol.*, 1905), pp. 91–92. See E. Ewig, 'Milo et eiusmodi similes', *Sankt Bonifatius Gedenkgabe* (1954).

[2] I understand *sermonicari* in some such technical sense.

[3] H. Fichtenau, *Das karolingische Imperium* (1949), p. 146 (Munz's trans., *The Carolingian Empire*, p. 138) notes the flourishing of feud in the Carolingian age and sees no general prohibition; Goebel, op. cit. p. 26, thinks that the Carolingians did curb feud to some extent, and used their power to enforce final concords (p. 33). See also Olivier-Martin, *Histoire*, p. 82.

[4] Beyerle, op. cit. p. 439; cf. also 319.

[5] Brunner, *DRG.*, i, 329, 410, discusses the evidence.

[6] *M.G.H., Capit.*, i, 59, esp. §§ 66, 67. Cf. F. L. Ganshof, 'Charlemagne', *Speculum*, 24 (1949), 520 ff.

indication of policy, then it may be that Charlemagne, viewing his kingly rôle in the light of an Augustinian *pax*, saw feuding as a positive evil and, further, as eminently undesirable by reason of its private nature.[1] But even his friend Alcuin, we must remember, did not always see things thus.[2] What Charlemagne never experienced was a distaste for the bloodshed of the process. Royal justice could be savager than feud. There may, then, be a positive change of outlook here, such as no Merovingian evidence can plainly be seen to bear traces of; at once the culmination of a process of practical delimiting of feud that was centuries old, and a special development of the late eighth century. Feuding in the Carolingian world nonetheless had a long future before it.

What this paper has had to express is a view of the feuding of the Frankish age that is the reverse of clear-cut. There is no evidence that contemporaries saw it otherwise. To legal historians feud dies a slow, inevitable death, yielding to the superior equity of royal justice; chaos and bloodshed give place to good order because they must. But it is possible to see the matter otherwise: feud, as a means of obtaining redress, is already a various, elaborate procedure by the time we first meet it in barbarian sources, long since linked with the payment of compositions, in kind or money; the two are inseparable. Records of feud repeatedly betray the drift from fighting to composition, the vagueness of the line separating them. Always it is touch-and-go what will happen; it will depend on what the kins think, how extensively they or their followings are mobilizable, how rich they are or how ready to pay or to receive payment, how much the bishop or the king feels disposed to intervene. The royal position as expressed in legislation is not as a rule clear; and, when it is it does not always correspond to practice. Kings may sometimes have judged feuding proper to their immediate followers when they would have disallowed it to a wider circle. Royal justice and the local courts are still far too unsettled in function and fluid in procedure to offer a clear alternative to feud. They are more concerned with com-

---

[1] E. Ewig, 'Zum christlichen Königsgedanken im Frümittelalter', *Das Königtum* (1956), p. 63. Goebel, op. cit. p. 94, summarizes the evidence for an articulate penal theory, aimed at the suppression of wickedness, in Charlemagne's legislation.

[2] *M.G.H., Epist.*, iv, 376.

promises than with principles.[1] What, in fact, we do find is the movement of men and their troubles between the two. We may agree with Goebel that the process of composition 'remained essentially an alternative rather than a successor to settlement by violence'[2] though the reality of the bloodier alternative was the sanction that made composition possible at any stage. Except generally where honour was obviously involved, kins and families would find reasons and excuses to look to composition first, whether of their own making or under the protection of the courts. Their efforts might break down, and often did; and so might the efforts of the courts. There is no strong and continuous royal pressure against the principle of feud. There is no 'Kampf gegen die Fehde'.[3] Even the pressure of the Church should be subject to most careful interpretation. Feuds that wiped out whole kins it is impossible to believe were ever common.[4] Feuding in the sense of incessant private warfare, is a myth; feuding in the sense of very widespread and frequent procedures to reach composition-settlements necessarily hovering on the edge of bloodshed, is not. The marvel of early medieval society is not war but peace.

[1] The point is well expressed in Lot, Pfister and Ganshof, op. cit. p. 310: the spirit of the times showed 'l'horreur de l'arrêt qui tranche comme un couperet'.
[2] Op. cit. p. 38. See also Beyerle, op. cit. p. 261.
[3] As Beyerle holds, op. cit. p. 264.
[4] Beyerle, op. cit. p. 523, cites *Hist.*, VII, 47, but this does not show that Gregory thought such feuds common. All the narrative evidence points to the difficulty of enlisting the feud-service of more than the closest kin or a very restricted *ad hoc* force.

# CHAPTER SEVEN

# The Long-haired Kings

\*

## I · REGES CRINITI

No tradition of significance survives to illuminate the tribal origins of the Franks.[1] Who they thought they were, and what they called themselves, cannot be known or inferred. Perhaps, as their wanderings drew to an end, they had no name for themselves, and no sense of being different from other West German peoples. Romans of the third century, adept at naming and defining peoples and things, reflecting upon the meaning of their inclusion in the Empire, used the name 'Franci' to describe an agglomeration or confederation of tribes gathered on and near the east bank of the Rhine. It was a term of convenience. Archaeological evidence, plentiful enough and systematically studied, confirms this view. As we find them in their graves, we cannot as a rule distinguish the Franks of this age from Saxons or Frisians, let alone from each other. The Romans were turning to good use a

---

[1] One group of Frankish genealogies deriving from the early sixth century but appearing in no manuscript earlier than the ninth, attaches the Franks to a division of the Germanic peoples enjoying a common ancestor called Escio. Their immediate kindred are the Alamans, the Brittones and the Romani, which suggests less a blood-grouping than a contemporary's view of the political situation as he saw it in the early sixth century. Their connection with the Istaevones of Tacitus (*Germ.*, 2) seems to be purely nominal. The matter has been adequately dealt with by G. Kurth, *Histoire poétique des Mérovingiens* (1893), pp. 87, 96 and 520; but H. M. Chadwick, *The Origin of the English Nation* (1924), pp. 195 ff., gave considerable weight to the evidence of these genealogies in his classification of the Germani, and he has been followed by C. Hawkes in *Dark-Age Britain* (1956), pp. 106 ff. The case for regarding 'the Franks' as a term of historical convenience rather than as an ethnical reality is argued by W. J. de Boone, *De Franken van hun eerste optreden tot de dood van Childerich* (Amsterdam, 1954). 'Germani' is itself more likely to have been in origin a Celtic word to describe new neighbours than a Germanic word for which there was no need (L. Schmidt, *Geschichte der deutschen Stämme bis zum Ausgang der Völkerwanderung: die Ostgermanen*, 2nd ed., pp. 40-45).

word of Germanic origin that may have had reference to a savagery or bravery that seemed to characterize these particular Germans.[1]

One group of Franks, and that not the largest, was known to the Romans as the Salians. Whatever the size, the term 'Salii' is likely to have been used by the Romans as a description of an *ad hoc* association thrown together by warfare or chance, and perhaps not even closely linked by kinship. 'Salii' identified the Franks who lived near the sea, in the general area of the mouth of the Rhine. Not blood, nor way of life, but geography distinguished them from other Franks. It is Ammianus who reports that it had become the custom to call these particular Franks 'Salii', and he goes on to describe how the Emperor Julian received their surrender and permitted them to settle in Toxandria.[2] We cannot tell if the ancestors of these Salians had played any part in the general Frankish and Alamannic attack of 253, which it had taken Gallienus five years to stem, nor whether they were to be found in the repeated Frankish sallies into Gaul of the following century; but it seems likely. Some of them would then have shared the fate of their kindred, who were exiled by Probus to the shores of the Black Sea.[3] Probably they were allies of the Sicambrians, or Sugambri, whose main field of activity in the third century was also the Rhine mouth, and whose ancestors had been permitted by Augustus and Tiberius to settle in small numbers on the left bank.[4] With others, they would have taken advantage of imperial distractions during the time of Carausius's revolt (286–93) to cross to the left bank and settle tribally. By 297, they were established on the 'island of the Batavians' – that is, Betuwe. If the Empire looked askance at them, it was less as settlers than as a reservoir

[1] Some historians prefer to interpret 'Franci' as 'free men', a meaning which it certainly came to acquire at a later date. It might thus betray a very early Frankish sense of the need to fight for freedom against the Romans (cf. Otto Höffler, in *Das Königtum, seine geistliche und rechtliche Grundlagen* (Konstanz, 1956), p. 103.
[2] *Rer. Gest. Lib.*, XVII, 8.
[3] Sir Samuel Dill suggested that there might be some connection between this exile and the tradition reported by Fredegar that the Franks had come from Troy (*Roman Society in Gaul in the Merovingian Age*, 1926, p. 6). See also chap. iv, above.
[4] It is well to keep the two distinct, for later on the Merovingians are referred to by Gregory as Sugambri (*Hist.*, II, 31) whereas their subjects live under the law of the Salians. (G. F. Petri, 'Stamm und Land im frühmittelalterlichen Nordwesten nach neuerer historischer Forschung', *Westf. Forschungen*, 8, 1955.)

of manpower on which independent-minded generals might draw; so, at least, one may account for the time and energy devoted by Constantius Chlorus to the driving-back and pinning-down of the Franks: they were *barbari*, whom Constantine did not hesitate to throw to his wild beasts at Trier; but they were also warriors experienced in Roman military techniques, and dangerous at a time when Gaul was far removed from speedy reinforcement of the legions. Not many years later, Franks were to be found in high office in the imperial service – as masters of cavalry, counts of the largesses, even as consuls; Ricimer, Arbogast, Merobaudes and Bauto were great men in their day.[1] First-rate 'fantassins', it was the potential military value, and, equally potential, the military threat of the Franks that struck the imagination of the Romans. This is the background to the events that led up to the arrival of the Salian deputation at the camp of the Emperor Julian in 358. Ammianus is not entirely clear here, but he seemed to understand that the Salians had come to ask for terms because they were living in lands that were already their own, and that they therefore had some right to be left in peace, so long as they did not attack the Romans: 'ut quiescentes eos, tanquam in suis, nec lacesseret quisquam nec vexaret'. Julian prevaricated, perhaps fearing for the safety of communications with Britain. But circumstances compelled him to march south again, leaving the Salians established as *dediditii* in the approximate area of modern Dutch Brabant, and presumably entrusted with the protection of Rome's northern frontier. This was the beginning of full-scale tribal colonization.

Julian's concession was not enough. It is difficult to see how it could have been, so long as it confined the Salians to lands that it took the entire Middle Ages to render habitable; lands, moreover, from which there was an easy way out along river-courses into richer country to the south, where the Romans had grown corn and bred horses. Moreover, the Salians had no means of checking the arrival of kindred from across the Rhine, to share with them

---

[1] Sir Samuel Dill's masterly summary of the evidence (op. cit., chap. 1) should be read in conjunction with K. F. Stroheker, 'Zur Rolle der Heermeister fränkischer Abstammung im späten vierten Jahrhundert', *Historia*, IV, 1955. At the same time, we should not press too closely for a precise meaning of 'Franks' in such a context.

whatever the bogs and heathlands of Toxandria might yield by way of livelihood.[1] It was not, then, so much greed that led these warrior-pastoralists to penetrate south, into the valleys of the Scheldt and the Lys, as necessity. The move was made easier, though there was nothing to show that it was caused, by the thinning-out of the legions along the Lower and Middle Rhine. The Romans would probably have said that the threat from the Salians was a thing of the past. Claudian describes how in 395 Stilicho travelled down the Rhine to renew Rome's treaties with the German tribes. The Alamans, he says, were refused permission to send a contingent to serve with the legions; by implication, that privilege was reserved for the Franks, and notably for the loyal Salians, who had beaten their swords into sickles and were devoting themselves to tillage.[2] Archaeology and place-name study suggest that this was not wholly wishful thinking. But what also struck Claudian was the contrast between these Salians and their fiercer kinsmen, the Ripuarian Franks of the Middle Rhine, who had lately revolted under Marcomer and Sunno; and, bad as the Ripuarians were, no Frank was as bad as an Alaman. In so far as they were heirs of Roman Gaul, the Franks may well have been heirs to this feeling about Alamans.

Infiltration into the territory of what is now Belgium brought the Salians into Belgo-Roman farmlands that had partly lapsed into scrub, partly been left clear of settlers by the Romans, particularly in the area just north of the Boulogne–Cologne road,[3] and partly passed into the hands of earlier Germanic *laeti*, among whom we should include the pirates, whether Saxons or Franks, who were trying to establish colonies along the coast and in the river estuaries. Competition of this kind meant war. There was no turning back.

One group of Salians set up a headquarters of sorts at Thérouanne (formerly Roman Taruenna) in *Belgica II*; and this is the first town in which we know them to have shown an enduring interest.

---

[1] I do not know on what evidence Ferdinand Lot based his calculation that fourth-century Toxandria would have accommodated between 100,000 and 150,000 Salians (*Les Invasions germaniques*, 1945, p. 128).

[2] *De Consulatu Stilichonis*, I, ll. 218 ff.

[3] Cf. G. Faider-Feytmans, 'La frontière du nord de la Gaule sous le Bas-Empire', *Mélanges Marouzeau* (1948), pp. 161–72.

They had moved within range of city walls, of what the Anglo-Saxons termed 'the work of giants'. Thérouanne lay on the system of Roman military roads that ran from Boulogne through Tournai and Bavay to Tongres, Maastricht and Cologne. It was less a Roman barrier of defence than a lateral communication running behind a no-man's land furnished with advance defence-points. Today, the road marks a clear linguistic frontier, though this may have very little to do with any Salian settlement of the fourth or fifth centuries. Heli Roosens has catalogued something not far short of five hundred Frankish cemeteries in Belgium; and many are closely associated with what had been Roman *villae rusticae*.[1] Some of those that are certainly of the fourth or fifth century are to be found near Tongres, Tournai and Liége; but mainly they are in the province of Namur, comfortably south of the road. It can be no accident that Romans and Franks, together or successively, chose to live in the same south-east corner of Belgium and to neglect the lands immediately to the north and west which, though unprotected, had once been rich. They were not again to be occupied till the sixth century. The relation of these earliest Salian settlements in Wallonia to the *villae* has not yet been enough investigated to enable us to know how the Belgo-Roman landlords reacted to the newcomers. There would plainly have been fighting here and there; but Romans and Franks do not seem always to have coveted the same kinds of property; and, further, the Salian Franks had a good name, and might afford protection in a time of trouble. They were not so numerous as to affect seriously the development of the spoken Latin of the area. The greatest degree of doubt must exist over the Roman re-action to the Salian occupation of successive cities, such as Arras, Cambrai and Tournai. Did the Salians respect towns? Did they use them for cantonment purposes? Four centuries later, Arch-bishop Hincmar reported, in his *Vita Remigii*, that Clovis had waited with his army outside Rheims rather than damage the city.[2] He did not find this comment in the earlier *Vita*; neither do I

---

[1] *De Merovingische Begraafplaatsen in België* (1949); with which compare R. De Mayer, *De romeinsche Villas in België* (1937). A useful résumé is given by Mme Faider-Feytmans in *Études Mérovingiennes* (*Actes des journées de Poitiers*, 1952), pp. 103–9.

[2] *Vita Remigii*, chap. XI (*M.G.H., S.R.M.*, III, p. 292).

think that he invented it. In the context, it has much more the complexion of a Rheims tradition. Hincmar knew more about the Franks than we do, and it struck him as plausible that Clovis would have spared Rheims; and, if Rheims, may we not suppose Arras, Cambrai and Tournai also? It is another matter to determine how much there was to spare.

Tournai had been a Roman garrison-town of some importance, and its trade and industry had helped to supply the needs of the legions stationed on the Lower Rhine. It had suffered under the Vandals in 407, and some at least of its inhabitants were deported into Germany.[1] As imperial *foederati*, the Salians may have been not merely permitted but encouraged to garrison this and other strongholds of *Belgica II*; and conceivably they were expected to protect the imperial fisc.[2] Nothing of their movements and attitude between 358 and their arrival at Tournai suggests awareness of any break with Rome. No Germans were town-dwellers by preference. Even the Romans showed an increasing disinclination to live in towns. We must, then, suppose that some compelling reason moved the Salian chieftains to enter the walls and set up their headquarters inside them.

These Salian chieftains were known to Roman contemporaries as *reges*. Among themselves, they would have used the word *kuning* (Anglo-Saxon *cyning*) – the man of, or from, or representing the kin. No military function was thereby implied, any more than in the closely-allied title of *thiodan*, which it seems to have replaced; but we should not, on the other hand, assume that the *kuning* was ever debarred from war-leadership on account of his representative or sacral functions within the tribe. The Salian *reges* we know of were mostly of one kindred – the Merovingians. Their rôle was to be such that it is worth inquiring what Frankish society of the fifth century expected of its kings. Most, but not

[1] According to St Jerome, *Epistolae* CXXIII (ed. Hilberg, *C.S.E.L.*, LVI, p. 92). Why does Fernand Vercauteren consider this tendentious (*Étude sur les civitates de la Belgique Seconde*, 1934, p. 236)?

[2] Pirenne has pointed to the unusual care with which the Frankish kings preserved their royal fisc of Tournai and has suggested a direct continuation of the imperial domains controlled from the *Civitas Menapiorum* ('Le Fisc royal de Tournai', *Mélanges Ferdinand Lot*, 1925, p. 648); but he has failed to notice what might be thought a plausible explanation of their attitude – that their ancestors had been officially charged with the preservation of the fisc.

all, of the evidence comes from the second book of Gregory of Tours' *Libri Historiarum*, and in particular from his long chapter (9) on the Franks in Germany. Among the historians of Germanic peoples settled in Roman provinces, Gregory displays unusual curiosity about the origins and nature of barbarian kingship, and in this respect, if in no other, is a second Tacitus. His sifting of the evidence, written and oral, is technically skilful. It is extremely unlikely that he ever read Tacitus' *Germania*, but, even so, his comments on early kingship read rather like an unconscious gloss on the famous distinction of the Roman historian, 'reges ex nobilitate, duces ex virtute sumunt'.[1] Whether or not this implied that Tacitus or his informants distinguished the functions of *reges* and *duces*, it certainly implied a distinction in qualification. Dr Sisam, with an eye to the genealogical implications, has urged that Tacitus makes a fair generalization, so long as the meaning of *rex* is not pressed too closely.[2] How closely can we press it? There is always a temptation to see pagan Germanic kingship in terms of Scandinavian practice, to give weight, where we cannot give much meaning, to the magic element in royal initiation-rites,[3] or to picture the *reges* as kings of 'the Golden Bough' – guarantors and distributors of prosperity for their social group, defenders of their people against famine, plague and defeat, scapegoats in time of trouble. If such, in whole or in part, are the *reges* of Tacitus, he would have been distinguishing between the war-leader chosen for particular campaigns (the *truhtin*) and the king of a whole people (the *thiodan*) who indeed may have had a sacral function; but neither by himself can be the immediate ancestor of Gregory's *reges criniti*. Even allowing for some residual sacral element in Frankish kingship, *reges* of the Later Empire must surely be something else.

We shall probably be coming near the truth if we start from the fact that movements of big integrated tribes (*gentes*) were not at all common after the first century A.D. In face of Roman opposition, the *gentes* showed some disposition to break up into

---

[1] *Germania*, chap. VII. See the commentary of Rudolf Much, *Die Germania des Tacitus* (Heidelberg, 1959), pp. 102 ff.

[2] 'Anglo-Saxon Royal Genealogies', *Proceedings, British Academy*, XXXIX, p. 322.

[3] As was done by K. Olivecrona, *Das Werden eines Königs nach altschwedischem Rechte: der Königsritus als magischer Akt* (Lund, 1947).

fighting bands. A group of such bands, perhaps from various *gentes*, might unite under one leader to seek its own fortune within the Empire, as mercenaries, as brigands in search of land and booty, or as both. The leader of such a confederation would owe his position to his own strong right arm: in a word, to *virtus*. But it is surprising how quickly *virtus* will lead to *nobilitas*. Many such leaders show a remarkable tendency to found a *stirps regia*, though not necessarily a very durable one.[1] They equally appropriate certain sacral qualities; perhaps not those of the former *thiodan*, but rather qualities that go with war-leadership in the cult of Woden and with oath-taking on the part of their followers. It is under Woden, the war-god *par excellence*, that such confederations of warriors set out to win their way in the world. Their leaders were prominent enough to be known to Tacitus when he came to consider the East German tribes, though, comparing them with the traditional kings of the *gentes*, they seemed ephemeral. If we turn to the evidence of Gregory of Tours in the sixth century and of Fredegar in the seventh, we shall see that the *duces* of Tacitus have developed into kings. Such development was not inevitable and not irreversible; kings of this kind could be dispensed with, as the Herules, the Gepids, the Lombards and others were to show; but the Franks did not dispense with them.

Gregory was a little confused by terms. Where his sources used the verb *ducere*, in the general sense of 'to command in the field', he saw a reference to a *dux*, whom he then proceeded to distinguish from a *rex* – not in Tacitus' sense but in the sense that there was a distinction between a Merovingian *rex* and his Frankish official, the *herizogo*, of which title *dux* was a Latin approximation. Hence, he is always worried to find that his source, Sulpicius Alexander, discusses the early Frankish leaders in terms of kingship while omitting to use the word *rex*. For Gregory, then, the problem is, when do the Frankish *reges* begin? He does not see

[1] If we except, at least provisionally, the Merovingians, I should agree with Mr Philip Grierson that 'there may have been a divinity attached to kingship, but it was attached to a particular king and not to any particular royal line; its sanction was always the tacit acquiescence or the express will of the people, and not a mystical right arising from a fictitious claim to divine descent' ('Election and Inheritance in Early Germanic Kingship', *Cambridge Historical Journal*, VII, 1941, p. 22).

that this is largely a problem of terminology, since the leaders he first discusses are neither *reges* nor *duces* in the sixth-century sense but *Heerkönige* – chieftains, that is to say, whose kingship was based on war-leadership of confederations. He writes:

> It is generally agreed that the Franks in question came from Pannonia, that they first settled on the banks of the Rhine, which they subsequently crossed to reach Thoringia; and here, in the *pagi* and *civitates*, they set over themselves long-haired kings of their first and, so to say, noblest family.[1]

There are no forest-depths in this account, or in the traditions of the Merovingian kings he knew so well. Perhaps we should see these kings as the first kings of a new series; they are war-leaders who have proved themselves in battle and now have other tasks. They are not there to rule a *gens* or to unite warriors of different tribes into a *gens*; they are more what continental scholars call *Kleinkönige*, chieftains of war-bands who subsist by tip-and-run raiding over the Rhine (the Ripuarian Franks were expert at this, in the district of Cologne). But they are in more or less continuous contact with the Romans. What difference this made to their ideas of kingship it would be impossible to tell, but it certainly gave them a new function. In negotiating tribute or terms of peace or conditions of service as *dediditii*, it was for the chieftains to deal, on behalf of their followers, with the Romans; and we must suppose that it was the Romans who sometimes took the initiative in grouping otherwise unconnected tribes into formations of auxiliaries and appointing a leader over them, possibly also taking the chance to teach them the value of imposing compulsory oaths of fidelity.[2] More than *virtus* was required in such chieftains; *nobilitas* might be a help; social standing, as much as magical properties,[3] may have been symbolized by their long hair. There are

---

[1] 'Reges crinitos super se creavisse de prima et, ut ita dicam, nobiliore suorum familia' (*Hist.*, II, 9).

[2] E.g. Tacitus, *Annals*, I, 7; I, 34; XVI, 22; Suetonius, *Caligula*, 15. The possibility of Roman influence on Germanic oaths of fidelity is discussed by P. W. A. Immink, *At the Roots of Medieval Society* (Oslo, 1958), pp. 42–44.

[3] Cf. P. E. Schramm, *Herrschaftszeichen und Staatssymbolik*, I (1954), pp. 118–27, who effectively solves some difficulties raised by J. Hoyoux, 'Reges criniti. Chevelures, tonsures et scalps chez les Mérovingiens', *Revue belge de philol. et d'hist.*, 26 (1948).

scholars who hold that hair was then commonly worn long by barbarians of rank, and that it only later acquired special significance because the Merovingian dynasty maintained a hairstyle long since abandoned by everyone else. This view has something to commend it. It is easy to imagine Gregory of Tours looking at his kings. Long hair, by his time exclusively Merovingian, long hair in Chilperic and Guntramn, would argue long hair equally exclusive in their ancestors. What other evidence would one need? The Romans, for their part, would have looked back to the tradition of the *rex datus*, the vassal-king officially recognized by the emperor,[1] and to such as Ariovistus, who dealt direct with Caesar and was recognized as *rex Germanorum* by the senate; and this, in its turn, would have helped to mould the functions of the *reges* they dealt with. Such contacts by no means necessarily meant a softening of military *virtus*; a *Heerkönig* surrounded by his faithful warriors – probably an *élite* comparable with the *berserkir* of the Scandinavians – was precisely what the Romans wanted. Small groups so led, and held together by some sort of military compact to aid one another, were likely to stabilize the troubled north, to protect rather than to threaten the landlords. Nor was their devotion to Woden any disadvantage. The last thing that the Romans expected was that the Franks would allow themselves to be quietly absorbed by the Christian and Latin-speaking populations among whom they settled. It is a fair guess that they were not so much interested in potential *coloni* as in the *élites* of young warriors, the men of *dura virtus* trained to special ferocity in war and set apart from their fellow-men.[2] Nonetheless, the *Heerkönig* needed to be rather more than a warrior. He was also the man who held together for a common purpose kindreds who otherwise would have fought each other; and he spoke for them at a higher tribunal. He was something of both *rex* and *dux* in the old sense of the words.

[1] On the Arch of Constantine can be seen the investiture of such a king by the emperor in the presence of the army; and an *aureus* of Lucius Verus shows the emperor giving a king to the Armenians in A.D. 164 (cf. P. G. Hamberg, *Studies in Roman Imperial Art*, Uppsala, 1945, plate 13). We may also recall the notable passage in Mamertinus, *Panegyricus Maximiano Augusto dictus* (Coll. Budé, *Panegyriques Latins*, I), p. 33.

[2] Cf. G. Dumézil, *Mythes et dieux des Germains*, chap. 6.

Gregory's picture of the establishing of the long-haired kings is in some essentials the picture of Fredegar. Fredegar relates that certain of the Franks escaped from 'Frigia' and chose a king named Francio, under whom they wandered, fighting their way west. When he died they decided to live under *duces*, since warfare had reduced their numbers.[1] We have the same movement west-wards, followed by fragmentation at a later stage, which we may identify with reaching the Rhineland. Whether Fredegar is right in his explanation of this fragmentation may be doubted; but in his *duces* we may surely see the long-haired kings of Gregory of Tours. So much that is characteristic of the Merovingians, but above all their initiation at a shield-raising and, when occasion demanded, the manner of their deposition, goes back to these *duces* – men whose authority was derived from some sort of elec-tion or contract made firm with oath-taking of a most solemn kind. Their sacral functions, if such there were, rested in part upon this,[2] though, if Gregory means what he says, they also de-rived, like the Merovingians themselves, from older times. It is just possible that, in the Merovingians, we may have a dynasty of Germanic *Heerkönige* derived from an ancient kingly family of the migration period; a dynasty that brought to its new tasks and responsibilities within *Romania* a fresh reputation for good generalship and a memory of patriarchal authority exercised in an older world. There may have been other dynasties that once could boast as much; but they failed to survive. Gregory was a little too keen to see his Merovingians as the only descendants of a line of kings that was once acknowledged by all his Germans; though he may have been right. Right or wrong, however, patriarchal roots, unremarkable in themselves, would gain in significance as the centuries passed and the family flourished.

Some of the Salian chieftains of the Toxandrian period are known by name: we need not doubt the existence of Faramund, Clodio, Merovech or Childeric I, even if their precise relationship is uncertain. Sidonius praises Aetius for having resisted a south-

---

[1] *Chron.*, II, 5-6.
[2] The best statement of the results of modern research into the origins of Germanic kingship is that of Walter Schlesinger, 'Über germanisches Königtum' in *Das Königtum*.

ward push by Clodio at *Vicus Helena*.[1] This would have been in
the year 446.[2] Gregory understood that Clodio had advanced
from his stronghold at *Dispargum*[3] to take Cambrai and conquer
land down as far as the Somme. Frankish tradition of the late
sixth century thus remembered Clodio as the chieftain who led the
first detachment of Salians into Gaul proper, perhaps leaving some
settlements and certainly meeting with scattered opposition from
the Gallo-Romans. Another chieftain of the same family, Merovech,[4] is found not much later fighting as a loyal federate of the
Empire under Aetius against Attila on the Catalaunian Plain. We
may conclude that Clodio had been over-zealous and interpreted
his privileges too liberally; but *Vicus Helena* still left the Salians
in good enough odour to be welcome and trusted in a major
engagement.

A change comes with the overthrow of Aetius in 454; it marked
the end of any semblance of military imperial command in the
West and afforded the chance for adventurers to make good.
Among these must be counted Aegidius, the independent *Magister
Utriusque Militiae per Gallias*, who ruled northern Gaul (or at least
southern *Belgica Secunda*) from the stronghold of Soissons, where
the Romans had not long since manufactured arms. His power
may have extended as far south as the Loire. Why he should have
chosen Soissons rather than Rheims is not clear; perhaps he had
family estates round Soissons; but it seems likelier that the grip
of the Church on property in and around Rheims was already such
as to make it unattractive to a military commander, who presumably had to buy loyalty with gifts of land on the spot. Aegidius
belonged to the senatorial family of the Syagrii, from the Lyon-
nais, and had some pretensions to being a latter-day Aetius. The
temptation to see him as little better than a barbarian should be

[1] *Carm.*, V, 212 ff. Where this place was is a matter of dispute: Hélesmes (Nord)
is to be preferred to Vitry or Vic-en-Artois (both in Pas-de-Calais).
[2] Cf. C. Verlinden, 'Frankish colonization: a new approach', *Trans R. Hist. Soc.*,
5th Series, vol. 4 (1954), p. 11; and A. Loyen, 'À la recherche de Vicus Helena',
*Rev. des études anciennes*, XLVI (1944), pp. 121–34.
[3] Probably Duisburg or Duysborch in Belgium.
[4] Merovech, the eponymous head of the Merovingian dynasty, is more likely to
have been the brother than the son of Clodio. Cf. L. Schmidt, 'Aus den Anfängen
des salfränkischen Königtums', *Klio*, 34 (NF 16) (1942), pp. 306–27, and E. Ewig,
'Die Civitas Ubiorum, die Francia Rinensis und das Land Ribuarien', *Rheinische
Vierteljahrsblätter*, 19 (1954), pp. 13 ff.

resisted. His friendship with the Emperor Majorian and his dealings with Burgundians, Visigoths and even Vandals, suggests a
man whose ambitions were considerably in excess of what he
achieved, but whose nature it was to be loyal to Rome. He ended
up, like Magnus Maximus in Britain, in the unenviable position of
a Roman commander whose effective power rested on what he
could make of it locally. He would have seen himself as a loyal
defender of imperial territory against Ripuarian attacks over the
Rhine, and against Saxon and Gothic pressure further south and
west. But, whether he liked it or not, he was as independent of
Rome as Alaric had been. Aegidius, and his son Syagrius after him,
ruled northern Gaul for something over twenty-five years; but in
what capacity it would be hard to say. They would, in practice,
have been *comites civitatum*, exercising civil and military command
in a vital frontier zone. Fredegar calls Syagrius 'patricius', though
to Gregory of Tours he was 'rex Romanorum'. The latter title
may have been that by which he chose to be known to the German chieftains with whom he dealt; at least it helps to emphasize
his intimate connection with them. 'Patricius' or 'rex', Syagrius
must have ruled independently of the Empire, and even while
acknowledging an imperial *auctoritas*, would inevitably have re-
warded his followers with presents of imperial lands under whatever guise of security. It is our misfortune that none of his notarial
instruments have survived; they would have been known to
Clovis.[1] Some of the Salian Franks must have regarded Syagrius
as their overlord, and thus taken him as their model of what a
ruler on Roman territory should be like. But in Byzantium the
doings of this remote 'patricius' may not consistently have looked
like loyalty.

The Salian chieftain most closely in contact with these *reges
Romanorum* of Soissons was Childeric I. By 457 he already ruled
over the Franks of Tournai and the Lys valley, though the extent
of his power towards the south can only be guessed at. There is

---

[1] I concur with the opinion of Peter Classen, 'Kaiserreskript und Königsurkunde',
*Archiv für Diplomatik*, I (1955), p. 81, though I could not go so far as to accept, as
he does, the judgement of Heinrich Mitteis that 'Syagrius regierte schon durchaus
in der Art eines germanischen Heerkönigs, gestützt auf seine Klienten und seine
germanische Trustis' (*Der Staat des Hohen Mittelalters*, p. 43). This implies a different
kind of adventurer from what the scant evidence suggests.

good reason to believe that Aegidius used him to keep at bay the Alamans, the Visigoths and possibly also the Saxons on the Loire, but was strong enough to push him back into the Tournaisis when his help as a federate was no longer required. A number of Franks remained behind in the south, perhaps in garrisons under the direct orders of the *rex Romanorum*. In some such way we have to interpret the conflated Frankish traditions known to Gregory of Tours. Childeric was ordered out of northern Gaul and exiled to 'Thuringia' (either Tournai or German Thuringia across the Rhine). Tradition explained this exile as the result of Frankish dissatisfaction with Childeric's private life: 'coepit filias Francorum stuprose detrahere'. No student of the later Merovingians could fail to detect here the royal practice of polygamy.[1] Is it possible that Frankish chieftains, observing the entourage of a Roman ruler for the first time, had lost faith in the way of life of their own warlord? At all events, they preferred to live under Aegidius for a few years; and they may in the end have incited Clovis to move south and to reassert his father's rule over his own people, in place of that of Syagrius.

But tradition has a little more to tell of Childeric. Gregory had heard, or read, that he was recalled during the eighth year of his exile, an unnamed friend having in the meantime pacified the offended Franks and then sent to Childeric the half of a divided *solidus*, which he would recognize as proof that it was safe to return from 'Thuringia'. Not long afterwards, however, the author of the *Liber Historiae Francorum* and Fredegar do rather better than this. Fredegar[2] in particular records an elaborate tale in which Godefroid Kurth[3] has detected a popular epic based on the adventures of Gundoald, who in 582 came to Gaul from Constantinople as a Merovingian pretender. Fredegar identifies the faithful friend as Wiomad, a Hun, describes circumstantially what steps Wiomad took to put enmity between Aegidius and his Franks, and finally brings Childeric home, by way of Constantinople, with a handsome subsidy from the emperor. Behind the improbabilities of this rigmarole may lie, it seems to me, not so

---

[1] *Hist.*, II, 12. We may recall Tacitus, *Germ.*, 17: 'prope soli barbarorum singulis uxoribus contenti sunt, exceptis admodum paucis qui non libidine sed ob nobilitatem plurimis nuptiis ambiuntur'.

[2] *Chron.*, III, ch. 11.     [3] *Histoire poétique des Mérovingiens* (1893), ch. 7.

much the career of Gundoald (whose end was quite unlike that of Childeric) as a kernel of historical fact. Even if Childeric never did go to Constantinople, may we not suppose that he could have been in the pay of Byzantium? What more likely than that the imperial court, finding him at loggerheads with Aegidius, should choose to support him against the latter? There is no reason why the rule of Aegidius should have pleased Byzantium more than that of the chieftain of a trusted federate people. On this interpretation, Aegidius was a rebel, and Childeric owed his rule in Gaul in part, at least, to imperial backing.

Here, then, we have a Salian chieftain who repeatedly brings his warriors into Gaul to fight the barbarian enemies of the *rex Romanorum* on whatever front, and who subsequently falls out with his employer and retreats to his stronghold of Tournai, perhaps with a pension from Byzantium. And there in Tournai he was buried. His grave, discovered in 1653, yielded treasure the small remaining part of which proves that he was laid to rest with magnificent wargear, a cloak embroidered with some three hundred gold 'cicadas', a fine gold bracelet and buckles, a crystal globe and a miniature bull's-head in gold, the severed head of his war-horse caparisoned in precious materials, a signet-ring bearing his name and showing him wearing his hair over his shoulders, a purse of one hundred gold coins and a box of two hundred ornamental silver coins.[1] In terms of wealth, we have come a long way from the German forests, and the world not merely of Clovis but of Dagobert and Charles Martel seems in sight. Childeric was more than a wanderer in search of a livelihood. His treasure was that of an established federate warrior. If the charger's head speaks for the barbaric customs of his fathers, and that of the bull for the good luck of the successful kingly family to which it conceivably stood as talisman, the ornaments of gold speak for Byzantium, whether or not by way of Soissons; and his seal-ring is engraved in Latin characters. The coins, moreover, argue substantial wealth of another kind in those who could afford to deposit them in his grave. What the grave does not reveal, at least so far as can now be told, is any certain mark of kingship. The

---

[1] This and comparable treasures are considered in my article, 'The graves of kings', *Nuovi Studi Medievali*, 3rd series, I (1960).

ring is a means of identification; the gold betrays favour and wealth; and the weapons, power. It is commonly held that war-gear distinguishes the barbarian king who fights under the aegis of Woden. It may do so; but we have no means of knowing whether Childeric and his men professed Woden's cult, and, if they did, whether this was to the exclusion of other cults (e.g. the cult of Tiwaz or Tiw, who was then something more than a war-god).[1] In short, Childeric's is the grave of a barbarian who has done well by the Romans; but his masters have not romanized him or converted him to their religion. Why should they have done? When his followers laid Childeric in his grave, in the year 481 or 482, he was no more and no less than chieftain of the Franks of Tournai, acknowledged by Romans. To Gregory, looking back over a century, he seemed to be a king; but the historian does not explain what he meant by this. *Virtus* was there, without a doubt, and *nobilitas* too; his authority may not have extended far in the Frankish world, and we cannot be sure that other Frankish kings would have allowed the pre-eminence of his blood; but he had known how to sell or withhold the striking-power of his warriors; in brief, to handle them like the commodity that, in Roman eyes, they were. We may best characterize him by borrowing a word from the Pegau annalist, who distinguishes two qualities in a king: *fortitudo* and *felicitas*. *Fortitudo* is plainly the *virtus* of Tacitus. *Felicitas* is not quite his *nobilitas*; but, nonetheless, it is that fruitful good-luck that stems from *nobilitas*. Childeric had it.

## II · PUGNATOR EGREGIUS

The importance of Clovis to the history of the practice of kingship depends in large part on the fact that Gregory of Tours chose to write about him. Like all good historical writing, Gregory's account of the great barbarian carries that kind of conviction from which the reader can never afterwards escape. Clovis is Gregory's Clovis, whether we like it or not; he is Gregory's 'magnus et pugnator egregius', the man who brought the Salians to Catholicism

---

[1] The very large literature on the pagan cults of the continental Germanic peoples is evaluated by Otto Höfler, 'Der Sakralcharakter des germanischen Königtums', *Das Königtum*, particularly pp. 102 ff. Höfler is, however, too ready to push back mythical genealogies to a remote past, and confuses the descent of peoples with the descent of kings.

and to a kind of *Romanitas*, the father of his dynasty. This must be accepted at the outset: there is no getting round the Bishop of Tours, however much we emend his chronology, and however often we impute to his hero motives that might have shocked him.[1]

Childeric's successor was a youth of 15; successor, that is, to the rule of Franks, Salian and other, settled round Tournai. There were plenty more *reges Francorum* scattered between Tournai, Toxandria, and the Middle Rhine. There is no knowing what he made of his southern neighbour, the *rex Romanorum* of Soissons, who since 476 had had no emperor he could call master, and whose legal position was thus finally exposed for the sham it was. It could have been this that brought down upon Syagrius the warriors of a king whose title to rule was as good as his own. If it was, it took Clovis nearly five years to argue his way to this conclusion, for it was not till 486 that he attacked Syagrius in the territory of Soissons, and routed his force. When he finally laid hands on the *Rex Romanorum*, obligingly betrayed by the Visigoths, he made short work of him. Gregory paints that engagement in the colours of a personal clash, and this may reflect the actual relationship between Clovis and Syagrius, and not the romantic way of epic tradition.[2] They may have seen each other as rivals for the floating loyalties of the warbands of *Belgica Secunda*. Some of these warbands, moreover, were Frankish and had been in the pay of the kings of Soissons since forsaking Childeric. Their natural inclination to return to the allegiance of their Frankish lord may have combined with Clovis' own wish to reclaim them, and, with them, his father's southern conquests. Yet another reason for the battle of Soissons may be found in the practical difficulty of controlling any considerable part of northern Gaul without at the same time controlling Soissons and Rheims.

Wavering loyalties had still left Syagrius ruler of what was worth fighting for. So far from collapsing before Clovis, he put up a stiff fight. Gregory's account can only mean that Syagrius thought he could win: 'sed nec iste distolit ac resistere metuit'.[3]

---

[1] General reference may be made to chapter III.
[2] H. Mitteis, *Der Staat des hohen Mittelalters*, p. 43, is sensible about this.
[3] *Hist.*, II, 27.

His defeat was on the field of battle: there was no question of any moral disintegration of a Roman frontier-province. Except, then, in so far as he may have been an imperial official, his power and his lands fell to Clovis, who would have regarded himself as his heir. The defeated warbands would have gone to strengthen the Frankish following; and Roman notaries and the like who had served Syagrius would have been ready at hand to constitute a writing-office for the new ruler.

The chronology of the next few years cannot be determined, but it does look as if Clovis gave his energies to the affairs of the conquered province, rewarding his followers with gifts of land from the disintegrated remnants of the imperial fisc and from whatever private properties he seized. A smooth transfer of *villae* from Gallo-Roman to Frankish ownership would be too simple a way to conceive either the changing nature of the *villae* or the needs of the newcomers, whose taste for hunting-lodges in forest-clearings may have left the Romans in possession of more culti-vated land than they had hoped for.[1] A large body of warriors always remained in attendance on the king, constituting his *trustis*, the nucleus of his field-force. In Clovis' day, if not later, this *trustis* may have formed a much higher proportion of the fighting strength of the Franks than is always allowed. With its help, the king browbeat his Frankish neighbours into subservience without, however, preventing that slow, unchronicled movement of Ripuarian Franks westward from the Cologne area to colonize northern Gaul, in a way that would have been impossible for the swift-moving and less numerous Salians.[2] Also with its help, he made sallies into the chaotic Armorican region of the Loire, the home of the Bacaudae. The subsequent history of that area does not suggest that he had any more success than the Romans in making his authority felt. Little as we know about them, these operations should be interpreted strictly at their face-

[1] The complex story of the nature of the Frankish settlement of northern Gaul is no part of this study. Its outlines have been firmly sketched by Alexander Bergengruen, *Adel und Grundherrschaft im Merowingerreich* (1958). The legal status of Roman *possessores* under the Franks is discussed by Heinrich Dannenbauer, 'Die Rechts-stellung der Gallorömer im Frankischenreich', *Grundlagen der mittelalterlichen Welt* (1958).

[2] I here accept the thesis of Charles Verlinden, 'Frankish colonization: a new approach', *Trans R. Hist. Soc.*, 5th series, vol. 4, 1954.

value. It was a time for rewarding followers and putting down rival claimants to the rule of Syagrius' rich kingdom. To see it as a 'period of consolidation' before another great advance goes contrary to the evidence. Opportunism, short-sighted and ruthless, was characteristic of every barbarian who made his way in the Roman world.[1]

These early years were also a time for learning to know the Romans. Their tone is set by a famous letter addressed to the new king by Remigius (St Rémi), bishop of Rheims.[2] The bishop has learned, without being officially informed, that Clovis has taken over the administration of *Belgica Secunda*: 'non est novum ut coeperis esse sicut parentes tui semper fuerunt'. He goes on to speak of 'tua provincia', 'cives tuos' and 'praetorium tuum', which has led some scholars to think that the letter must have been written after the defeat of Syagrius;[3] but the case for dating it to 481 or a little after seems the stronger. It is a hortatory letter of a recognized pattern; the bishop acknowledges the effective rule of Clovis over part at least of *Belgica*, without foreseeing its extension south and without supposing that it is at all likely to be detrimental to Roman interests. The tone of the letter is patronizing: the pagan barbarian will wish to reflect on the advantages of having the Gallo-Roman Church on his side. It is not, in so many words, a warning against the Arianism of the neighbouring Visigoths and Burgundians, nor a direct appeal for conversion to Catholicism. It is rather a statement of fact: *Belgica* is Roman and is run by Roman bishops; and a prudent *rex* will wish to take note of this, since most of his subjects will be Romans. Clovis has crossed the frontier and is welcomed in, on terms. To bring about his conversion would be a matter of years: how could he think of flinging away the support of the tribal gods who had so plainly brought prosperity to him and his followers? The pagan Franks were a religious people. There is every indication that the Roman bishops also recognized this, and were much happier with

[1] In general the argument of this chapter will be found to run counter to that of A. van de Vyver, 'Clovis et la politique méditerranéenne', *Études d'histoire dédiées à la mémoire de Henri Pirenne* (1937), who sees planning and an inexorable advance in each step of Clovis' career.

[2] *M.G.H., Epist.*, II, 113.

[3] Notably J. B. Bury, *The Invasion of Europe by the Barbarians* (1928), pp. 244-7.

a pagan overlord than they would have been with an Arian. Clovis gave them further proof of his goodwill by marrying the only Burgundian princess who was a Catholic;[1] but however his wife and Bishop Remigius may have worked to bring him nearer conversion, he saw no reason yet to risk a breach with ancestral tradition. He took his time, as the Kentish husband of his great-granddaughter, Bertha, was to take his, a century later.

A consequence of marriage was the involvement of Clovis in Burgundian family affairs. It was the fact of kinship, not of his wife's Catholicism, that caused Clovis to intervene in the fratricidal quarrels of her uncles. The account of the intervention given by Gregory of Tours[2] is tricked out in the frills of saga, and this invites the historian to dismiss the whole as a latter-day invention, behind which lies the more prosaic truth that Clovis was fishing in troubled waters. But the fact is that the springs of action in these remote times lay more in kinship and its claims than in statesmanlike calculations as to the main chance. I therefore accept Gregory's statement that Clovis marched into Burgundy at the invitation of one of his kinsmen by marriage, Godigisel, caring little where it might lead.[3] The outcome of a series of sorties into territory more romanized than any he had known was the linking, not merely of the dynasties, but of the Frankish and Burgundian peoples, in an uneasy relationship that was to last centuries. They hated each other with the hatred that barbarians reserved for barbarians; but the Franks had discovered that their new properties were exposed on the south-east frontier to a people formidably

---

[1] I see no reason to disturb the traditional chronology, which places the marriage before the Burgundian war. This is the point where I find the arguments of M. Van de Vyver least conclusive. Reference should be made to his three important studies in the *Revue belge de philol. et d'hist.*: 'La victoire contre les Alamans et la conversion de Clovis', XV (1936) and XVI (1937), and 'L'unique victoire contre les Alamans et la conversion de Clovis en 506', XVII (1938), the last being a rebuttal of criticisms advanced by Ferdinand Lot, ibid., XVII (1938). Van de Vyver was also attacked by J. Calmette in *Acad. des Inscr.* 1946 and *Le Moyen Age*, 53 (1947). While I see no convincing reason for placing the marriage as early as 493–94 (the traditional date), I accept the arguments of C. Courtois for placing it before 500. ('L'avènement de Clovis II et règles d'accession au trône', *Mélanges Halphen*, p. 164). Van de Vyver's date is 502–3. It is fair to say that in most respects van de Vyver's chronology has withstood criticism. It is the motives he attributes to Clovis and his contemporaries that inspire more serious doubts.

[2] *Hist.*, II, 32.

[3] But cf. van de Vyver, *Rev. belge*, XVI, pp. 84 ff.

befriended by the Goths, whom they could never again afford to forget. The Merovingians were seldom astute in their handling of the Burgundians, but they had every excuse to go on trying.

Where Frankish territories approached the Upper and Middle Rhine, contact could not be avoided with the Alamans. Here, the immediate threat was to the Ripuarian Franks; but these, too, tended to fall under the kingship of Clovis, either because he was a great warrior or because he was successor of Syagrius. All the Franks looked upon the Alamans as a natural threat and as competitors for Roman territory. Though West Germans like the Franks, the Alamans were perhaps a more primitive people: their horsemen certainly struck terror into the Franks, among whom only the chieftains were mounted; they seemed to belong to another world.[1] In addition to this antipathy, the Franks were heirs and defenders of Roman territory, even if they had it without permission. The very structure of the *regnum* of Syagrius could be overthrown by a successful Alamannic drive across the Rhine into eastern Gaul. Fear for this frontier was a constant preoccupation with Clovis, and it can hardly be doubted that Franks, whether his or those of the chieftains of *Francia Rinensis*, would have been dealing with Alamannic sorties for years before the great engagement of Tolbiac (Zülpich), when a confederation of Franks routed the Alamans, and Clovis was accepted by the Alamannic remnant as king in place of their fallen leader.[2] We need not see Tolbiac as part of a Frankish plan to stabilize the eastern frontier and neutralize the barbarians of the Rhine and the Rhône before attempting a more ambitious push against the Goths. Such concepts belong to the sixteenth century; hardly to the sixth. Nonetheless, it is true that Tolbiac marks a turning-point in the relations of Franks with Goths. The southward flight of some at least of the Alaman host to the protection of the Ostrogoth Theodoric comes too soon after a Visigothic warning

[1] As late as the eighth century, the abbot Pirmin denounced the Alamannic rites of prayer and magic that propitiated the secret powers of the forest and its soil (*Dicta Pirminii*, ch. 22).

[2] I accept van de Vyver's date of 506 for Tolbiac and agree that it was the only major engagement involving Franks and Alamans. It is also quite clear from Ennodius that it was the Alamans who provoked the final campaign. Even Theodoric, warning Clovis to lay aside 'vindicta' against the fleeing Alamans, speaks of their host as 'acerrimum' and 'innumerabilem' (Cassiodorus, *Var.*, II, 41).

to Clovis to leave the Burgundians alone to allow any escape from
the conclusion that the Arian, and equally the East German,
dynasties of the West were aware that Syagrius had a successor
who might endanger their own position. He had already put his
own house in order to the extent that all the Frankish settlers
between the Loire and the Rhine acknowledged his kingship. Here
was a 'Bretwalda' if ever there was one. It seems also very probable that Clovis was already in touch with Byzantium, and that
this would have been known to the Goths.[1] Enough had happened to cause the Visigoth Alaric II to make preparations for
war so extensive as to bring down a rebuke and a warning from
the more prudent Ostrogoth, Theodoric.[2] The Goths were presumably worried at news of Byzantine curiosity at the altogether
unexpected success of Clovis against the Alamans. What could be
done with Clovis was more interesting than what Clovis could do.

The victory of Tolbiac, whether we date it early or late in
Clovis' career, was associated by Gregory with his conversion to
Catholic Christianity. The pattern is familiar. Defeat stares him in
the face and his gods have deserted him; his thoughts turn to his
wife's god, to whom he prays in his heart for victory; and victory
is his. Like Constantine in a similar predicament, Clovis knows
that he must throw in his lot with the new god.[3] This was no total
conversion, for it did not imply that the myths and rituals of
ancestral heathen piety were to be swept aside. The barbarian is
not aware of being offered a new way of life complete with a
theology of its own; at most, he sees it as an additional cult. It is
a supplement, not a substitute; adhesion, not conversion.[4] His
private decision calls for no dogmatic preparation, for which indeed there is no evidence, but rather for a conviction that the
territorial god of *Belgica Secunda* must be added to his people's
pantheon, perhaps in a commanding position. We are still some
way from the bigger decision implied by the catechumenate and

[1] The *aliena malignitas* of *Var.*, III, 1 and 4, is probably an allusion to imperial
machinations, as van de Vyver claims.

[2] *Var.*, III, i.

[3] The parallel with the battle of the Milvian Bridge does not disprove the later
story. His wife and St Remigius were there to remind Clovis of Constantine, if he
needed reminding.

[4] A. D. Nock, *Conversion*, p. 7, makes this general distinction.

by baptism: the decision to abandon, at least officially, all other gods but the Christian god. This final transition is softened by acceptance of the cultus of local saints, who must have appeared to Clovis very like demi-gods. But even adhesion calls for conviction of right, and it is no belittlement of Clovis' act to term it a political decision, taken after weighing Frankish pagan conservatism[1] against the assured approval of the Gallo-Romans. We cannot tell whether the support of a Gallo-Roman episcopate, long prepared to work with Clovis without any assurance of his ultimate conversion, was at last demanding positive action. Nor can we know if he hoped that conversion would buy active imperial intervention against the Goths. The fact of conversion cannot be dissociated from the circumstances. Without Tolbiac, the proof would have been lacking that the Christian god gave victory over other Germans; there might have been no conversion, and no desire for it. Victory over enemies, victory over rebels; this, and not administrative help, is what would tempt a *rex barbarorum* to conversion. It is Christ the warrior, the defender of a chosen people, who is revealed on Frankish grave-stones in the Rhineland.[2] The feeling is authentically conveyed in a Merovingian prayer for victory over rebels, based on Nehemiah's great invocation (2 Maccabees i. 24 ff.) beginning 'Domine, deus omnium creator, terribilis et fortis'.[3] Clovis would have understood Nehemiah. The risk was great, however, and not much precision can be attached to Gregory's statement that three thousand warriors were baptized with their king:[4] the figure comes from Acts ii. 41. A people is not converted in a generation. The hardheaded nature of the king's decision, singularly free from miraculous atmosphere, comes out well in a letter addressed to him by

---

[1] Note the king's doubts, as expressed to Remigius: 'sed restat unum, quod populus qui me sequitur non patitur relinquere deos suos, sed vado et loquor eis iuxta verbum tuum' (Gregory, *Hist.*, II, 31). The result was not a foregone conclusion.

[2] Cf. Kurt Böhner, 'Die Frage der Kontinuität zwischen Altertum und Mittelalter im Spiegel der fränkischen Funde des Rheinlandes', *Trierer Zeitschrift*, Heft 1/2, 19 Jahrgang (1950), p. 99.

[3] The prayer survives in a Reichenau manuscript. Cf. A. Holder, *Reichenauer Handschriften*, 1, pp. 568 ff., and A. Dold, *Texte und Arbeiten* I, 12 (Beuron, 1925, pp. 35–37).

[4] *Hist.*, II, 31. Compare Avitus to the hesitant Gundobad, urging him that people should follow kings, and not kings people, in religion as in war (ibid., II, 34).

Bishop Avitus of Vienne.[1] The bishop (who has one eye on his own Arian master, Gundobad of Burgundy) praises the king's *subtilitas*, as well as his courage, in abandoning the faith of his ancestors. Herein lies the miracle, that without the aid of preachers Clovis has chosen the right way, at the right time for himself. He has broken with his ancestors, so that his posterity must look back to him alone as the source of their excellence:

> Vos de toto priscae originis stemmate sola nobilitate contenti, quidquid omne potest fastigium generositatis ornare, prosapiae vestrae a vobis voluistis exsurgere. Habetis bonorum auctores, voluistis esse meliorum.[2]

It is the first appearance of 'le roi très chrétien': 'instituistis posteris ut regnetis in caelo'. Avitus, like Remigius, has a clear notion of what he expects a Catholic barbarian king to be, and we should not underestimate this tenacity of viewpoint in the slow evolution of Merovingian kingship. Clovis must make a sacrifice and take a risk; his heathen *fortuna* will go, and in its place he must believe that the rite of baptism will substitute a Christian *fortuna* in battle, with a fine new field of foes in God's Germanic-pagan enemies, to say nothing of heretics.[3] Avitus further compares the Frankish king with the Byzantine emperor. Clovis must now become a kind of western emperor, a patriarch to the western Germans, reigning over, though not governing, all peoples and kings:

> Quatenus externi quique populi paganorum, pro religionis vobis primitus imperio servituri, dum adhuc aliam videntur habere proprietatem, discernantur potius gente quam principe.

One catches an echo of the tone of Remigius, writing to the young warrior twenty years earlier; there is a disposition to lecture

[1] I follow van de Vyver's interpretation but cannot agree that it excludes the essentials of the Tolbiac victory reported by Gregory. It does exclude Nicetius' version of the story, on which I comment below.

[2] Letter 38 in the edition of Chevalier, 46 in that of Peiper. I quote from Chevalier.

[3] Cf. Karl Hauck, 'Die geschichtliche Bedeutung der germanischen Auffassung von Königtum und Adel', *Rapports du XIᵉ congrès international des sciences historiques* (Stockholm, 1960), p. 113. It is, however, difficult to follow Hauck and others in their contention that Clovis was worried about the effect of conversion on his descent from the gods, and that Avitus intended a compromise whereby the names of the pagan gods were to remain in the Merovingian genealogy, but without cult-significance.

and to patronize the child of nature, as well as some anxiety to be known for his friend. But there is also awareness of wider horizons. By the mere fact of conversion to Catholicism Clovis is a new kind of barbarian king. He stands apart from and in opposition to the Gothic kings. His natural ally and his model will be the orthodox emperor. He is Gregory's 'novus Constantinus',[1] a figure of speech that recalls not merely the first Christian emperor but the acclamation that had for long greeted the Byzantine emperors. The break with the past is as complete as the bishops can make it; Avitus insists on it, and Remigius has nothing less in mind when he baptizes Clovis at Rheims with the words:

Mitis depone colla, Sicamber, adora quod incendisti, incende quod adorasti![2]

The mere use of 'Sicamber' with its reminder of small tribal origins, sharpens the contrast and points the moral. It is almost as if, without this emphasis, the king might have had something else, and something less, in mind. The subsequent history of the Merovingians, who owed almost nothing to Byzantine example, strongly suggests that he did. No sharp break seemed apparent to Bede's Redwald, with his prudent arrangement of a heathen and a Christian altar in one and the same building,[3] or to Gregory's Spanish visitor, who reported that in his part of the world it was usual to pay one's respects to both heathen and Christian altars, if one happened to pass between them.[4] Clovis presumably abandoned his heathen cultus, but the memory remained of victories, his own and his ancestors', not won under Christ; it

[1] Gregory may have found the acclamation-formula in a written source or may be making use of the reported plaudits of easterners who witnessed the ceremony and instinctively employed it. Cf. E. Ewig, 'Das Bild Constantins des Grossen in der ersten Jahrhunderten des abendländischen Mittelalters', *Historisches Jahrbuch*, 75 (1956), p. 28. That his mind was running on the legend of Sylvester and Constantine is further shown by the reference in the same sentence to cleansing from leprosy (*Actus S. Silvestri*, ed. B. Mombritius, *Sanctuarium seu Vitae Sanctorum*, Milan, 1480, vol. II, p. 281). See also W. Levison, 'Konstantinische Schenkung und Silvester-Legende', reprinted in *Aus rheinischer und fränkischer Frühzeit* (1948), esp. p. 434.
[2] *Hist.*, II, 31. It seems to me that the force of St Remigius' remark is not affected by whether or not one accepts the view of Jean Hoyoux that Clovis was being asked to dispense with his magic necklaces ('Le collier de Clovis', *Rev. belge*, XXI, 1942). It should be added that the form of the baptism, as we have it, is nothing more than the normal admission of a catechumen. Legend was to treat it quite differently.
[3] *Hist. Eccl.*, II, 15.      [4] *Hist.*, V, 43.

was a long way from Soissons to Tolbiac, as his warriors well knew, and Frankish graves of much later date than Tolbiac yield amulets and charms and offerings that are anything but Christian. At least for a time, the core of Merovingian kingship remained heathen in some indefinable way, even while it benefited from the baptism at Rheims.[1]

Clovis fought his last campaign, against the Visigoths in 507, as a Catholic. Gregory reports that many in Gaul wanted the Franks as overlords, and gives as one example the Bishop of Rodez. We are left to infer that what the 'many' objected to were the Arian Goths, which is not quite the same thing as the Arianism of the Goths.[2] But Gregory makes Clovis take it as a religious challenge to conquer Alaric II. Clovis set forth under the aegis of St Martin of Tours, whose sanctuary had not long since been freed from the Visigoths; and he returned there to give thanks for his victory at Vouillé. Historians of the Church did not invent this. But there are other factors, too. Aquitaine was an indivisible part of Roman Gaul, and the peace of the new Frankish conquests south of the Seine was bound up with mastery of the Loire valley. More important still, the Goths were hereditary enemies of the Franks. Childeric had fought the Goths round Angers and Tours for years. Clovis himself had spent a decade skirmishing against them in the same area, and may even have got as far south as Bordeaux.[3] Looked at in this way, Vouillé marks a culmination in a long series of raids and sorties in which religion can have

[1] I accept without reservation the tradition of baptism at Rheims and reject the tradition of baptism at Tours, which has no more factual support than a misreading in the text of a letter written about 565 by Bishop Nicetius of Trier to Clotsinda, granddaughter of Clovis and wife of the Arian Alboin, king of the Lombards (*M.G.H., Epist.*, III, pp. 119–22). If one were needed, an additional argument in favour of Rheims would be the will of Remigius himself (cf. A. H. M. Jones, P. Grierson, and J. A. Crook, 'The authenticity of the testamentum S. Remigii', *Revue belge de philologie et d'histoire*, XXXV, 1957, no. 2, pp. 368, 371).
[2] Gregory, *Hist.*, II, 35–37. Professor E. A. Thompson writes: 'It might be truer to say that the Roman landowners, who as a class had not been dissatisfied with the rule of the barbarian kings, gave considerable support to the Visigothic king Alaric II in 507, whereas the poorer classes had now lost their earlier enthusiasm for the conditions of life under Visigothic rule and stayed neutral in 507' ('The Conversion of the Visigoths to Catholicism', *Nottingham Medieval Studies*, IV, 1960, p. 6). I do not know that we can divide up support for the Franks in this way.
[3] These early skirmishes into Visigothic territory are known from two notices in the Copenhagen continuation of Prosper's chronicle under the years 496 and 498

played no part. The difference that religion made may have been more apparent after the battle than before.

Allowing for the fact that Vouillé did not permit Clovis to annexe Visigothic Gaul,[1] and afforded him little more than a much-needed replenishment of his treasure[2] and relief from the threat of eclipse, he still did remarkably little with his victory if we suppose that the Mediterranean was his goal. It is not enough to see Theodoric with his Ostrogoths in Provence as too formidable to take on, especially since the Ostrogoths were themselves threatened in the rear by an imperial naval expedition to Italy, of which Clovis cannot have been ignorant. A threat had been lifted, great treasure collected, old scores wiped off, the Church delighted; and Clovis, after wintering in Bordeaux, made off north to Tours and thence to Paris. There seems never to have been any question of his transferring his headquarters from Soissons or Rheims to Toulouse. What his latest victory chiefly gave him was a free hand in the north.

The victorious Franks bestowed treasure on St Martin's Church at Tours, for to this saint, according to Gregory's account, they thought they owed their victory. St Martin is adopted, his cult appropriated. Henceforth this most Gallic of saints belongs to the Merovingians; his *cappa* or soldier's cloak is soon their most treasured relic, from the seventh century at latest, and probably earlier.[3] The soldier-saint of Gaul is not the least of the Merovin-

---

(*M.G.H., Auct. Ant.*, IX, 331), and must presumably be associated with the banishment of Bishops Volusianus and Verus of Tours on charges of treasonable association with the Franks (Gregory, *Hist.*, II, 26, and X, 31). Cf. Stroheker, *Der senatorische Adel*, though it does not follow that we see in this Frankish activity 'den Weg nach Süden bis zum Mittelmeer' (p. 106).

[1] Septimania and the Spanish March remained in Visigothic hands till the Arab invasion. The rest of the Midi was only slowly conquered by Clovis' successors, though some Frankish settlements in Aquitaine must date from the early sixth century, as Broëns has shown. Cf. E. Ewig, 'Die fränkischen Teilungen und Teilreiche, 511–613', *Akad. der Wissen. und der Lit.*, Mainz (1952).

[2] Gregory says (*Hist.*, II, 37) that Theuderic, Clovis' son, captured all the Gothic treasure in their capital of Toulouse, though parts of it were certainly in Gothic hands in Spain in the seventh century, as a story in Fredegar's chronicle, Book IV, ch. 73, will show. However, the Franks may have supplemented the haul from Toulouse with more from Carcassonne, including 'the treasure of Solomon' taken by Alaric I from Rome (Procopius, *Bell. Goth.*, V, 12, 42).

[3] Josef Fleckenstein, *Die Hofkapelle der deutschen Könige*, I (1959), esp. pp. 12 ff., traces the growth of the Frankish *capella* from these beginnings.

gian gains from the field of Vouillé, and, in the eyes of many, would be the first solid compensation for the loss of the heathen gods. The gift of treasure to his sanctuary was thus rather more than a polite way of thanking the bishops for favours received. It marked a submission. Moreover, inside St Martin's Church, Clovis received from a representative of the Emperor Anastasius I a diploma, bestowing on him the title of consul: 'et ab ea die tanquam consul aut augustus est vocitatus'.[1] He was then vested in a purple tunic and a chlamys, placed a diadem on his head[2] and rode from the church into the city of Tours, scattering gold and silver among the crowd as he went. Much has been written about this incident. In general, there is a disposition to belittle it. But Gregory does not belittle it, and the facts as he states them are at least intelligible.[3] They mean that the emperor had bestowed on Clovis an honorary title, probably of consul though possibly of patrician. He could scarcely have bestowed on him a Byzantine rank inferior to that already held by the Burgundian king;[4] and the diploma (*codicilli consulatus*) was the essential preliminary to such an honour.[5] The tradition of Clovis' dress is at once too exact and too misleading to be acceptable as reported by, and probably to, Gregory. It suggests rather a literary source in its details; for the *tunica blattea* and the chlamys and the diadem were all part of imperial, not of consular, ceremonial. Furthermore, a consular procession should have been in a chariot and not on horseback. Only

---

[1] Gregory, *Hist.*, II, 38. Ensslin (*Historisches Jahrbuch*, 56, 1936, p. 507) reads *ut* in place of *aut*, though there is no manuscript justification for doing so. The sentence would then be translated 'he was henceforth called consul, like the emperor'.

[2] P. E. Schramm, *Herrschaftszeichen und Staatssymbolik*, I, p. 137, is uncertain whether the diadem was part of the regalia bestowed by the emperor or belonged to Clovis as king. Can there be any doubt that Gregory understands the former?

[3] A fair statement is that of E. Stein, *Histoire du Bas-Empire*, II, p. 150. See also P. Leveel, 'Le consulat de Clovis à Tours', *Études Mérovingiennes, Actes des journées de Poitiers, 1952*, pp. 187–90.

[4] Gundobad was *magister militum Galliarum* (Stein, op. cit. p. 59), and Sigismund a *patricius* (Avitus, *Epist.* 7 in Chevalier, 9 in Peiper). The Ostrogoth Theodoric had been consul in 484 (W. Liebenam, *Fasti consulares imperii Romani*, p. 50), though he came to Italy as *patricius* and *magister militum* to displace the *patricius* Odovacer. Theodoric is described in one contemporary Italian inscription as *semper augustus*. Imperial practice in the bestowal of titles of honour on barbarian rulers seems not to have been governed by hard and fast rules, and it is hardly surprising that western commentators sometimes gave misleading accounts, particularly of insignia. Cf. W. Ensslin, *Theodorich der Grosse*, esp. pp. 82 ff.

[5] So, at least, *Cod. Just.* XII, 3, 3, pr. See, too, Jordanes, *Getica*, 57.

the throwing of gold and silver was typically consular.[1] Whatever
the rank, we may be perfectly sure that Clovis and the imperial
representative were not in any doubt about it. The significant
point is, perhaps, not that the Byzantine envoy was on the spot
with imperial approbation of the blow against Gothic power in
Gaul, but that Clovis was willing to accept the public mark of
that approbation. It makes him no vassal of the Byzantine court;
he remains a *rex* and his own master; but he has acknowledged
imperial *auctoritas*, the moral ascendency of Rome over Gaul. This
is no small matter. It makes one think again of the strange tale
of Childeric and Byzantium and the possible significance of the
succession to Syagrius; it forewarns one of exchanges between
Frankish kings and emperors; and it lends weight to the opinion
of Procopius, that the Franks never felt that they held Gaul
securely unless the emperor had ratified their title.[2] Clovis would
have agreed with his contemporary, Theodoric, that, leaving
aside the question of function, the title of consul was supremely
worth having; it was 'summum bonum primumque in mundo
decus'.[3] No wonder that the people of Tours hailed the purple-
robed barbarian as if he were a kind of Augustus; he probably felt
that he was.[4] He had received his title in a part of the world where
Roman titles counted for something. The Aquitanian senators
were proud of their descent. They attached importance, as did the
Germans, not merely to ancestors as a class but to ancestors who
were regarded as sanctified. They were confident in the future.
How should they not have been, having survived the century of
Visigothic rule? The Ostrogoths, moreover, were on the point of
re-establishing many of the forms of imperial rule in Provence.
It was the world, furthermore, of *Lex Romana Visigothorum* and

[1] I am grateful to Mr Philip Grierson for advice on this point. Mr Grierson also
questions where Clovis could have obtained silver coins for distribution, since
there was no regular imperial silver coinage at this time. Some were being struck by
the Ostrogoths, and he may have had some of these. Or was there a Merovingian
silver-hoard, from which, e.g., the two hundred ornamental silver coins in Childeric's grave had come?

[2] *Bell. Goth.*, VII, 33, 4.

[3] Jordanes, *Getica*, 57.

[4] This is as far as I can go towards the theory of P. Courcelle, *Histoire littéraire*,
p. 204, that the church of Tours had the intention to revive the western empire in
the person of Clovis, and that this intention is later reflected in Gregory of Tours
and in Alcuin.

*Lex Romana Burgundionum*, both of which were to leave an in-
delible mark upon the laws of the Franks. Thus, law and titles
speak jointly for an active ideal of authority, of *imperium*, that
might at any time have assumed a practical, political shape. It
would be rash to assert that the investiture of Clovis had no effect
upon his subsequent acts.

We have to wait three years after Vouillé for a statement of the
king's relationship with the most Roman of his institutions, the
Church. This is comprised in the canons of the council of Orleans,
which are dated 10 July 511 and are subscribed by thirty-two
bishops, who represent, largely but not exclusively, the sees of the
lately-conquered region of the south.[1] They are no manifesto of
royal power. Had they been intended as such, they would surely
have been promulgated immediately after Vouillé. Instead, the
king waits three years, till a number of practical problems require
attention. As for his choice of Orleans, it can at least be said to be
further removed from Gothic influence than are the canons themselves, which at several points reflect the work of the council of
Agde, summoned by Alaric II the year before Vouillé. The
bishops admit that the initiative has been with the new king: he
has summoned them and has directed their attention to some of
the problems they have tried to solve. They have faithfully dealt
with 'titulos quos dedistis'.[2] Which *tituli* are meant is unclear, but
they probably include most of the first ten canons, which cover
matters where royal authority is interested: namely, the right of
asylum; royal permission for ordinations; the uses to which royal
largesse to churches may be put; the frequenting of the royal
court by clerics with favours to ask; the ordination of slaves; the
appropriation of Arian churches taken from the Goths, and the
employment of their ministers.[3] To this extent, the king is exercising authority over his bishops and showing how a king may
intervene; but not in a way that would have seemed excessive to
bishops who remembered the voice of the Visigoth Euric. Not

[1] The canons have been analysed by C. de Clercq, *La législation religieuse franque
de Clovis à Charlemagne*, pp. 8–13.

[2] *M.G.H., Concilia*, I, p. 2.

[3] Such is the view of L. Duchesne, *L'Église au VIᵉ siècle*, p. 501, with which I
concur. De Clerq, op. cit. p. 13, limits the *tituli* to canons 4 to 7. However, I would,
with Krusch, exclude canon 9 (*Nachr. d. Göttinger Gesell. d. Wissen.*, 1934).

even the Gallo-Romans need have found it so. So powerful a pre-
late as St Remigius had to consecrate a priest, at the king's wish,
whom all knew to be canonically unfitted. It is an authority,
moreover, that tacitly accepts that Roman Law by which the
Church lived. The 'saeculari lege' of canon 23 and the 'lex
romana' of canon 1 are alike the Theodosian Code.[1] It further sup-
poses the involvement of the Frankish king in that ferment of
local loyalties, that crystallization of affection round the shrines of
saints, that is the truly significant advance of the Gaulish Church
in the sixth century. An aspect of this advance in which the king
is necessarily involved is the rapid increase of gifts of land and
money and the flow of men to churches and to monasteries. It is
an increase, however, and not a beginning, since the Roman
*potentes* had also been in the habit of founding churches on their
estates.[2] The grants, or some of them, involved authentication
in writing; and this meant the help of Roman officials. (One such
grant is the *praeceptum de rege* of *Lex Salica*, XIV, 4.) But the
measures he takes to safeguard his interests say less to the historian than the fact of acquiescence,[3] which is apparent from the
moment of Vouillé and is immediately afterwards confirmed in a
letter addressed to certain unknown bishops.[4] We may detect in
this letter, and in the canons of the council, a groping for a relationship, but certainly not an endeavour to theorize. The king
accepts the bishops; and they accept him as yet one more *rex*. This
one, indeed, is a *rex catholicus*; but there is no disposition to treat
him cavalierly because of that. A king is expected to have his own
way. If he believes that Tolbiac and Vouillé have made him a great
Christian king, still more so do the bishops. This is perhaps as far

---

[1] Respectively *Cod. Theod.* IV, 14, 1, and IX, 45, 4. Canon 4 may reflect XVI,
2, 8, 9.

[2] Cf. *Cod. Theod.*, XVI, 2, 33 and 5, 14.

[3] The growth of ecclesiastical property under Clovis and his successors is treated
by E. Lesne, *La propriété ecclésiastique en France*, I, pp. 143 ff. It should be noted that
Clovis did not restore to the Catholic Church all the property it thought it
was entitled to, for the first canon of the council of Paris (568–70) alludes to
the spoliations of 'bonae memoriae domni Clodovei regis' (*M.G.H., Conc.*, I,
p. 143).

[4] It is the first letter in *M.G.H., Capit. Regum Francorum*, I, and the first official
document of a Frankish king to survive. Its form presupposes Roman drafting,
whether clerical or secular, and at more than one point is strongly reminiscent of
the style of the Burgundian Law.

as we can go in determining what difference his conversion made to the kingship of Clovis.

Royal authority is soon expressed in another way, if it is right to assign to these last years of his reign the promulgation of *Lex Salica*. The customary and unwritten laws of the Franks must be supposed to go back at least a century before this, and portions of them are to be seen in the *Lex*. But, as it stands in what seems to be the oldest recension, that of 65 titles,[1] *Lex Salica* is new law; and it is royal law. Clovis was here following the example of his Visigothic and Burgundian near-contemporaries. Not long before, Euric had legislated for the Visigoths, probably following the example of predecessors;[2] and Gundobad and Sigismund for the Burgundians. In addition, both Visigothic and Burgundian kings had legislated separately for their Roman subjects. Clovis did not legislate for his Gallo-Romans, perhaps because they were understood to live under the protection of Roman Law that needed no clarification; but he did offer his Franks the *Lex Salica*. It is a waste of time to debate how narrowly 'Salic', in a tribal sense, this law is. Perhaps it may be defined as that body of Frankish Law which any Frank choosing to acknowledge the kingship of Clovis was bound to live by. What holds it together is the king's will. Its contents are various in date, in provenance and in matter. They are largely concerned with what we should call criminal law, and hardly at all with civil. Indeed, the civil side of Frankish legal life must be supposed to have been determined by Roman practice. Predominantly, the matter of the *Lex* is Germanic, though here and there can be found certain traces of Roman legislation.[3] The true indebtedness of *Lex Salica* to the Romans lies, however, less in specific borrowings than in the fact of composition. Only lawyers familiar with the practice of Vulgar Law in the West could have compiled *Lex Salica*. It is a compilation

---

[1] Cf. chapter V. Even so, the 65-title text that has come down to us is rather a private, clerical compilation than the text as known to Clovis.

[2] See chapter II.

[3] E.g. title XIII, 11, which reflects *Cod. Theod.* III, 12, 3, by way of *Lex Romana Visigothorum*. Other possible borrowings are discussed by F. Beyerle, *Das Entwicklungsproblem im germanischen Rechtsgang*, 1 (1915), pp. 384–85. The 65-title text is best studied in the edition of K. A. Eckhardt, *Pactus Legis Salicae*, II, i (1955) and the most convenient summary of research is that of R. Buchner, Wattenbach-Levison, *Deutschlands Geschichtsquellen, die Rechtsquellen*.

for barbarians, but not by barbarians. Clovis may have inherited his learned helpers from Syagrius; but there is equally the likelihood that they came to him from Burgundy; and there could have been help from Toulouse. As it originally stood, *Lex Salica* would probably have boasted some royal prefatory matter,[1] such as figures in the Burgundian *Lex Gundobada*; and there are still traces of title-headings in the epilogue which suggest the same kind of Roman influence that moulded Visigothic law. All in all, *Lex Salica* is a fairly complex legal statement that covers a large range of the needs of Franks settled permanently among or near the properties of Christian and Latin-speaking Gallo-Romans. It accords them special privileges not because they are Franks but because they are the king's Franks; and when one considers the disparate nature of their own quite recent origins one appreciates why this protection was more important than any protection against Romans. *Lex Salica* has a practical purpose: it gathers together certain traditional Frankish practices – and these are signalized in the text by the so-called Malberg glosses, which are in the nature of scribal cross-references to aural tradition in the Frankish courts; and it adds to them other, more recent, practices that have come to be accepted on Roman soil, whether directly by the Franks themselves or indirectly, through their Germanic neighbours living in comparable circumstances; and all this matter is promulgated by the authority, the *verbum*, of the Frankish king. It has the further practical advantage of making available to the Church, and in a language it understood, the law by which the Franks chose to be judged in the criminal field. Here and there in *Lex Salica* we can see the king himself arbitrating, judging, extending his protection, when necessary over Romans as well as Franks,[2] watching his own interests, fiscal, military, and territorial. He does not see his subjects as of one blood or appear

[1] The shorter and longer prologue belong to a later date. Though the former may contain some earlier material, I cannot agree with F. Beyerle (*Rheinische Viertel-jahrsblätter*, 21, 1956, p. 384) that it could be assigned to the fifth century.

[2] E.g. titles I, i; III, ii; XIII, 6, 7; XIV, 4; XVIII; XXV, 2; XXVI, 1, 2; XXXVIII, 4; XLI, 8, 9; XLII, 1, 2; XLVI, 3, 6; XLVII, 1, 2; LIV, 1, 2; LVI, 1, 4, 5, 6; LXIII, 1, 2. The Roman *possessores* of Frankish enactments are the cultivators of the curial class and should be distinguished from the senators, a smaller and altogether more privileged class of Roman. The latter, not the former, would be the *potentes*, whose wide estates and big followings were not at first interfered with by the Franks.

to desire their fusion; but he is the king of them all, and a very busy man. More than this, the mere fact of his law-giving makes him more of a king. It puts him on a level with men like Alaric II, and it even recalls to his Romans, little though they benefit from *Lex Salica*, the legislative activity proper to the emperor himself. Paradoxically, Roman lawyers have helped him to be a more powerful Germanic king than he was before; they have shown him one way of drawing together his fighting-bands into a Frankish people. The kind of power that he is now able to exercise over them lies in a field where his ancestors would have had little or none; for he and his subordinates are judges in matters that would once have been left to free men in their own gatherings; and it is not to be taken for granted that the tariff fines and compositions laid down in *Lex Salica* might not be overruled by his royal will. Clovis has kept his fighting force intact about his person; he is rich enough in treasure and land to secure fidelity; his rule over Romans is acknowledged by the emperor and encouraged by the Church; and, significantly last,[1] he has collected his Frankish followings into a people that accepts the law that he says is their own.

Clovis did not remain long at Tours. His headquarters, which it would be going too far to call his *sedes regni*, were to remain in the north. His choice was not Tournai, the family property, or Rheims or Soissons; it was Paris. Two emperors, Julian and Valentinian, had made their winter-quarters there, in the walled Île de la Cité; and it was a convenient place from which to control *Belgica Secunda* without losing touch with the Loire valley. But its greatest attraction was its position in the heart of the newly-conquered lands – Neustria – which the Franks of Clovis saw as their own particular settlement-area, as distinct from Tournai. It might, then, seem strange that the toponymy of the Paris region should show no sign of heavy Frankish settlement in the early sixth century. The picture is much more of the continuing predominance of the Gallo-Roman inhabitants of the countryside.

[1] *Lex Salica* can be dated between 508 and 511 by titles XLVII; XIV, 4; XXVI; XLVI; and LVI—the first showing that Frankish conquests had reached south of the Loire, and the rest showing a unitary *regnum* such as ceased to exist with the death of Clovis. I do not think that any date later in the sixth century is a serious possibility.

Probably, Clovis came to Paris with no more than his private army, or *trustis*, and preferred to keep his men cantoned within the walls, as the Romans had done, and as the Visigoths did at Toulouse. Only later would they have been assimilated into the countryside of the *civitas*, where their properties lay.[1] Two-thirds of the *civitas* were covered by forest, full of game, except where the Gallo-Romans had made clearings to grow corn and wine. Possessor by confiscation of much of this *territorium*, Clovis would have moved from one *palatium* or hunting-lodge to the next. Such movement would slowly cause some increase in population at the *villae* or *vici* concerned, and there would also follow the creation of new parishes dedicated to the tutelary saints of the dynasty. Much of this Parisian property was to go to religious houses over the succeeding three centuries. But, at the centre, lay the stronghold of Paris on the Île de la Cité and an established town on the hilly left bank of the Seine; a place, moreover, of churches where, as dedications bear witness, the cults of St Martin and St Marcel were flourishing before the Franks arrived. Six miles away to the north, but well within the *territorium*, was the Roman *castellum* and Christian shrine of St Denis; the site, equally, of one of the earliest Merovingian *palatia*. We need not be concerned with the legendary story of the martyrdom of St Denis in the third century. What does matter is that, at about the time when Clovis succeeded his father as king in Tournai, St Genovefa (Geneviève) was building a church over the remains of St Denis and his companions. Here, then, was another Parisian cult with which Clovis could hardly avoid contact. The earliest Merovingian associations with that cult and its shrine stretch back far behind Dagobert, to whom the abbey was to owe a new lease of life. At least one of the burials at Saint-Denis recently investigated by M. Salin could belong to the early sixth century.[2] What part was played by the

[1] How slow this process was has been shown by A. Bergengruen, *Adel und Grundherrschaft*. An excellent study of the Frankish occupation of the *civitas* of Paris has been made by M. Roblin, *Le Terroir de Paris aux époques gallo-romaine et franque* (1951). M. Roblin argues, against Ferdinand Lot, for a continuous occupation of the Rive Gauche and an overall population of around 20,000, from the Later Empire to the Middle Ages ('Cités ou citadelles? Les enceintes romaines du Bas-Empire d'après l'exemple de Paris', *Revue des Études Anciennes*, LIII, 1951).

[2] Cf. his *Les Tombes Gallo-Romaines et mérovingiennes de la basilique de Saint-Denis* (*Mémoires de l'Académie des Inscriptions*, 44, 1958).

cult of St Denis in drawing the neophyte to Paris? The biographer of St Genovefa, writing also in the sixth century, affirms that it was at the request of his queen, Chrotechildis, that Clovis built a church on the site of what is now the Panthéon.[1] He dedicated it to St Peter and St Paul, the patrons of Rome. It was further claimed that the king marked out the extent of land for the church by throwing his hatchet, according to normal Frankish practice when taking possession. It does not follow from this that the area was uninhabited or without parochial organization. The evidence is rather of flourishing life on the Rive Gauche. Perhaps the dedication betrays a directer personal submission to the papacy than any written source bears witness of; it would be quite likely, and would be in keeping with the present tendency of scholars to think that early Merovingian contacts with Rome were numerous and natural. Clovis' church was 200 feet long (longer, that is, than St Martin's church at Tours); and it had marble columns (of which traces have been found) and mosaics representing the history of the patriarchs, the prophets and the martyrs.[2] It may not have been completed when, in 511, Chrotechildis buried her husband there, 'in sacrario' according to Gregory of Tours, who had good reason to know of what most concerned Chrotechildis.[3] It must have been a very different burial from that of King Childeric at Tournai, thirty years earlier. Here was a warrior of Beowulf-like stature, who yet forewent the barrow and the windy headland and was content with a Christian grave in a Parisian church. All the same, finds in later Merovingian graves would warrant the guess that the *novus Constantinus* would have been laid to rest with at least a selection of the pagan symbols dear to his race.

Clovis left behind him a Christian *regnum* that was Roman in expression. This implies that he viewed it in terms that were not

---

[1] *M.G.H., S.R.M.,* III, p. 237. The authenticity of this *Vita* was successfully defended against the attacks of Krusch by Godefroid Kurth, 'Étude critique sur la vie de Saint Geneviève', *Études Franques,* II. Cf. Émile Mâle, *La Fin du paganisme en Gaule et les plus anciennes basiliques chrétiennes* (1950), p. 161.

[2] Cf. Émile Mâle, op. cit., pp. 161 ff.

[3] *Hist.,* IV, 1. She herself, having died in retirement at Tours, was buried by her sons at her husband's side. Gregory adds that it was the queen who had built the church (possibly she completed it?) and that St Genovefa was also laid to rest there. This would, at least, account for the subsequent dedication of the church to St Genovefa.

wholly barbarian. It was his own conquest, his to do as he wished with; and the subsequent partition of the soil between his sons would support the view that the Franks conceived their conquests as something private to themselves. But the *regnum* itself was not divided, and there remains the possibility that Clovis had already reached an elementary concept of public law, based on his *de facto* succession to Syagrius and his control of Roman territory through Romans and with imperial sanction.[1] But his kingship, by contrast, remained Germanic in essentials. His prestige as a warrior was what most struck the Romans about him; they admired him for being precisely that kind of shield that the Syagrii and the Visigothic kings had failed to be. He afforded them that guarantee of safety from peasant upheavals, pirates' raids and barbarian sallies that had threatened all property-owners in the fifth century, even though he himself was apparently unbound by any treaty with the Empire to respect their lands. He did not marry a Roman, as he might have done, and his children all bore Frankish names redolent of the past. Already, there is that strong Merovingian family-feeling that was to defy stress and strain in the following centuries; there is about it something that the Church was quick to foster as a mystique. Clovis summons his kindred to battle and takes vengeance on them if they fail him. He also fears that they may supplant him. Merovingian blood is fairly widely dispersed among the Frankish kinglets of the north.[2] He does not make the mistake of some of the later Gothic kings, of appearing so Roman as to lose the sympathy of his Germanic followers. Indeed, his preoccupations were with the north, with the safeguarding of his Neustrian territory against all comers from across the Rhine. There is little enough trace of any ambition to make himself a power in the Mediterranean world.

Inevitably, one contrasts the success of Clovis in Gaul with the failure of Theodoric in Italy. The simple solution to the problem of their differing fates would lie in religion. Certainly the Arianism of the Ostrogoths, like the heathenism of the Franks, becomes a decisive factor comparatively late in the story. Both kings sup-

[1] Furthermore, Burgundian legal practice continued to distinguish between private and public law; and so did Visigothic (cf. Isidore, *Etymol.*, V, 8, *de legibus*).

[2] Cf. Gregory's curious account (*Hist.*, II, 42) of Clovis' relations with his kindred: he needs them, and yet they are in his way.

posed that their Germanic and Roman subjects could in many respects live under a common law; and both were liberally served by Roman administrative skill. Laden with imperial titles, Theodoric yet seemed to have ambitions for his people in the Mediterranean world that no emperor could long approve. The effect on his prestige of the withdrawal of imperial approval was incalculable but real. Clovis, on the other hand, remained sufficiently on the fringe of the Empire to offer no threat, and obtained a mark of imperial esteem at the moment when it could most affect the sympathies of the Gallo-Romans. Each claimed a Roman victim. Clovis' was Syagrius, a forgotten marcher-lord; Theodoric's was Boethius, *anima santa* of a civilization.

## III · GREGORY'S KINGS

The four sons of Clovis divided his property between them as shares of a great spoil. But this may not be the whole story. Their partition of Gaul, or of such parts of it as they were masters of, showed some respect for established political divisions, and in particular for the divisions of the *civitates*.[1] Within these limits, they felt free to make what provision they chose for the upkeep of each. None was more a king than his brothers, legitimate and illegitimate alike,[2] and none appeared to feel that the *regnum* of his father had been shattered or even weakened by division of property. No Gallo-Roman voice was raised in protest. Neither now nor in 561, when the grandsons of Clovis came to their partition of Gaul, can it be claimed that partition produced a situation unexpected or unwelcome to the Merovingians; it in no way modified the Merovingian notion of what a king was, and what he was meant to do. Partition strengthened the sense of family. Indirectly, however, it did produce a situation which led to change, for it led to quarrels and to feuds within the dynasty, characterized by

---

[1] E. Ewig, *Die fränkischen Teilungen*, p. 655, draws attention to the basis of Aetius' reorganization of provincial administration, and is particularly useful for an understanding of the apparently complicated partitions of 511 and 561. See also H. Mitteis, *Der Staat des hohen Mittelalters* (6th ed.), p. 41.

[2] 'Praetermissis nunc generibus feminarum, regis vocitantur liberi qui de regibus fuerant procreati' (Gregory, *Hist.*, V, 20). Neither the rank of his mother nor the legitimacy or otherwise of his birth necessarily affected the standing of a Merovingian prince.

Gregory of Tours as 'bella civilia'; and these, in their turn, made the Merovingians look at others, and sometimes at themselves, in a new way.

The absorption of the remaining parts of Gaul into the *regnum* presented another set of problems in kingship. Aquitaine was finally secured from the Visigoths at the cost of campaigning that lasted till the middle of the sixth century; so that, to begin with, the heirs of Clovis could not partition Aquitaine as they partitioned what Clovis had held firmly. Similarly, Provence and, with it, Marseilles fell to the Franks; Burgundy ceased to be independent, in the sense that Burgundians acknowledged a Merovingian for king, whether resident in Burgundy or Francia; and Thuringia, east of the Middle Rhine, became a Frankish bridgehead into Germany. These expansions caused the Merovingians to think in broader terms about their new kingship, and caused the outside world to look more seriously at them. The developments that were to make most difference to the extent of the power of Charlemagne occurred in the sixth century. All this, however, is only relevant here in so far as it makes the kings of that century reveal what they felt that rule entailed.

> Like the man at the helm of a ship, the mind of a king, with its many eyes, is always on the watch, keeping a firm hold on the rudder of enforcement of the law and sweeping away by its might the currents of lawlessness, to the end that the ship of the State of the world may not run into the waves of injustice.

These words were not written in the Barbarian West. They occur in an 'Exposition of Heads of Advice and Counsel' addressed to the Emperor Justinian by the deacon Agapetus.[1] But they would not have seemed entirely strange to the western kings who were that emperor's contemporaries. The mind of the king, many-eyed and watchful, is all that holds law on its course, whether eastern or western, Roman or Germanic. The initiative and force of that mind, crude or subtle, must at once strike the reader of the sixth-century narratives and letters and legal instruments of the Franks. It will strike him the more because of the combination of states-

[1] The translation is that of Sir Ernest Barker, *Social and Political Thought in Byzantium* (1957), p. 55.

manship of a kind with gross savagery in personal relations. To understand how these two were necessary parts of the same mind is perhaps to come near to understanding the nature of Merovingian kingship.

Clovis' *Lex Salica* was reissued twice in the sixth century, once by his sons and once by his grandsons. This is a way of saying that his successors recognized the *Lex* as valid, and made it their own by reissuing it as their royal law, emended where necessary. This was normal barbarian practice and will be familiar to students of Anglo-Saxon Law. On one of these occasions a short prologue was added, which reveals a little about the tribal origins of law-giving as understood in the sixth century.[1] More important, it plainly states that the object of this kind of lawgiving is that 'pro servandum inter se pacis studium omnia incrementa virtutum rixarum resecare deberent'. From these and similar words, historians have compounded the theory that bloodfeud was the traditional force of disorder, against which a succession of kings struggled manfully to create the good order of medieval kingship. But there is another way of looking at bloodfeud.[2] It can be seen as society's only defence against chaos, a hard but clearly-understood answer to the problem of where responsibility lay in a society organized on the basis of kindred. Feud, so far from being a crime or an admission of procedural defeat, was the way to the settlement of differences between kins. The way might lie through blood, in which case it was controlled by taboos and traditions of several kinds; or it might lie through peaceful settlement brought about by arbitration between kins, and the payment of a composition in kind or money that wiped out old scores. The forces making for settlement were strong, and one of these was the ultimate sanction of bloodshed. The presence of this sanction, as something right and necessary, lies behind every successful endeavour to patch up a feud. We can study the Merovingian kings as they participate in feuds, but more often as they intervene to limit their effects or to bring them to a close. The teaching of the Church against feud was listened to, without in the very least persuading the Merovingians that feud was immoral. So also was the practice

[1] See p. 202. The style recalls that of the so-called Treaty of Andelot.
[2] A longer statement of this view is in chapter VI.

of Roman Law. But the very desirability of finding some other answer to disputes, less wasteful, at least potentially, than feud, would have forced the Merovingians in the same direction, once the Franks had settled permanently among the Gallo-Romans. Despite these natural pulls against the solution of feud, however, the Merovingians were slow and unwilling to take steps, profitable to themselves, that could be interpreted as a blow against the principle of feuding. The feud thus continues to underlie all their piecemeal and groping efforts after good government. Not even Charlemagne saw feuding as a positive evil in the empire of his Augustinian *pax*. In the last resort, royal justice could be more savage, and more arbitrary, than any feud. We may, then, in the Merovingian period, find clear cases of a king overruling feud with his royal *verbum*[1] or, more often, intervening in a feud when he sees a reasonable chance of being listened to.[2] Sometimes, particularly in a case of hot blood, there will be no chance, and he might even think it immoral to attempt intervention. The greatest feuds of all involve the kings as principals.

*Lex Salica* provides, with royal approval, a generally-acceptable tariff of compositions for certain common injuries, personal and other, that might lead to bloodshed between kindreds. Royal approval is itself a kind of sanction; but behind it, and much stronger, is the sanction of bloodshed. The king is not compelling his subjects to a new, unwelcome alternative to feud. He is lending the force of his new authority to an old alternative with which they are quite familiar. Peaceful settlement is the solution that most kindreds, and many individuals, would prefer, when it could be managed without disgrace. The king makes it easier for them to manage it: composition is a part of feud;[3] and he will not object to collecting his *fredus*, or payment for intervention, so long as people do not confuse it with any penalty for the offence.

[1] A case in point is Gregory, *Hist.*, IX, 27. I must add that I see no evidence of any right possessed, or thought to be possessed, by the Franks to oppose the practical despotism of their kings. Fritz Kern and other supporters of *Widerstandsrecht* go too far.

[2] Ibid., V, 32, contains an example.

[3] For much of this I am indebted to Julius Goebel's brilliant study, *Felony and Misdemeanor*, 1 (1937). Though I do not follow him in regarding feud as 'an interminable antiphony of violence', I think that his attack on Brunner's theory of the Germanic 'peace' and of outlawry carries conviction.

The legislation of the Merovingians deals with problems as they arise. It does not pause to explain what principles have inspired or permitted this or that decision. Inference alone can guide us here. What principles lie behind the *carta* of Childebert I, King of Paris, issued between 511 and 558?[1] Its purpose, quite simply, is to back up the Church in its war against the idolatry of the countryside and to act upon the 'quaeremonia' that have reached the king's ears. The situation sounds familiar enough; but only in the light of subsequent history. Why should this Frankish king interest himself in such matters, when about his person he probably carried the phylacteries and charms of heathenism? The answer lies in the first sentence:

Credimus hoc, Deo propitio, et ad nostram mercedem et ad salutem populi pertenere, si populus cristianus, relictam idolorum culturam, Deo, cui integram promisimus fidem, in quantum inspirare dignatus fuerit, purae deservire debeamus.

A Christian king must, like an emperor, enforce the observance of Christianity upon his people and exterminate other cults. He must take action 'ut plebs . . . nostro etiam corrigatur imperio'. His clergy would have told him this, and imperial precedents could have been cited; but here, nevertheless, is a new kingly function for the Merovingians: they rebuke sin. In Childebert particularly can be seen that blending of piety with savagery, of kingliness with whim, that distinguishes his house. At one moment he is massacring his nephews;[2] at another, he is approving the election of bishops as outstanding as Germanus of Paris and Leobinus of Chartres, or the Breton bishops, Paul-Aurelian and Tugdual; or he is making munificent gifts to the churches of Amiens and Lyons[3] and founding monasteries in Arles, to which see he encouraged the popes to restore the vicariate over Gaul;[4] or he is helping monks at Beauvais, Bayeux, Avranches, Orleans, Micy, Châteaudun, Angers and elsewhere; or building Saint-Vincent in Paris, later to be called Saint-Germain-des-Prés. Here is a king

---

[1] The text is in *M.G.H., Capit*, I, pp. 2–3. It is incomplete.

[2] Gregory, *Hist.*, III, 18. All the same, there is a chance that Childebert and his brother Chlotar regarded themselves as instruments of divine vengeance, as is noted by J. Laporte, 'Le Royaume de Paris dans l'œvre de Fortunat', *Études Mérovingiennes, Actes des journées de Poitiers* (1953), p. 172.

[3] *Gallia Christiana*, X, col. 1152; IV, col. 33.      [4] Ibid., I, col. 537.

who goes a long way towards being the kind of king Remigius wanted: pious, generous and active. But his *trustis* comprises warriors who demand activity of another kind as the price of continued loyalty. When he marches to Spain to avenge his sister, wife of the Visigoth Amalaric,[1] he returns with a fine collection of loot. Gregory specifies 'sexaginta calices, quindecim patenas, viginti evangeliorum capsas . . . omnia ex auro puro ac gemmis praeciosis ornatas'. These, like the all-important relic of St Vincent, were for presentation to churches; they symbolized the acquisitive loyalty of the king to the shrines of his Church. But they were only 'inter reliquos thesauros', and we may be sure that his warriors had their share. Plunder-raiding remained a principal occupation of the Merovingians; it was expected of them – without it, they sometimes found it difficult to control their warriors; and it could conveniently be combined with raiding on behalf of the rightful Church, if necessary within a part of the *regnum* controlled by someone else, but for preference in Spain or Italy. However, Gregory of Tours had reservations about Childebert, and did not qualify him as 'magnus' as he did his nephew, Theudebert I.[2] What distinguished Theudebert was that he ruled justly, honoured the bishops, endowed churches, helped the needy and was generally free with his gifts. These are the virtues one would expect a bishop to emphasize. They sound more commonplace than they really were. They are the virtues of a strong and wealthy king, advised by Romans – married, moreover, to a Roman lady – whose power stretched over the northern Frankish world[3] and reached eastward over Germanic tribes who were not Frankish. These tribes are enumerated in a letter from Theudebert to Justinian.[4] Small wonder that the historian Agathias had his suspicions

[1] The call of blood is quite sufficient to account for this intervention, but it need not exclude the explanation of Gregory (*Hist.*, III, 10) that the princess had suffered for her orthodoxy at an Arian court, especially since this is ratified by Procopius (*De Bell. Goth.*, V, 3, 10).

[2] *Hist.*, III, 25.

[3] That it embraced some kind of lordship over the Anglo-Saxons is implied in a letter from Gregory the Great to the kings Theuderic and Theudebert (*M.G.H.*, *Epist.*, I, pp. 423 ff.), but the pope may not clearly have understood the political niceties of life in the Germanic world.

[4] *M.G.H.*, *Epist.*, III, p. 133. This is by no means the letter of a vassal, but it is couched in respectful terms and does not suggest a conscious attempt to break with the emperor. It may be compared with the preceding letter (No. 19)

about the intentions of a king who resented the implications of the imperial titles of Francicus, Alamannicus, Gepidus and Lango-bardicus.[1] Agathias knew of the solidus struck with the king's effigy and name – the first time that any Frank had dared to usurp this imperial privilege. He could have read of it in Procopius, who learned much from the Frankish ambassadors to Byzantium.[2] It was bound to give offence, especially when it closely followed a Frankish expedition into Italy that had not turned out in the way Byzantium had expected. Whether intended to supplement or to supplant imperial coinage, an issue in fairly large quantities of solidi and tremisses, meant for currency, plainly betrayed a pleasure in imperial forms, not a desire to be free of them;[3] and Theudebald, son of the daring innovator, was only too gratified by the kind wishes and presents of the emperor on the occasion of his succession.[4] Barbarian kings everywhere must have trembled when Justinian's mercenaries reached Italy and Spain. The first reaction of any such might excusably have been a little sabre-rattling, even if he felt in his bones that the emperor was his 'Domnus et Pater'. This is a typical instance where we are too far away to decide for ourselves that polite phrases have no bearing on the way their users acted. Gregory, it must be repeated, considered that King Theudebert had come some way along the road to the right kind of kingship. At least he could rule 'cum iustitia'. Another believer in Theudebert's sense of direction was Bishop Aurelian of Arles, from whom there survives, among the

---

of excuse to the emperor for having failed to supply reinforcements to the patrician Bregantinus. I have no notion what the foundation is for E. Stein's assertion that Theudebert 'n'aspirait à rien moins qu'à s'installer lui-même à Constantinople comme chef d'une grande coalition germanique' (*Histoire du Bas-Empire*, II, p. 525).

[1] *Hist.*, Bk. 1, chap. 4 (ed. L. Dindorf, Teubner series, *Historici Graeci Minores*, II, p. 146).

[2] Cf. *De Bello Gothico*, VIII, 20, 10.

[3] I am obliged to Mr Grierson for advice on this issue, which is illustrated in M. Prou, *Les monnaies mérovingiennes* (1892), nos. 38 ff. Mr J. P. C. Kent, 'From Roman Britain to Saxon England', *Anglo-Saxon Coins* (1961), p. 8, states that the king's transient attempt to issue coins in his own name 'failed in the face of diplomatic and no doubt commerical opinion'. Opposition on diplomatic grounds may perhaps be deduced from Procopius; but I know of no evidence of opposition on commercial grounds.

[4] *M.G.H., Epist.*, III, p. 131. See also the lecture read to the new king by the imperial ambassador, Leontius, and Theudebald's justification of his father's actions in Italy (*De Bell. Goth.*, VIII, 24, 12 ff.).

*Epistolae Austrasicae*, a most curious letter to the king.[1] This letter is just what the editor calls it – a letter of adulation and exhortation. Theudebert has all the virtues:

> Praetereo generis tui stimma sidereum; taceo et illud, quod unicus sceptris, multiplex populis, gente varius, dominatione unitus, solidus regno, diffusus imperio.

Then, a little later, the warning to do better:

> a christiano principe inestimabilis ratio Deo reddenda est. Cogita semper, sacratissime praesul, diem iudicii.[2]

There are, too, references to the dignity of his blood. Altogether, Aurelian's letter is a complete little Mirror of Princes, reflecting genuine pleasure at the progress so far made, as well as sanguine hopes for the future. There may be good imperial precedents behind this, and one thinks of the panegyrics of a time not so long past; but, much more, of Eusebius' picture of the pious prince, as he chose to present it to Constantine, and of the serious purposes underlying that presentation.[3] It is no ordinary man who is being exhorted to good works, but a king, who, if he does as he is told, will become more powerful and certainly no tool of any bishop. Thoughts such as these may have lain behind the writing of Aurelian's letter, which merits careful analysis. They may also have crossed the mind of the recipient.

Might it not also have been claimed for Theudebert's uncles, Childebert I and Chlotar I, that they ruled 'cum iustitia'? Between them, they thought out an agreed solution to some of their differences that could well be called a step towards 'iustitia'. This survives as the 'Pactus pro tenore pacis', though in fact it is a *pactus* of Childebert, a *decretio* of Chlotar and a joint statement by both.[4] It has been pointed out that the *pactus* is best understood as a measure to secure international, not domestic, peace. It permits bands in pursuit of thieves to cross with impunity from one king's territory into the other's; in a word, it aims to prevent war.[5] But

---

[1] *M.G.H., Epist.*, III, pp. 124–6.

[2] Important corrections to the text are made by Dag Norberg, 'Ad epistulas varias Merovingici aevi adnotationes', *Eranos*, 35 (1937), pp. 105–19.

[3] Cf. D. S. Wallace-Hadrill, *Eusebius of Caesarea* (1960), esp. chap. 9.

[4] *M.G.H., Capit.*, I, pp. 4–7.

[5] Goebel, *Felony and Misdemeanor*, I, pp. 67 ff.

it also aims to stop thieving and to protect the community against swift-moving bands of robbers. To do this effectively is not possible for the kindred; the problem must be faced territorially; so, King Chlotar imposes the burden of hue-and-cry on the community at large; the *centena* is directly involved and the *centenarius* given a new job;[1] there is a penalty for disobeying the king's orders in such matters; and the problem of the suspect, of determining what part character plays in assessing responsibility for crime, is boldly faced,[2] even to the extent of curtailing the suspect's normal procedural rights of purgation by oath. Can there be any doubt that what lies behind this innovation is the Roman law of infamy, as known to the Burgundians and the Visigoths, and as adapted to canonical procedure?[3] The Merovingian sees the problem, understands why the Germanic kindred have failed to solve it, and turns to his Roman advisers for a way out. It is a first step only; but the way out has been discovered, and it would be entirely superficial to argue that increase of royal power at the expense of the kindred was the object of the authors of the *pactus*. The gainers are the community, even to the level of the *potentes*, 'qui per diversa possedent'. There is something very moving about these brave first strokes; they are a consequence of that involvement in romanizing solutions through royal initiative that started, for the Merovingians, with *Lex Salica* itself. It is no accident that the text of the *pactus* is well-represented in the groups of manuscripts that preserve *Lex Salica*. Moreover, the Church was behind them, much as Remigius had wished it, to show the way to keep, 'propiciante Domino, inter nos germanitatis caritas'.

[1] By *centena*, I understand a Frankish settlement, part military and part colonizing in function, living under a royal official (of imperial origin) called the *centenarius*, upon land of the Merovingian fisc. How widesprad these *centenae* were in the sixth century cannot be determined; but, so far as the territories of these two kings were concerned, they were clearly not new at the date of the *pactus*. Cf. H. Dannenbauer, 'Hundertschaft, Centena und Huntari' (*Grundlagen der mittelalterlichen Welt*), and Theodor Mayer, 'Staat und Hundertschaft in fränkischer Zeit' (*Mittelalterliche Studien*).

[2] Perhaps on the analogy of the treatment of *latrones* in *Lex Burg., Const. Extr.*, 19, 1.

[3] The point is made by Goebel (op. cit. pp. 70 ff.), though he seems still to pay overmuch respect to Zeumer's assertion that Visigothic infamy was Germanic, not Roman, in origin ('Geschichte der westgothischen Gesetzgebung', II, *Neues Archiv*, 24, 1899, p. 99).

One could hardly guess from this that Chlotar I was the simple Frank of Gregory's history, with his 'Wa! Quid putatis qualis est illi rex caelestis, qui sic tam magnos reges interfecit!' [1] His heart seems still to be somewhere in the forests, though his companion is St Médard of Noyon, whom he buried with honour outside the walls of Soissons, in a place that was soon to become a second Saint-Denis to his family.[2] Not only this: Chlotar also paid a special visit to the shrine of St Martin, in the last year of his life, before returning to die in the north and to be buried at Soissons. He was thus placating the miracle-working god of battle of his father's choice, and honouring the saints that had the Merovingians under their protection. Already we can see the emergence of the great quartet of patrons: St Martin, St Denis, St Vincent, and St Médard; patrons of the Merovingians, not of the Franks. Chlotar places the Church, its officers and its properties under his special care, and issues a *praeceptio* to his agents to take note of this, and likewise to protect the interests of his Roman subjects.[3] This he achieves in thirteen neat clauses that waste no words. They depend directly on Roman legal practice, and they cite *Lex Romana Visigothorum*. Most significant, they do this at the point where the king states the authority by which he acts: it is, he says, inseparable from princely clemency that it should look after – 'provida mente tractare' – the interests of *provinciales*. 'Ideoque per hanc generalem auctoritatem praecipientes iubemus' . . . Roman Law has given King Chlotar an *auctoritas* to formulate his wishes, and to compel their observance, that his ancestors knew nothing of. Those who drafted his *praeceptio* could find what they needed in the phraseology of Roman Law, but could alter an important word, to make better sense than what they thought was in front of them; so that the classical *humanitas* of the original (which, to the Merovingians, would here mean 'provisions', 'entertainment') is changed to royal *integritas* in the *praeceptio*.[4] One has to bear in

[1] *Hist.*, IV, 21. Some further flavour of the man may be had from Baudonivia's *Vita Radegundis* (*M.G.H.*, *S.R.M.*, II).

[2] Cf. Clovis Brunel, 'Les actes mérovingiens pour l'abbaye de Saint-Médard de Soissons', *Mélanges Louis Halphen*, pp. 71–81.

[3] *M.G.H.*, *Capit.*, I, pp. 18–19. I agree with H. Dannenbauer that this instrument should be attributed, as Sirmond attributed it, to Chlotar I and not, as by Boretius, to Chlotar II (*Grundlagen der mittelalterlichen Welt*, p. 104).

[4] Cf. H. Fichtenau, *Arenga*, pp. 46–47.

mind that several of these high-sounding Roman words in Merovingian documents (*felicitas*, *pietas*, *fortuna*, *virtus* are among them)
may, by analogy with Frankish words, have had special Germanic
meanings to the earlier Merovingians. At all events, Chlotar has
been given a king's tongue.

The third generation of Merovingians were the contemporaries of
Gregory of Tours. He did not think much of them. He was distressed by their 'bella civilia' (as perhaps they, too, were) and he
thought they compared ill with Clovis and his sons. The failings
he detected were moral failings: failure to turn their energies into
the right channels; failure to be whole-hearted in approval of the
great wealth of the Frankish Church, already a rival to their own
wealth; failure to listen to the bishops. We are reminded that the
Church had developed as fast as the monarchy in the century
since Clovis. Story after story in Gregory's history drives home
his point and leaves the reader wondering what Remigius would
have made of Charibert, Guntramn, Sigebert and Chilperic. Each
in his own way was a wild man: fierce, bloodthirsty and the slave
of whim; also, master of much treasure, and thus of many followers. This wealth came from taxation, subsidies, loot, inheritance and other sources, and, altogether, it made these early
Merovingians very rich men. Their vices were the vices of their
age, and had nothing to do with their being Franks. A barbaric
licence was a feature of the new kingship; this was plain to Gregory, though he had no motive for exploring its possible origins.
Chilperic, Gregory's pet aversion, was an able man of a certain
cultivation, capable of acquiring some loosely heretical ideas in
the field of theology. In him one detects, not perhaps a groping
towards the ideal of the philosopher-king, but at any rate some
notion that a taste for letters was proper for a king. It fitted in
with carousing and hunting and vendettas, along with reverence
for the shrines of saints and dependence on a Roman civil service
still largely in the hands of laymen. There survives, in a tenth-
century manuscript of St Gallen,[1] one sad attempt at poetry by
King Chilperic. It is a hymn in honour of St Médard. 'Chilbericus

[1] Now Zürich, *Zentralbibl.* C. 10. It has most recently been edited by K. Strecker,
*Rhythmi aevi Merovingici et Carolini*, *1*, pp. 455 ff.

rex composuit istud ymnum', adds the scribe. Dag Norberg has shown[1] how the king was imitating an epitaph of Jovinus, consul in 367, which he could have seen in the church of St Agricola at Rheims. He was also using a *Life* of St Médard now lost, and perhaps Sedulius. The result is bold, if barbaric, and on the whole confirms Gregory's disdainful opinion of his literary capacity, rather than the kindlier judgement of Venantius Fortunatus.[2] But it betrays a Merovingian with his wits about him, moving in a field where kings are not often found. One could instance barbarian kings outside Francia, notably Anglo-Saxons and Visigoths, as literate as Chlotar, and more so; but they were uncommon. As master of Soissons, Chilperic thought it well to celebrate the cultus of the saint that his father, Chlotar I, had specially honoured. Perhaps it was less native barbarity or unteachableness that held back other Merovingians from following Chlotar's example than the reluctance of the Church to encourage literacy among kings, at least beyond a certain point. Gregory of Tours would possibly have preferred kings to keep off poetry. Gregory the Great praised Brunechildis for the way in which she had brought up her son, Childebert;[3] but would such a prince's *educatio* have included the study of poetry? Would that have been proper to laymen which the pope denied to bishops?[4] The interest of Fortunatus' eulogy of Chilperic, written, it may be, to soothe the king's feel-

---

[1] *La Poésie latine rythmique du haut môyen age* (*Studia Latina Holmiensia*, II, Stockholm, 1954), pp. 31–41.

[2] Gregory writes 'confecitque duos libros quasi Sedulium meditatus, quorum versiculi debiles nullis pedibus subsistere possunt, in quibus dum non intellegebat, pro longis sillabis breves posuit et pro breves longas statuebat; et alia opuscula vel ymnos sive missas quae nulla ratione suscipi possunt' (*Hist.*, VI, 46). Fortunatus writes thus, in his panegyric of Chilperic (*Carmina*, IX, i):

> Regibus aequalis de carmine maior haberis,
> Dogmate vel qualis non fuit ante parens.
> Te arma ferunt generi similem sed littera praefert:
> Sic veterum regum par simul atque prior.

As in his other Merovingian panegyrics, Fortunatus was not portraying the king as he actually saw him; that was not the purpose of panegyric. The poem is meant to please and to flatter; but it equally aims to set a standard. It cannot have seemed obviously satirical. Fortunatus never failed to combine scholarship with service.

[3] 'Excellentiae vestrae praedicandam ac Deo placitam bonitatem et gubernacula regni testantur et educatio filii manifestat' (*Reg.*, VI, 5).

[4] Cf. Gregory's letter of rebuke to Bishop Desiderius of Vienne for teaching classical literature (*Reg.*, XI, 54).

ings after a brush with his bishops, does not lie in the truth or falsehood of the poet's picture of the learned king, but in the possibility of presenting such an ideal to a sixth-century court:

> Admirande mihi nimium rex, cujus opime
> Proelia robor agit, carmina lima polit.
> Legibus arma regis et leges dirigis armis:
> Artis diversae sic simul itur iter.[1]

Gregory's Chilperic was not in the least like that, but he may have enjoyed thinking of himself thus.

Chilperic promulgated an *edictum*[2] that is really a further gloss on *Lex Salica*. Again, it faces the problem of the malefactor who evades the normal processes of the kindred, and in particular the professional malefactor who is here today and gone tomorrow. What is to be done about him? Or, which is much the same question, what can the king do about him? Chilperic starts from the position that a complaint about him will be taken before the *rachimburgi*, and that it can be established on oath that he is locally known as a bad man, has no substance and is in hiding.[3] The matter will then be referred to the king, 'et ipsum mittemus foras nostro sermone, ut quicumque eum invenerit, quomodo sic ante pavido interfitiat'. He is fair prey to anyone, and no feud will ensue. This altogether exceptional procedure is meant to deal with an exceptional situation; the king stretches his authority very far to bring about an end that can only be desired by all. The limitation of feud is incidental to the underlying purpose of protecting property. In consequence of this action, the power of the crown is increased and the seriousness of contempt of its authority is made plainer. That is the light in which a constitutional lawyer would view it. The subjects of King Chilperic would have felt gratitude for his solution without bothering their heads about crowns and precedents. Kings, not crowns, were what mattered to them, and there is no ground for arguing that, behind a veneer of Latin created by clever Romans, there merely lurked royal men of the woods innocent of any thought beyond the chase, the treasure-hunt and the banquet. Chilperic might have had much support

---

[1] *Carm.*, IX, 1.    [2] *M.G.H.*, *Capit.*, I, pp. 8-10.
[3] I here follow Goebel, op. cit. p. 53.

when he rounded on the bishops for the disproportionate share of royal wealth that had come their way. But he accuses them of stealing something more: 'periet honor noster'.[1] What is this *honor* that the bishops have stolen? Can he mean less than the right to do as he wished with his own? Something has been lost that was there before, and, in consequence, he feels himself less strong as a king. Gregory goes on to say that, with such thoughts in his mind, Chilperic would tear up wills made in favour of churches and trample on his own father's diplomas, 'putans quod non remanerit qui voluntatem eius servaret'. There seem, then, to have been two grievances in his mind: loss of income, and loss of servants. Free disposal of these two constituted an important part of royal *honor*. He was a man who took unconventional decisions; and such men need a free hand. One sometimes has the impression that he acted on Roman advice where he seems most unconventional. A case in point is his abolition of the right of *vicini* to inherit, in certain circumstances, land bordering on their own (*Edict.* 3); the rights to succession of the kindred are thereby strengthened. Doubtless he acted so because it seemed to serve his purpose; but where did he get the idea? Ernst Stein has pointed to a possible parallel in the legislation of Chilperic's contemporary, the Emperor Tiberius II.[2] It was Tiberius who abruptly terminated the Byzantine practice of 'epibole', which corresponds at some points to the custom (itself Roman) terminated by Chilperic. The likelihood that Chilperic had some knowledge of Tiberius' *novella* is increased when one recollects that the two rulers had already been in friendly contact.[3]

The best of the brothers, if Gregory is right, was Guntramn of Burgundy. No other of them stands out in the same way as a personality – passionate, cunning, doubtful of himself, suspicious of all. But this is not what matters in the present context. By devoting much attention to him and by recording many of his comments on the political scene, Gregory conveyed an idea of what kingship held for Guntramn. King of the most romanized and least Frankish part of the Merovingian *regnum*, Guntramn felt

---

[1] *Hist.*, VI, 46.

[2] 'Des Tiberius Constantinus Novelle περὶ ἐπιβολῆς und der Edictus domni Chilperici regis', *Klio*, XVI (1920), pp. 72–74.

[3] Cf. Stein, *Studien zur Geschichte des byzantinischen Reiches*, 108.

insecure, and consequently emphasized family-ties. The insecurity
had more to do with his being far from his relatives than in being
among Burgundians, who thought well of him. Guntramn was
for ever exhorting his relations to unity, and patching up vendettas where he could. He was very conscious of his blood and of
the danger of its extinction. In a hostile city he was not above
begging to be spared the assassin's knife: 'me defuncto, simul
pereatis, cum de genere nostro robustus non fuerit qui defensit';[1]
and thereupon the people put up a prayer to God for the king.
Does this suggest a flaw in Merovingian kingship, or does it raise
a suspicion that the Merovingians were more dispensable than we
like to think them? Certainly there is no evidence that the individual Merovingian was at all safe; he had to be a *homo utilis* to
survive and look after himself as best he could, particularly
against other Merovingians. Perhaps this was especially true of a
Merovingian like Guntramn, whose devotion to Christian piety
may not always have pleased his *trustis* as much as it pleased the
bishops. The dynasty, however, and not the individual is what was
in Guntramn's mind when he made an appeal that otherwise
would have been too ignoble for his admirer to record. He is
appealing directly to the Frankish sense of dependence upon the
Merovingians for protection: in them alone will the Franks
recognize a defence that is *robustus*. Again, is it dynasty or personality that lies behind Gregory's curious account of Guntramn's
thaumaturgical power?[2] There is nothing else like it in Frankish
literature, Merovingian or Carolingian. Gregory says that, according to the reports of the faithful, a woman with a sick son once
approached the king from behind, removed a few fringes from
his royal robe, soaked them in water and gave the potion to her
son to drink, with excellent results. The bishop, for his part, was
prepared to accept this tale, since he had himself often heard how
evil spirits had been exorcised by the invocation of the royal
name, and the *virtus* residing in it. The intention of Gregory in
this chapter was to illustrate the personal sanctity of the king, and
Marc Bloch may well have been right to insist that this, and no
family-virtue, was what Gregory saw in Guntramn.[3] All the same,
sanctity and miraculous power are not identical graces; and it may

---

[1] *Hist.*, VII, 8.    [2] Ibid., IX, 21.    [3] *Les Rois thaumaturges*, pp. 33–36.

have helped Guntramn on the road to both that he was of the right race of kings. Gregory was hoping that his Merovingian readers might be moved in the same direction. There is good evidence for a Burgundian cult of Guntramn, inspired no doubt by his good works in endowing churches and his rôle in furthering the decisions of church councils. (Indeed, we owe to him a clear statement on the principle of collaboration between church and state: 'distringat legalis ultio iudicum quos non corrigit canonica praedicatio sacerdotum'.)[1] Gregory may also have had in mind the repute of Sigismund, also king of the Burgundians in his day, founder of Agaune, opponent of Arianism and curer of fevers; the object of a cult more widespread than Guntramn's was ever to be. These two kings, the one a native Burgundian and the other a Merovingian, are important in the history of royal saints; but they owed their sanctity to their willingness to conform to the Church's pattern of the good king, and not to the magic of their blood or any natural goodness.[2] Sanctity, moreover, was not weakness. When the need arose, Guntramn could pursue his enemies with relentless hatred, as the Visigoths well knew;[3] he could defend himself in the field against the usurper Gundoald; and, in an emergency, he could close all the roads in his kingdom.[4]

Guntramn speaks for himself in two instruments. One, an edict, was given under his hand at Péronne, on 10 November 585, and is addressed to all his bishops and civil officers.[5] His purpose is to commend the stricter observance of a Christian life to his people, to insist that his bishops shall look to this, and to order his judges to administer justice directly and not through delegates, 'nam non dubium est quod acrius illos condemnabit sententia nostri iudicii a quibus non tenetur aequitas iudicandi.' He further introduces his instructions with a more general paragraph of moralizing.

[1] *M.G.H., Capit.* I, p. 12.
[2] The matter is excellently treated by Robert Folz, 'Zur Frage der heiligen Könige', *Deutsches Archiv*, 14 (1958), who, however, shows some disposition to read into Gregory's words a belief that the magic *virtus* of Sigismund had somehow passed to Guntramn. Neither can I agree with him that Guntramn's sanctification owed anything to the myth-making mentality of his contemporaries, nor that there was a magical significance in the fringes of the royal robe.
[3] I discuss some instances of Guntramn's participation in vendetta in chapter VI.
[4] *Hist.*, IX, 32.
[5] *M.G.H., Capit.*, I, pp. 11–12.

This begins, 'per hoc supernae maiestatis auctorem, cuius universa reguntur imperio, placari credimus, si in populo nostro iustitiae iura servamus'. Empty words, put into his mouth by an active clergy or by an efficient writing-office furnished with good imperial models? It could be so; the edict is a consequence of a synod held at Mâcon earlier in the same year. But Guntramn speaks of his *facultas regnandi* as God-given, and nothing that is known of him suggests that he did not, directly and actively, believe that he had a kingly duty to enforce Christian morals and to interpret *iustitia* in a Christian way. If we find it hard to square this sense of divine mission with a good Merovingian career in the field of vendetta, the fault may be ours, not his. When this friend of bishops is after the blood of an assassin, he declares that he will pursue his kindred 'in nonam generationem',[1] and will not count himself a man if he fails to take vengeance within a year.[2] On another occasion, he spurns a Visigothic embassy 'donec me Deus ulcisci iubeat de his inimicis';[3] and the Church keeps quiet. When he transmits sovereignty to his nephew, the symbol he uses is the symbol sometimes associated with Woden: the spear.[4] Gregory finds nothing strange in this. Two years after the edict, at Andelot, the king makes a *pactum* with Childebert II, his nephew. Gregory of Tours preserves the text, which he had from some 'exemplar pactionis'.[5] It embodies the terms of a peace sworn to by both kings to end a state of feud between them, to restore properties to their rightful owners and to stabilize the shifting loyalties of their followers.[6] The substance of it is not really beyond the ingenuity of two barbarians who have had enough of fighting. However, the Roman lawyers have got it down in writing and expressed it in an orderly fashion that should make sense of the details to interested parties in years to come. We can even guess the identity of the Roman most directly responsible: it was Asclipiodotus, referendary first to Guntramn and later to Childebert II,[7] and, very likely,

---

[1] Gregory, *Hist.*, VII, 21, 29.     [2] Ibid., VIII, 5.

[3] Ibid., IX, 16.     [4] Ibid., VII, 33.     [5] Ibid., IX, 20.

[6] Goebel, *Felony and Misdemeanor*, p. 32, seems to consider the last clause of the *pactum* a clause of security to ensure observance of a final concord.

[7] Such is the view of Franz Beyerle, *Zeitsch. der Savigny-Stiftung, Germ. Abteilung*, 49 (1929), pp. 330 ff. and 409 ff. Merovingian referendaries are discussed by H. Bresslau, *Handbuch der Urkundenlehre* (3rd ed.), I, pp. 360 ff., under the title, 'Merovingische Reichskanzlei'.

the author of the shorter prologue to *Lex Salica*.[1] Such were the civil servants who gave shape to the wishes of the Merovingians. They no doubt also suggested expedients to them, as did their colleagues, the bishops, in another sphere.

Is it fanciful to see, in the pacts and edicts of this time, a growing disposition to settle differences by arbitration and by royal initiative? One is more struck by the spirit in which these matters are settled than by the machinery that settles them. It is clear enough in the shorter prologue to *Lex Salica*, where, even if we accept the basic facts as traditional, the language and the spirit belong to the sixth century: 'placuit atque convenit inter francos et eorum proceres ut pro servando inter se pacis' is a formula that is found elsewhere in Frankish documents; and already there is a hint of pride in being Frankish that is not at all traditional, and, indeed, could only have been possible after the Merovingians had made the Franks politically self-conscious.[2]

In 859, Charles the Bald took occasion to remind a church synod of the hereditary basis of Frankish kingship, quoting the words of Gregory the Great: 'in Francorum regno reges ex genere prodeunt'.[3] The Church acknowledged that, in fact, Frankish kingship was a matter of blood. We should remember this when examining the canons of Merovingian church councils, which sometimes express a hostility to kings that is, however, particular, not general. The Gallo-Roman bishops may have smiled at Merovingian boorishness, and frowned on activities hurtful to their own interests, but there is nothing to show that they did not accept the principles of barbarian kingship. The Frankish Church was still feeling its way; it needed masterful kings; and certainly it recalled no tradition of overmuch freedom from imperial control. A Merovingian was a great man, even to a bishop. If, like Guntramn, he had bishop-like qualities, this did not make him indistinguishable from one; there was no confusion. Guntramn feared that his dynasty faced extinction because

[1] Cf. K. A. Eckhardt, *Pactus Legis Salicae, 80 Titel-Text*, pp. 170 ff.

[2] It is this pride, though he calls it the pride of Gaul, that Julian of Toledo attacks in his *Historia Wambae* (*M.G.H., S.R.M.*, V, p. 526). To Cassiodorus, native of a land threatened by Franks, the national Frankish characteristic was rather weakness for robbery with violence (*M.G.H., Auct. Antiq.*, XI, *Chron.* s.a. 508).

[3] *M.G.H., Capit.*, II, N$^r$ 300, cap. 1, p. 450.

of its sins,[1] but did not say that the dynasty had ever owed its authority to good moral qualities. When St Columbanus suggested that King Theudebert might become a monk, the reaction was decisive: 'quod et regi et omnibus circumstantibus ridiculum excitat, aientes se numquam audisse, Mervingum in regno sublimatum, voluntarium clericum fuisse'.[2] Neither the office nor the character of the churchman was that of a king in fact or ideally. The answer to Canon Delaruelle's question (put, it is true, in a rather different context), 'l'idée de la sainteté et du pouvoir royalty est-elle la même'?[3] is that they were not the same, although Merovingian attachment to the saints of the dynasty brought in a rich harvest of another kind. We have got no great way towards an understanding of the Merovingian grip on society if we represent the Frankish Church as struggling slowly uphill against a pressure of barbaric despotism that was nearly too much for it. The despotism would be unrecognizable if we tried to rid it of what it owed to the Roman Church and to imperial precedent.

The epoch of Frankish history that opens with the defeat of Alaric II at Vouillé closes with the murder of Galswintha, daughter of another Visigoth, Athanagild of Toledo, and with the execution of her sister, Brunechildis. Between the murder and the execution there lies a family feud of great bitterness. Paradoxically, this reveals the closeness of the family, the moral uncertainty into which feud plunged its members and its fumbling attempts to patch up the quarrel; if the 'bella civilia' distressed the Church, they distressed the Merovingians no less. Bitter words were exchanged, and chronicled, that afford more than one insight into their view of kingship. For one thing, the feud betrays something of how queens fitted into royal life. The Merovingians indulged a weakness for paramours that shocked the Church and seemed not to be characteristic of the ways of the Frankish nobility as a whole. Why should this have been persisted in against the opposition of powerful bishops? Why was it tacitly approved by the Franks themselves? We may here be in the presence of ancient usage of polygamy in a royal family – a family of such rank that its blood

[1] Gregory, *Hist.*, VII, 33.
[2] *Vita Columbani*, M.G.H., S.R.M., IV, p. 105.
[3] In *Études Mérovingiennes* (*Actes des journées de Poitiers*), p. 66.

could not be ennobled by any match, however advantageous, nor degraded by the blood of slaves. The Merovingians saw no gain of prestige in their marriage-alliances with the civilized, byzantinizing Visigoths of Spain, and were quite prepared to murder an unwanted princess from those parts. From this point of view, it was a matter of indifference whether a queen were taken from a royal dynasty, or from among courtesans, or the unfree. Her husband's name, not that of her father, was the only protection a Frankish queen had in Frankish territory, as Brunechildis learned too late. Her children, on the other hand, male and female, had in their own Merovingian blood a prestige the queen must always lack. Royal bastards were never at a discount because they were bastards, any more than they were to the societies over which ruled the bastards Theodoric the Great, Geiseric, Charles Martel, Arnulf of Carinthia, William the Conqueror and Manfred. Merovingian princesses owed nothing to their mothers.[1] Hence the language of Rigunthis to her mother, Fredegundis: 'cum saepius matri calumnias inferret diceritque se esse dominam, genetricemque suam servitio redeberit'.[2] A Merovingian, she could afford to taunt her mother with her low birth. Gregory of Tours states the matter plainly, if also with undertones of some surprise: 'praetermissis nunc generibus feminarum, regis vocitantur liberi qui de regibus fuerant procreati'.[3] Hence, too, the anger of the Merovingians when St Columbanus refused to bless two young princes because they were illegitimate.[4] The *fortuna* of the dynasty, though not the *raison d'être* of Frankish kingship, rested in its blood and was shared by all who were of that blood.

Sometimes it is said that these years of feud reveal a growing hostility between the Merovingians and the aristocracy, and that Brunechildis, as she fought for the rights of her children and grandchildren, was opposed by magnates who hated her as much for her attempts to restore royal absolutism as for her foreign,

[1] Cf. Fritz Kern, *Gottesgnadentum und Widerstandsrecht* (ed. R. Buchner, 1954), 'Das germanische Geblütsrecht'. Both Kern and his editor are firmer than I should care to be about the specifically Germanic traits of Merovingian kingship in the sixth and seventh centuries.

[2] Gregory, *Hist.*, IX, 34.

[3] *Hist.*, V, 20. Cf. J. P. Bodmer, *Der Krieger der Merowingerzeit und seine Welt* (1957), pp. 18, 31 ff.

[4] *Vita Columbani*, I, 18, 19.

Gothic blood.[1] It is not clear in what sense royal absolutism stood in need of restoration. However, Brunechildis did sponsor an unwelcome attempt to return to the Gallo-Roman system of taxation. Her contacts with Byzantium, both direct (as witness the *Epistolae Austrasicae*) and indirect, through her father's court, may explain this step, though neither is really necessary. There is no solid evidence of byzantinizing tendencies at her court. We can make Brunechildis a good deal more civilized than she really was, and imagine her battling in vain against the barbarism of northern warriors who would sooner have been without any king at all. Equally, we can, if we wish, dismiss the account of her reign given by the chronicler Fredegar; though, if we do, we must allow that his frightful description[2] of the old queen's capture and arraignment before Chlotar II (son of her rival, Fredegundis) and her subsequent execution, contains something other than malice. It is plain evidence that the troubles through which the Merovingians had been passing had been the outcome of feud. The matter was personal, though it rent Francia. The intensity of its violence reveals savagery indeed, but of a special kind: the savagery of outraged feelings. The moral intensity of this kind of reaction is extremely hard for the modern mind to grasp; but it is there. If one can explain these grim days without resort to a monarchy-versus-aristocracy struggle that is surely anachronistic, one still cannot leave aside the effects of a growing sense of provincial, territorial, divergence of interest within Francia. In this sense, it is true enough that a hardening of aristocratic interests is discernible, in Neustria, in Austrasia and particularly in Burgundy with its strong Roman family-traditions.[3] The great men of Austrasia felt the pull towards Rhenish Germany and Italy, and their traditional interests in the Midi gave them no special dislike of the Visigoths; the Burgundians, on the other hand, had ambitions in the Midi that directly conflicted with Visigothic control of Septimania, as well as deep distrust of the Franks of Neustria. The degree of romanization of these *Teilreiche* may have had something to do with their

[1] Ferdinand Lot, in Lot, Pfister and Ganshof, *Les Destinées de l'Empire* (1941), p. 266.

[2] *Chron.*, book IV, chap. 42.

[3] This is well treated by E. Ewig, *Die fränkischen Teilungen und Teilreiche*, esp. pp. 704 ff.

attitude towards each other and towards each other's kings. But
kingship itself did not seem to be threatened, or to be passing
through a crisis brought about by its over-romanization. To us,
the complexities of early Merovingian history appear as growing-
pains, or as movement towards a known solution – Carolingian
rule and the early medieval state. But this was not so to Gregory's
contemporaries. To them, there was no transition and no problem, at least of this kind; and no dichotomy of Roman and German in their kingship.

## IV · FREDEGAR'S KINGS

Twenty-five years is not long in Merovingian history. It is all the
time that was allowed to the two kings, Chlotar II and his son,
Dagobert I, successively rulers of a united *regnum*. Contemporaries do not say whether either king considered this brief unity to
be the realization of a dynastic dream; it may be doubted; although,
in those twenty-five years, royal rule did develop in ways that
unity favoured. The Burgundian chronicler, Fredegar, who wrote
in the second third of the seventh century,[1] was not much interested in unity, but he was fascinated by what kings did, and by how
they behaved; and the most perceptive part of his chronicle is
devoted to the doings of Chlotar and Dagobert. We can still
watch them, through his sometimes unfriendly eyes, as they
moved about their kingdom, and as they reacted to events in
Europe at large. Fortunately, there are other routes to a knowledge of their doings; but Fredegar's picture of them is vivid
enough to justify our calling them 'his' kings.

As Fredegar saw the matter, Merovingian power was anchored
firmly in Neustria. The greatest estates of the kings, their wealth
in so far as it depended on land,[2] the mass of the fidelity they
attracted among *potentes* of every kind, lay in the Seine basin. Here
were their principal residences and hunting-lodges, and the shrines
that were holiest to them. Clichy, in particular, was to them almost

---

[1] I discuss Fredegar's identity and work in the introduction to my edition, *The Fourth Book of the Chronicle of Fredegar with its Continuations* (1960).

[2] In Pirenne's opinion, Merovingian wealth depended more on *telonea*, that is, upon commerce (*Mahomet et Charlemagne*, esp. pp. 40, 88, 90, 170 ff.); but whether more or less, I see no means of determining.

what Aachen was to be to the Carolingians:[1] much of their history was determined at that *villa*. Outside Neustria, however, their authority was what they could make of it; and it was often flouted, when their backs were turned, in Austrasia, in Burgundy and in the Midi. How to get over this difficulty was a problem to which no Frankish king, not even Charlemagne, found a better solution than the binding of men to himself in a personal bond of fidelity, supported by the unswerving service of a few lieutenants and spiced by the fear that his constant movement inspired. But if royal authority was flouted, it was not replaced. The great men of Austrasia and Burgundy could express a fierce independence at times; Fredegar is full of this; but it was independence of the Neustrian rulers and their hangers-on, not of the Merovingians as such. The argument that kingship itself was at stake, that the very nature of Merovingian rule was being challenged by a new aristocracy, has often been advanced. But it seems simpler to account for the events we know of in terms of local hostility to Neustrian officials, Neustrian advisers, Neustrians on the make, in territories of quite other traditions. Chlotar and Dagobert, then, exercised and defined their power in territories and among magnates that reacted to them in quite different and distinct ways.

Leaving aside Fredegar, the Merovingians of the seventh century stand out most sharply in their legal instruments. After the kings of the sixth century, it is almost like leaving the Norman for the Angevin kings of England. Here at last begin the impressive series of extant Merovingian diplomas, starting with that of Chlotar II for Saint-Denis in 625.[2] But extant diplomas form only a small part of the evidence. Diplomas and other instruments no longer extant can be found in later copies, more or less concealed under matter that has been added. An earlier generation was perhaps quicker than we are to dismiss as forgeries charters to which interested parties had at some later time made additions of their own. An instance of how careful one must be is provided by the charters of Saint-Calais. The hermit, St Calais, was accidentally discovered during a hunt in the forests of Maine by Childebert I,

[1] The comparison is made by E. Ewig, 'Die fränkischen Teilreiche im 7 Jahrhundert, 613–714', *Trierer Zeitschrift* (1953), p. 93.

[2] These are reproduced in facsimile by Ph. Lauer and Ch. Samaran, *Les Diplômes originaux des Mérovingiens* (1908).

who, after some initial irritation, was won over by the holy man, and shortly afterwards endowed him with the extensive nucleus of lands from which the future monastery of Saint-Calais was to grow and flourish. This story is told in the *Vita Carileffi* and in the earliest charter of the house. *Vita* and charter are later confections, and so the story itself has been dismissed as make-believe; but the likelihood that it is true has recently been shown, after all, to be serious.[1] In just such haphazard ways did kings grant large properties to casual acquaintances who took their fancy.[2] Collections of charters kept as *formulae* also contain invaluable information about the Merovingians of the seventh century. The greatest of these, Marculf's Formulary, was compiled not to provide a convenient work of reference for scribes in search of models but, in the compiler's own words, 'ad exercenda initia puerorum'.[3] Law and teaching were associated still; youths in some monastic or cathedral school benefited from the fact that the monk Marculf had access to a well-kept collection of documents. His prefatory letter gives no hint that he thought he had chanced upon an unusual treasure or had had a special stroke of luck. The truth is rather that documentation was on the increase; and royal activity played its part in this. Thus, the monk can divide his documents into two groups – 'royal' charters and 'rural' charters. The former, however, are not just 'cartae'; they are 'praeceptiones', and as such they would have been understood by the king, by the beneficiaries and by Marculf's *pueri*.[4] The peremptory note of authority is what first strikes the reader in these royal charters. Whatever the message conveyed by the charter – a simple administrative order to an official, a donation, the grant of a privilege or a con-

---

[1] By A. Bouton, 'Saint-Calais: histoire et légende', *La Province de Maine*, XL, 1960. Krusch, who edits the *Vita* (M.G.H., S.R.M., III, pp. 386 ff.) and J. Havet, who edits the charter ('Les chartes de Saint-Calais', *Questions Mérovingiennes*, pp. 103–54) attach no historical importance to the story.

[2] M. Latouche points out that most French monasteries that survived to the Revolution were founded in Merovingian times, and rightly stresses Merovingian generosity (*The Birth of Western Economy*, p. 89); but none of the historians who emphasize the woeful consequences of alienation has shown that contemporaries thought the Merovingians reckless, or that the Merovingians themselves had no care for what became of their gifts.

[3] *M.G.H., Leges*, V, p. 37.

[4] An early instance of the prestige of a royal *praeceptio* over other documents is Gregory of Tours, *Hist.*, IV, ch. 12.

firmation – a direct, personal order is involved.[1] The circumstances of donation or confirmation are recalled, and the king gives his instructions that what was then approved in his presence shall be observed or carried out. Hardly surprisingly, *Lex Ribvaria*, which is of the early seventh century, exacts the death penalty for whoever shall contravene or challenge a royal *testamentum*.[2] One is struck, too, by the growing number of occasions when the king is sought out by parties to an agreement that would be legally valid without his intervention. There is no greater protection to property, secular or ecclesiastical, than a royal writing. The writing will in many respects follow the format of an imperial rescript; and one is again reminded of the complex heritage of Roman Law in Gaul. Papyrus, the material proper to Roman Law, is sought out and bought by the Merovingian chancery, and continues to be used till the late seventh century, when, at last, it yields to parchment; and the format, script and word-order of the royal commands, down to details of witnessing, dating and authentication, tell of writing-offices properly conducted by officials trained in old traditions of administration. This is not to say that there is nothing 'German' about Merovingian charters; it can, for instance, be argued that interest in the relative age of conflicting grants is Germanic rather than Roman. But the whole developing shape of Merovingian practice makes it hard to attach much meaning to racial distinctions that belong to the time of Clovis. The new kingship, like the new age, is neither specifically Germanic nor Roman. An age of social movement and of the foundation of many new landed fortunes is given coherence and direction by royal decisions; and these are ratified in much sought-after writings, which bear the royal image on a seal, not to authenticate the document but to represent the king's authority in the most direct way possible: it is a kind of magic, showing the king front-face, eyes staring, as if he were there to speak for himself. Not magic, but commonsense, is the attempt on the king's part to introduce into the *arenga* of his written instruction something amounting to royal propaganda. This was not new; Late Antiquity made the same use of the *arenga*, and so did Byzantium, though each reflected

---

[1] Cf. the excellent comments of P. Classen, op. cit. II, p. 62.
[2] Ed. Beyerle and Buchner, 59, 3.

a local view of a ruler's functions.[1] For instance, here is the *arenga* of Dagobert's charter for Desiderius of Cahors, in 630:

> condecet clementiae principatus nostri sagaci indagatione pro-
> sequere et pervigili cura tractare, ut electio vel dispositio nostra
> dei in omnibus voluntati debeant concordare . . .[2]

The 'cura pervigil' of the king is not yet the royal and ecclesiastical commonplace that it was to become, though it will be found in imperial inscriptions of the third and fourth centuries, and was known to Avitus of Vienne.[3] Perhaps the influence of the Gallo-Frankish clergy in the Merovingian chancery was stronger and earlier than some believe.[4] Again, in a charter for Saint-Denis, in 629, Dagobert devotes an *arenga* to the transitory nature of rewards in this life and the solid gain of eternal reward:

> optabilem esse oportet de transitoria promere eterna vel de
> caduca substantia erogandum lucrare gaudia sempiterna.[5]

If the drafting originated in the Saint-Denis *scriptorium*, the king still understood what sentiments were being attributed to him, and he approved them. It is hardly possible to picture the numerous legal instruments of the period as so many tunes called by a set of wily referendaries who had no need to consult the tastes of their savage masters. The chances are rather that the masters knew very well what was said and written in their names.

Even more than their predecessors, the seventh-century Merovingians were preoccupied with Europe east of the Rhine. It was the time of the great Slav settlements and Avar advances in central Europe, with consequent disturbance of the Germanic peoples; the time, also, when the Lombards effectively closed the

---

[1] Cf. H. Fichtenau, *Arenga* (1957), *passim*.

[2] *Vita Desiderii* (*M.G.H., S.R.M.*, IV, p. 571). The texts of Pardessus, *Diplomata*, II, no. 246, p. 3, and of Pertz, *M.G.H., Diplomata*, I, no. 13, p. 15, are taken from the *Vita*.

[3] *Œuvres complètes*, ed. Chevalier (1890), no. 32d (Peiper's ed., no. 41).

[4] H. Bresslau, *Handbuch der Urkundenlehre*, I, p. 649, drew attention to the likelihood that the Church influenced Dagobert's diplomatic practice.

[5] J. Havet, *Œuvres*, I, p. 264. Havet, who rescued this charter from Pertz's *diplomata spuria*, also observes, at the end of the *arenga*, 'des signes au crayon, se rapportant évidemment à l'étude métrique des fins de phrase'. The employment of *cursus* by Merovingian scribes remains a largely unworked field.

Mediterranean to the Franks, and Byzantium turned to face Persia and then Islam in her rear. Much of this finds an echo in the confused accounts of Fredegar who, for all his shortcomings, can safely be said to have had a sense of a Europe alive and moving beyond the borders of his own small world. The Emperor Heraclius struck him particularly. He describes him with some care and gives an account of an imaginary duel between the emperor and the Persian ruler;[1] and, more important, refers, tantalizingly, to a request from Heraclius to Dagobert, that the latter should forcibly baptize all Jews in his kingdom – which he promptly did.[2] Fredegar and his readers saw nothing unusual in this connection between the two rulers: indeed, there is no evidence that Dagobert or any subsequent Merovingian considered himself outside imperial authority. This may be why their diplomas avoided exclusively imperial marks of authentication. Imperial approbation may have been an added source of strength, or at least of prestige, to a king who needed to stand well with the chieftains of west-central Europe. This need is vividly illustrated by the adventure of the Frankish merchant Samo, who set up a Slav kingdom of his own, in the general area of Bohemia, where he was ready to defy Dagobert.[3] But the startling fact is that Dagobert felt that he had a serious claim to overlordship in those parts, and should be ready to protect the many Frankish merchants travelling there. After this, it is less surprising to watch him enforcing his authority over independent tribal rulers nearer home, in Germany. Most of the Franks and Germans saw him as the one man who could save them from the Avars, the masters of the Slavs. The Austrasians alone had their doubts, which cannot easily be accounted for. It looks as if the Austrasian magnates felt less apprehension of the dangers facing them across the Rhine

---

[1] *Chron.*, IV, 64.

[2] Ibid., IV, 65. Bernhard Blumenkranz, *Juifs et chrétiens dans le monde occidentale, 430–1096* (1960), p. 100, considers that, if this tale is not pure invention, then it is a generalization from the forced conversion of Jews by Bishop Sulpicius of Bourges, between 631 and 639. However, *Gesta Dagoberti*, 24, looks like independent confirmation of Fredegar's source, if no more.

[3] Fredegar, *Chron.*, IV, 68. Paul Lemerle suggests that Heraclius may have encouraged Samo and his Slavs to attack the Avars ('Les répercussions de la crise de l'empire d'Orient au VIIᵉ siècle sur les pays d'Occident', *Settimane di Studio del Centro Italiano di Studi sull'alto medioevo*, V, p. 719).

than they did of domination by the Neustrians. The Burgundians, too, were suspicious of Neustrian power and pretensions. It seems that the magnates of eastern Francia were beginning to feel and to express a sense of not belonging to the Franks of the Seine basin. They were strong men, warriors and settlers on their own account,[1] finding one focus for local loyalty in the family of the Arnulfings; and they were not pleased to be part of the belt of marcher-lordships favoured by the Neustrians. But they were not 'anti-Merovingian'. When Chlotar II gave them his young son, Dago-bert, for their king, he was acknowledging a separatism of interest and outlook, while probably considering that the arrangement strengthened his dynasty.[2] Whatever their wishes, Chlotar II and Dagobert were caught up in political problems resulting from the movement of peoples and the shifting of loyalties across the Rhine. Their activity sometimes took the shape of diplomacy, backed by a wealth to which no other Frankish family could pretend. It also took the shape of military expeditions on a larger scale than the type of expedition normally mounted against the Visigoths or the Lombards, when treasure-hunts or the pursuit of private vendettas were the objectives. The German expeditions were for the defence of what amounted to the territorial interest of a settled people. This is how Dagobert, in particular, reinforced the military content of Merovingian kingship that men missed under his successors. In intention, at least, it was not the old Frankish war-leadership, but in retrospect it could look much the same.

Territory, lands old and new, endowments, run like a refrain through Frankish documents of the time. New land is being won for cultivation, even in the heart of Neustria; new families are settled on property; new churches and monasteries look for endowments; and royal initiative lies behind much of it. The Merovingians endow, confirm, witness, sanction. They always did; but now, much more. We may take as typical, while not tying it down to any particular king, the 'confirmacio ad secularibus viris' of Marculf's *Formulary* (I, 17), with its succinct reminder that the

[1] The significance of the Frankish colonizing movement of the seventh century is well brought out by A. Bergengruen, *Adel und Grundherrschaft im Merowingerreich* (1958).

[2] Cf. Fredegar, *Chron.*, IV, 47, 52–53, 56.

beneficiary has taken the first step in 'suggesting to our clemency' that we should confirm the grant made from the fisc by 'quondam rex, parens noster', and that he should hold it 'in integra emunitate, absque ullius introitus iudicum de quaslibet causas freta exigendum'. The beneficiary is himself the royal agent within the terms of the concession. Or we may take the sharp instruction (*Marc. Form.*, I, 28) to a count, to look into a complaint about an unjust seizure of property; and if this is not put right by a certain date, the culprit is to be sent forthwith 'ad nostram presentiam'. Most of the confirmations and grants that survive are for the benefit of the Church, though laymen had their full share of these colonizing activities and acquisitive energies. All were Merovingian *fideles*.

Lawgiving played its part in the Merovingian wooing of marcher-peoples. The *Pactus Alamannorum* can reasonably be assigned to the early seventh century.[1] It is lawgiving for the Alamans, certainly, but lawgiving by the Franks – or, more accurately, by a Merovingian, and in his chancery. The borrowings from *Lex Salica* are numerous; and, like *Lex Salica*, the *Pactus* has the appearance of a code the matter of which is not specifically of one people. It is specifically Merovingian, and its acceptance implies the acceptance of Merovingian rule. Perhaps it should be assigned to the decade 613–23, at some time when Chlotar II was holding his court at Marlenheim in Alsace, and was generally concerning himself with law and order among the Alamans.[2] There are, too, striking similarities between the *Pactus* and the *Lex Ribvaria*, which in its first recension belongs to the reign of Dagobert. In the *Lex*, again, the content of the tariff of offences is not peculiar to the Ripuarian Franks, whether by them we mean Germans of the *civitas* of Cologne or of Rhineland Austrasia in a wider sense.[3] Allowing for some modifications, not all of which are local, *Lex Ribvaria* is the work of lawyers at the Merovingian court, including

---

[1] Most recently edited by K. A. Eckhardt in the series *Germanenrechte, Westgermanisches Recht* (1958). I agree with Theodor Mayer, *Mittelalterliche Studien* (1959), p. 121, and others, that the *Lex Alamannorum* has less strong claims than the *Pactus* to so early a date.

[2] Fredegar, *Chron.*, IV, 43.

[3] Cf. E. Ewig, 'Die civitas Ubiorum, die Francia Rinensis und das Land Ribuarien', *Rheinische Vierteljahrsblätter*, 19 (1954), esp. pp. 26 ff.

Burgundian lawyers skilled in Vulgar Roman Law. Some of its titles suggest the special interests of Chlotar II[1] and of Dagobert.[2] As originally promulgated, this collection could have been a concession to the separatist feelings of a group of Rhineland Franks, who had to be placated. On the other hand, the mere fact of its reception may have marked a surrender. The same can be said of the Bavarian *Lex*, parts of which may very well go back to the reign of Dagobert.[3] One is left with the impression of policy: Chlotar and Dagobert make these peoples their own by the simple expedient of admitting their distinct existences and by defining for each in turn its Law; and by drafting each Law in a chancery that could command some impressive talent.

In the Edict of Paris,[4] following quickly upon his assumption of sole rule, Chlotar II made, 'Christo praesole', twenty-four provisions. They have been interpreted as a royal surrender to the new power of the landed aristocracy, to which the king owed his victory over Brunechildis, and have even been referred to as a French Magna Carta.[5] Nobody would deny that magnates, lay and ecclesiastical, were the gainers by some of these provisions; Chlotar did not forget his friends – particularly, it may be, his Austrasian friends of the Arnulfing clan. But it is hard indeed to discover any evidence that the magnates stood, as a group, to gain by bargaining with the king to reduce his power. The Burgundian magnates had been weakened, not strengthened, by *bella civilia*;[6] and the rest were divided, as magnates are, by age,

---

[1] e.g. titles 57–62 (60–65 in the edition of Beyerle and Buchner). Cf. K. A. Eckhardt, *Lex Ribvaria*, I (*Germanenrechte*, 1959), pp. 142 ff.

[2] Title 88 (= 91).

[3] Note the words of the prologue: 'Haec omnia Dagobertus rex gloriosissimus per viris illustribus Claudio, Chadoindo, Magno et Agilolfo renovavit et omnia vetera legum in melius transtulit et unicuique genti scripsit tradidit, quae usque hodie perseverent' (ed. K. Beyerle, 1926, p. 8). The widely-differing views of the origins of *Lex Baiuariorum* are summarized by R. Buchner, *Deutschlands Geschichtsquellen, die Rechtsquellen* (1955), p. 26.

[4] Text in Boretius, *M.G.H., Capit.*, I, pp. 20–23. I follow C. de Clercq, *La Législation religieuse franque* (1936), p. 62, in supposing that Chlotar assembled all the magnates of the territories united under him; that, first, the bishops met and promulgated the canons of the Council of Paris (*M.G.H., Conc.*, I, pp. 185–92, a truly remarkable programme of reform); that, afterwards, Chlotar and his magnates joined the bishops in discussions; and, that finally, the king published his Edict.

[5] An extreme statement of this view is that of H. Mitteis, *Der Staat des hohen Mittelalters* (1959), pp. 52 ff.

[6] For what follows, cf. A. Bergengruen, *Adel und Grundherrschaft*, pp. 174–76.

wealth, temperament and place of residence. If they had a unity, it
was that of serving one king – and he the greatest of the magnates,
one of themselves. Nor is it any easier to find evidence that the
king sought shelter from them behind the Church. What the king
was concerned to do was, not to safeguard his power against
magnates, but to use them in the elaborate business of ensuring
law and order over a huge area. He does not, as has been argued,
make an unwilling concession to the magnates when he ordains
(clause 12) that

> nullus iudex de aliis provinciis aut regionibus in alia loca[1]
> ordinetur, ut, si aliquid mali de quibuslibet condicionibus per-
> petraverit, de suis propriis rebus exinde quod male abstolerit
> iuxta legis ordine debeat restaurare.

He is giving his support to the law against misuse of office by
*iudices*. Again, clause 19 does not 'surrender' the appointment of
*iudices* to magnates or bishops. It reads:

> Episcopi vero vel potentes, qui in alias possedent regiones,
> iudices vel missus discursoris de alias provincias non institu-
> ant, nisi de loco qui iusticia percipiant et aliis reddant.

This is more likely to be a reminder than a concession: the magnates must look after the *iudices*; and Burgundy was the place
where this would apply with special force. Throughout his Edict,
indeed, Chlotar is peremptory in reminders about the duties of
others and his own authority. The 'felicitas regni' will depend on
his own 'acta, statuta atque decreta';[2] bishops will be consecrated
'per ordinationem principis', though naturally 'si de palatio eli-
gitur, per meritum personae et doctrinae ordinetur' (1); priests are
not to come bothering the king or his magnates with their com-
plaints without leave of their bishops, but 'si pro qualibet causa ad
principem expetierit et cum ipsius principis epistola ad episcopo
suo fuerit reversus, excusatus recipiatur' (3); *telonea* will be levied
as in the time of 'parentum nostrorum Gunthramni, Chilperici,
Sigiberthi' (9); our *praeceptiones* shall be carried out by all, now and
in the future;[3] whoever shall challenge this *deliberatio* shall be
sentenced to death as an example to others (24); and so 'pax et

---

[1] 'Loca' is not the equivalent of 'pagus', as Boretius believed.
[2] Cf. Fichtenau, *Arenga*, p. 67.
[3] Cf. *Cod. Theod.*, I, 2, 2 and elsewhere, and the *Praeceptio* of Chlotar I, 5.

disciplina in regno nostro sit, Christo propiciante, perpetua, et ut revellus vel insullentia malorum hominum severissime reprimatur' (11). Altogether, the Edict fits comfortably into the series of Merovingian 'capitularia', of which it happens to be the last survivor. If it reads like a jumble of legislative, administrative and fiscal decisions interspersed with threats, hopes and prayers, it should not on that account be despised. It says what it means, and it represents a genuine effort to enforce law and order, to secure good appointments to a variety of offices and to make all men aware of their responsibilities in a large, loose-knit community. It calls to mind, furthermore, the spirit of contemporary Visigothic legislation, and in particular the reflections on the king as legislator that will be found in the first Book of the *Leges Visigothorum*. Visigothic lawyers went further than the Franks in defining the objects of legislation and the rôle of their king; but close analysis of the laws of the two peoples would probably reveal a common inspiration.

In practice, how far was 'disciplina' realized? Fredegar was clear that Chlotar's sixteen years of sole rule were, on the whole, a happy time: he reigned 'feliciter'.[1] The chronicler seemed to think it no bad thing that he had begun by striking bargains with the 'maiores palatii' of Burgundy and Austrasia. When the Burgundian mayor died and Chlotar summoned the 'leudes' of Burgundy to Troyes to tell him if they wanted a successor, 'they unanimously decided that they would never have another mayor of the palace and earnestly begged the king of his goodness to deal direct with them'.[2] Perhaps this was the outcome of his having already dealt direct with them; for in 616 he had summoned the mayor, together with all the Burgundian bishops and notables, to his villa of Bonneuil, near Paris, where he had listened to all their just petitions and confirmed his concessions in writing.[3] One has the impression that Chlotar had something of the English Edward I's capacity for handling public occasions, as when, in 627, he summoned all his great men to meet him at Clichy, 'pro utilitate regia et salute patriae'[4] – words that would be less surprising in a

[1] *Chron.*, IV, 42.   [2] Ibid., IV, 54.   [3] Ibid., IV, 44.
[4] Ibid., IV, 55. Part of the assembly's time was taken up with a church council, the canons of which are in *M.G.H., Conc.*, I, pp. 196–201.

thirteenth-century English context than in that to which they actually belong. An ugly quarrel broke out on this occasion. This was quelled by Chlotar's decisive intervention, and by the fear his authority inspired.[1] He was that kind of man: sufficiently uxorious and keen on the chase to excite comment even among the Franks, but ruthless and vigorous, so that, as Fredegar remarks, he stood well with the Church;[2] and to this we shall return.

Dagobert shared his father's taste for public performances of a kind that Clovis never knew. Until the promptings of cupidity (that is, his need to seize Church property) intervened to cost him Fredegar's good opinion, he was a great one for 'disciplina'. Fredegar's account of his Burgundian progress must be quoted in full:

> The profound alarm that his coming caused among the Burgundian bishops, magnates and others of consequence was a source of general wonder; but his justice brought great joy to the poor. On arrival at the city of Langres he gave judgement for all, rich and poor alike, with such equity as must have appeared most pleasing to God. Neither bribe nor respect of persons had any effect on him: justice, dear to the Almighty, ruled alone. Then he went to Dijon and spent some days at Saint-Jean-de-Losne, and did what he could to bring justice to his people throughout his realm. Such was his great goodwill and eagerness that he neither ate nor slept, lest anyone should leave his presence without having obtained justice.[3]

Allowing for exaggerations, Dagobert had made an impression. He was the sort of king whose image is propagated in a curious list of office-holders and their functions that has survived in a single manuscript of the tenth century,[4] which seems to be a copy of a Merovingian original. It is a muddled list, and no clear statement of practice, but the writer at least manages to arrange his

---

[1] Ibid., IV, 55.    [2] Ibid., IV, 42.

[3] Ibid., IV, 58. I quote from the translation in my edition of the Fourth Book of Fredegar's chronicle (1960).

[4] MS Vatican Lat. Reg. 1050, a legal collection of considerable interest. The relevant part has been edited by Max Conrat, 'Ein Traktat über romanisch-fränkisches Ämterwesen', *Zeitsch. d. Sav.-Stiftung, Germ. Abt.*, 29 (1908), pp. 239–60. I cite the text as emended by Conrat, though the punctuation is largely mine. Beyerle, ibid., 69 (1952), pp. 1 ff., argues inconclusively for an Ostrogothic origin.

officials in a sensible order, which places the king firmly under the emperor. He distinguishes them thus: 'Rex qui super unam gentem vel multas. Imperator qui super totum mundum aut qui precellit in eo'. He has, too, that omnipresent Frank, the 'potens, qui multas divitias habet'. But the royal functions are what are of significance here; and since the document is little known, it may be worth quoting the entire passage as it stands, in barbarous but intelligible Latin:

Obtimates rathinburgii acciones unum sunt, qui manducant cum rege et absente eo cum episcopis iudicant causas. Praeses multas divitias habet, qui iudicat ad presentiam regis et causas de scola regis et de domo palatii iudicat et damnat, ut voluerit, et solvit, sicut oeconomus sub abbate, et qui super duces civitatum longe. A rege ad facienda iuditia preses vocatur. Obtimates autem non iudicant ad presentiam regis, sed seorsum et forsan cum episcopis, et non possunt damnare vel solvere, antequam veniat rex. Sed episcopi et obtimates tantum iudicant, ut rex distinguat nisi per pauperibus, ut episcopis indulgeant pro vita, sed plus pauperes obtineant. Non de causis scole vel domus iudicant, ad quas preses sit, sed de causis deforis adlatis ab episcopis vel ducibus comitibus et ceteris. Consules et proconsules; sed consules qui dona regis consulunt et donant, cui voluerit rex. Interdum consul coram rege minutos argenteos super planam terram spargit, ut certatim pauperes propriis et velocissimis manibus sibi, ut valuerint, rapiant, ut letus rex aspiciat subridens. Prefectus qui precellit de obtimatibus.

The writer has not managed his notes with the skill that Hincmar was to show in a comparable piece, the *De Ordine Palatii*; and his meaning is unclear in more than one passage. However, he does give a sketch that would well fit the Merovingian court of the seventh century: the king among his poor, smiling approval as the *consul* (treasurer) distributes largesse; the disciplining of his *scola* (military establishment) and his *domus* by the *praeses*; the judicial duties of his bishops and his magnates; and, above all, the king himself, in judgement. The writer feels the need to be clear about the judicial side of the work of the king's officers, including bishops, because there is a possible field of conflict among them. He leaves plenty of latitude to the king and is aware of the difference that his personal presence makes. Fredegar's Burgundians, fresh from Dagobert's visit, would have borne this out. One could illustrate it, too, from many of the 'praeceptiones regales' of Marculf; for example, the prologue (I, 25) on the doing of royal justice; the plea (I, 34) of certain 'pagenses' to the king for justice; the instructions to officials to see that justice be done in particular cases (I, 29, 37); the royal protection of men whose properties and deeds to properties have suffered when 'exercitus noster domos suas incendium cremassent' (I, 33); the indemnification of such as pursue others on the king's orders (I, 32); and measures that concern fidelity – the conditions in which it is entered upon, its advantages to the 'fidelis', its seriousness (1, 8, 18).[1] The very spirit of royal rule of the early seventh century is caught in the simple opening sentence of I, 8:

> praespicuae regalis in hoc perfectae conlaudatur clementia, ut inter cuncto populo bonitas et vigilantia requeratur personarum, nec facile cuilibet iudiciaria convenit committere dignitatem, nisi prius fides seu strinuetas videatur esse probata;

and, to the men that show these qualities of 'fidelitas' and 'strenuitas' in action, 'rectum est, ut qui nobis fidem pollicentur inlesam, nostro tueantur auxilio'. Are we at grips here with 'Germanic' virtues fighting a rearguard action on 'Roman' soil? Is this the key to Merovingian capacity for survival? Some believe so. One may wonder, however, whether the bishops and priests and monks of the Merovingian world would have been quite happy to see 'fidelitas' as something 'Germanic'. Theirs was a Latin world, writing, speaking and thinking Latin.[2] Not many words in the Vulgate are commoner than 'fides' and its derivatives. The language undergoes strange processes of change, for example in the

---

[1] F. S. Lear, 'The public law of the Visigothic Code', *Speculum*, 26 (1951), has distinguished between the ideas of Germanic 'infidelitas' and Roman 'maiestas' as they emerge from Visigothic legislation on treason. There is a difference between 'infidelitas' and 'maiestas'; but what it has to do with 'Germanic' and 'Roman' is another matter.

[2] Ferdinand Lot's view that, by the sixth century, Latin in Gaul was dead has been controverted by Einar Löfstedt, *Late Latin* (1959), pp. 11 ff., who agrees rather with H. F. Muller (*Romanic Review*, 12, 1921, p. 330) that 'neither the Merovingian *capitula* nor the canons of the very numerous councils during the Merovingian period give any inkling that the spoken language was so essentially different from the written language that the latter was unintelligible to the people'.

pages of Fredegar, but it is still Latin, impoverished in some directions and enriched in others, the language of trade, of law and of administration as well as of literature. Notably, it is the language of charters, edicts and testaments, and therefore specially associated with the business of the royal court. It is the royal language, and, as such, one of the principal influences making for social homogeneity in early medieval France.

The Latin of the age could be used to convey a wonderfully effective idea of the Merovingians in search of an image of themselves. In Latin, Fredegar tells that, by the seventh century, the Merovingians had acquired a mythical ancestry, and were presumably content to have news of it propagated. The significance of his fairy-tale about the procreation of Merovech by a sea-monster[1] can be missed. Fredegar was not simple-minded. Not he, but someone nearer the Merovingian house, and better-read than he in the kind of literature that would produce a 'bistea Neptuni Quinotauri similis', had managed to associate the dynasty with a fabulous strain that emphasized its remoteness from other Frankish dynasties.[2] The Arnulfings, so far as is known, had no minotaurs in their genealogy. There is nothing 'popular' about the fable. It is a literary confection inserted in a serious chronicle of political events. Fredegar's Merovech, so fortunately conceived, gives his name to the dynasty – 'per quo reges Francorum post vocantur Merohingii'. Is it a coincidence that this is the very time – the first time, in fact, since the eponymous hero – that the name of Merovech appears among the Merovingians? It was borne by Chlotar II's eldest son (Dagobert's brother), by Theudebert II's elder son and by Theuderic II's youngest son, and does not appear to have been used again. This brief popularity is no part of that conservative tendency in nomenclature shared by the Merovingians with many of their contemporaries.[3] It is another act of

---

[1] *Chron.*, III, 9.

[2] Buchner, following Hauck, associates this minotaur with the bull's head in Childeric's grave and sees it as an embodiment of Merovingian power and ferocity in war ('Die römischen und die germanischen Wesenszüge in der neuen politischen Ordnung des Abendlandes', *Settimane di Studio del centro italiano di studi sull'alto medioevo*, V (i), p. 229).

[3] R. Buchner, 'Das merowingische Königtum', *Das Königtum*, p. 147, notes only two non-Germanic names in the entire Merovingian dynasty, from which he infers

policy, an echo of the success of which may perhaps be discernible in *Beowulf*.[1] The sense of *parentela* is reflected in the Merovingian manner of ratifying the concessions and the arrangements of forebears:

> principale quidem clementia cunctorum decet accomodare aure benigna, precipuae quae pro conpendio animarum a precidentibus regibus, parentibus nostris, ad loca ecclesiarum probamus esse indultum;[2]

or, more clearly still, 'Quem divina pietas sublimatur ad regnum, condecet facta conservare parentum'.[3] Slaves are to be manumitted to celebrate the birth of a son, 'iuxta votum fidelium et procerum nostrorum',[4] whereas a sterile queen is abandoned 'cum consilio Francorum'.[5] Now, too, comes the earliest extant genealogy of the Merovingian house, preserved today in a single manuscript of the ninth century (St Gallen 732).[6] It covers nine generations of Merovingians, from Clodio to Dagobert; and, though three of the names are hard to account for, none of them is mythical. It contains no gods, not even the Minotaur, and for the most part is safely based on Gregory of Tours.[7] As in the matter of nomenclature, it is difficult to consider this genealogy a coincidence. There is no evidence for the existence of such at any earlier time in Merovingian history. Some monk with his nose in legal texts (*Lex Burgundionum*, possibly) or Italian histories (Cassiodorus?) where genealogies could be seen, was curious enough to try his hand at a Frankish genealogy; to excerpt the names of the Merovingians from Frankish history and to construct a genealogy

---

a deliberate policy of keeping the family German. I doubt if enough can be known of comparable families to regard this as exceptional.

[1] *Beowulf*, lines 2910–2921, reading 'Merewīoingas', not 'mere-wīcingas'.
[2] *Form. Marc.*, I, 4.   [3] Ibid., I, 16.      [4] Ibid., I, 39.
[5] Gomatrudis, wife of Dagobert (*Gesta Dagoberti*, chap. 22, M.G.H., S.R.M. II, p. 408).
[6] The genealogy occupies foll. 154–55 and is placed between 'De VI aetatibus mundi' (a mid-ninth century miscellany) and 'De symbolo apostolici'. As so often, law appears in the same manuscript as genealogy – in this case, *Lex Alamannorum* – but they are not directly associated. In view of Merovingian activity in seventh-century Alamannia it seems likely that the original of St Gallen 732 belonged to the same area.
[7] It is printed by G. Kurth, *Histoire poétique des Mérovingiens*, pp. 517–18.

for himself. He happens, however, to do this in the reign of Dagobert.[1]

Paul Lehmann has remarked the distinctive religious bent of Merovingian culture.[2] It is time to see what this bent entailed for the kingship of Chlotar II and Dagobert.

Since the days of St Remigius, there had been a succession of bishops ready to point out their duty to the Merovingians; and sometimes they were listened to. All the same, those closest to the kings had been laymen. With Chlotar II there are signs of a change, and indications of the growing rôle of clergy at court. What this meant can be seen in the correspondence of Desiderius, bishop of Cahors. In a letter to Abbo, bishop of Metz, he reminds his friend of the days when 'nos sub saeculi habitu in contubernio serenissimi Chlothari principis mutuis solebamus relevare fabellis'.[3] They had been laymen then, perhaps youngsters attached to the *scola*. Not long afterwards, Desiderius is reminding the former referendary Dado (or Audoenus), now bishop of Rouen, of their happy times together 'quemadmodum in aula terreni principis socii fuimus' and of their friendship there with Eligius, bishop of Noyon.[4] Now, these were considerable men, who had earned their sees in the king's service. Kings who could find, educate and use men like Desiderius, Dado, Eligius, Sulpicius of Bourges and Paul of Verdun had no reason to be ashamed of their firm hold over the disposal of sees.[5] What is more, Desiderius remained in favour, as Abbo reminded him: 'vos enim et in palacio regis, ubi inutriti fuistis, bene cogniti estis'.[6] He was Dagobert's treasurer, well enough in with his king to be solicited

[1] Cf. the comments on barbarian genealogies of K. Sisam, 'Anglo-Saxon Royal Genealogies', *Proc. Brit. Academy*, 39, esp. p. 323. Otto Höfler made no progress at all with the matter, 'Der Sakralcharakter des germanischen Königtums', *Das Königtum*, p. 80.
[2] 'Das Problem der Karolingischen Renaissance', *Erforschung des Mittelalters*, II (1959), p. 120.
[3] *M.G.H., Epist.*, III, p. 198. Ed. Norberg (1961), p. 28.
[4] Ibid., p. 199.
[5] Ewig, 'Die fränkischen Teilreiche', p. 110, considers that appointments to sees may have been kept in the hands of the Merovingian *Gesamtherrscher* and denied to under-kings (e.g. in Austrasia or Aquitaine).
[6] *M.G.H., Epist.*, III, p. 210.

for support in approaching him.[1] His reward was the see of
Cahors, which he was not embarrassed to admit that he owed to
the king. Neither was he embarrassed to recall to the king their
good times together, 'recordatio contubernii et dulcido auspicatae
indolis pubertatis'.[2] Later on, he informs Sigebert III of his intimacy with his father, and begs for its continuance.[3] This must
have been conceded: at least, Sigebert wrote him one friendly little
note, to say that all went well – 'gentes patriae, nobis a Deo con-
cesse, pacifico ordine nobis oboediunt, gentes etiam barbarae
pagatismae nobis cohabitant' – and that he would attend to a
request of the bishop's.[4] This did not, however, save Desiderius
from a sharp warning to have nothing to do with a church synod
that the king had not been consulted about – not, the king adds,
that he has any objection to synods 'pro statu ecclesiastico an pro
regni utilitate', so long as he has been consulted in the first place.[5]
But the relationship was happy, on the whole. These kings of the
seventh century were as willing as their predecessors to be read
lectures on the proper behaviour of kings, on the lustre of their
forebears and on the examples of David and Solomon.[6] Wilhelm
Levison, who was much struck by this circle of bright young
men from the court of Chlotar II, considered it likely that they had
fallen under the influence of St Columbanus and his Irish monks.[7]
This same influence may have been felt by the lay magnates at
court, for among them were distinguished founders of monasteries. It makes one reluctant to believe that Chlotar and Dagobert encouraged their bright young men as a counter-balance to
the magnates. At all events, these same men formed the first
nucleus of the group of *Hofgeistliche*, who grew in influence under
the later Merovingians and came fully into their own under the
Carolingians. There was no Merovingian court-chapel for them,
not, at least, by the name of *capella*; but there was an *oratorium*, and
there was, by the seventh century, a court-cult of St Martin's *cappa*
as a principal relic. It may have been in the service of the *oratorium*,

[1] e.g. Bertigisel to Desiderius, Ibid., p. 204. Bertigisel had a case pending before
the king in person – 'placitum ante ipso domno habemus'.
[2] Ibid., p. 195.        [3] Ibid., p. 195.        [4] Ibid., p. 208.
[5] Ibid., p. 212.
[6] e.g. ibid., pp. 194, 457.
[7] *Aus rheinischer und fränkischer Frühzeit*, pp. 100, 119, 149.

rather than among the lay officials of the court, that the new churchmen found their natural home.[1]

Even at its strongest, the cult of St Martin did not satisfy the Merovingian need for the support of holy men. Oaths were taken on St Martin's *cappa*,[2] but they could be taken elsewhere. Chlotar II, convinced of the treachery of Godinus, ordered him to be conducted to swear fidelity to him at the churches of St Médard (Soissons) and of St Denis (near Paris), and afterwards at the churches of St Aignan (Orleans) and St Martin (Tours).[3] Relics were even despatched to suitable places for occasions of general oath-taking.[4] The point is best made in some words interpolated in a charter of Clovis II:

> oportet nos sedule secundum paternam institutionem locis venerabilibus sanctorum reverentiam exhibere, ut eos in die necessitatis, patronos et defensores contra visibiles et invisibiles hostes possimus habere.[5]

But the protector most favoured by the dynasty, at least from the seventh century, was St Denis, of whose earliest associations with the Merovingians something has already been said. In two charters granted to the community by Chlotar II, St Denis is characterized as 'peculiaris patronus noster'.[6] Dagobert went further – so far, that the future could mistake him for the founder of the house. His gifts in land cannot be computed: a well-known group of falsified charters stand between the historian and this particular truth. According to the ninth-century *Gesta Dagoberti*, which in this respect is above suspicion, Dagobert's last gift was

[1] Cf. J. Fleckenstein, *Die Hofkapelle der deutschen Könige* (1959), introductory chapter.

[2] *Form. Marc.* I, 38 ('tunc in palatio nostro, super capella domni Martini, ubi reliqua sacramenta percurrunt, debeat coniurare'), and, in much the same words, a confirmatory charter of Theuderic III (Pertz, *M.G.H., Dipl.*, I, p. 45) and a judgement of Childebert III (ibid., p. 69).

[3] Fredegar, *Chron.*, IV, 54. Chlotar also had a special reverence for St Vincent, in whose Parisian church he was buried (ibid., IV, 56). See Gregory, *Hist.*, III, 29 for the impression made on the Merovingians by the way in which a relic of St Vincent protected the city of Saragossa from their siege.

[4] *Form. Marc.*, I, 40.

[5] *Gesta Dagoberti*, chap. 51 (*M.G.H., S.R.M.*, II, p. 424).

[6] These are Pertz, *M.G.H., Dipl.*, I, p. 13, nos. 10 and 11, but a better text of 10 is Havet, *Questions Mérovingiennes*, pp. 226 ff. (facsimile, Lauer and Samaran, no. I).

to Saint-Denis, though he was so ill that he had to ask his son, Clovis II, 'ut per signaculum sui nominis istam cartam adfirmet'.[1] Saint-Denis also benefited under his will.[2] There is no reason to doubt the explanation for this special affection that appears in the *Gesta Dagoberti*: that he believed that the saint had once protected him from the dire consequences of a quarrel with his father.[3] What the author proceeds to make of the incident is another matter. The community itself seemed to feel that Dagobert's gifts of lands were of less importance than his embellishment of their abbey-church; and the story of this is told, soon after, in tones of wonder, by Fredegar.[4] He reports, not indeed that Dagobert had built or rebuilt the church, but that he had embellished it magnificently with gold and precious stones, 'et condigne in circoito fabrecare preceperat'; and all with the intention of ensuring the saint's precious patronage. The work was quite possibly carried out under the supervision of St Eligius, treasurer and goldsmith. Furthermore, the king so endowed the church that many marvelled. Nothing of what remains today of the Saint-Denis treasure is attributable to Dagobert.

One last benefit bestowed by Dagobert was a charter (no longer extant) granting the community the right to hold a fair, annually, on the day after the patron-saint's feast, 9 October.[5] On that fair-day, a market for winter provisions, crowds were drawn to the abbey by the cult of the saint. Whether it was Dagobert's intention to draw merchants to Paris, there is no way of determining.[6] But they came. The financial gain to the abbey increased with the popularity of the saint, and the occasion of this fair was to be one of the principal sources of the vast wealth of the medieval abbey.

[1] *M.G.H., S.R.M.*, II, p. 420. Cf. Bresslau, *Handbuch*, II, p. 202.

[2] Allegedly, the king wished Saint-Denis to keep a copy, 'alium vero Parisius in archivo ecclesiae commendamus' (*M.G.H., S.R.M.*, II, p. 417).

[3] Ibid., pp. 403 ff.

[4] *Chron.*, IV, 79. Cf. L. Levillain, 'Études sur l'abbaye de Saint-Denis à l'époque mérovingienne', *Bibl. de l'École des Chartes*, 86 (1925), esp. p. 22.

[5] This charter is summarized in *Gesta Dagoberti*, chap. 34. For what follows, see particularly L. Levillain, *op. cit., Bibl. de l'École des Chartes*, 91 (1930). Exemption from control by the bishops of Paris followed in 653, and the grant of full immunity was made by Clovis II. Dagobert's fair (that of St Denis proper) should be distinguished from the later fairs of the 'Lendit' and of St Matthias.

[6] Cf. A. R. Lewis, *The Northern Seas* (1958), p. 125. Lewis is in general content to be conjectural about Merovingian trade.

There may have been older fairs – the fair at Troyes may date from at least the sixth century[1] – but this fair is notable for being entirely due to Dagobert's action. It is one aspect of rapidly-increasing Merovingian interest in religious communities at large (an interest that they shared with other magnates). Charters, or copies of charters, exist to show how much the Merovingians felt that *stabilitas* depended on such communities, and on the mutual help that they could give one another.[2] It would be unwise to question the sincerity of any seventh-century king who required his monks to intercede with prayer 'pro aeterna salutae vel felicitate patriae seu regis'. Another aspect of this interest is Merovingian encouragement of the missionary enterprise in northern Francia and the Rhineland, which laid the foundations of the better-known work of St Willibrord and St Boniface in Carolingian times. The era of St Vedast, St Amand, St Ouen, St Wandrille and St Eligius has justly been called 'le siècle des saints'.[3] As in Alamannia and Franconia, so in the territory of present-day Belgium, the political grip of the Merovingians was steadied by the Church. Dagobert, perhaps consolidating the work of the Rhineland missions of men from the Midi, conferred the *castellum* of Utrecht, together with a ruined church, on the bishopric of Cologne, to be a centre for missionary work.[4] Prosperity was likely to follow. Coin-finds suggest, though they do not prove, some increased movement of trade in the Rhineland of the seventh century, in which Franks, Frisians and Anglo-Saxons took part. The Merovingians had no concept of commercial policy, and knew little or nothing of what might encourage or damage their subjects' prosperity; and in this they were not alone; but they were quick enough to see where

[1] Cf. R. Bautier, *La Foire* (1953).

[2] e.g. *Form. Marc.*, I, 1 and 2. See also Dagobert's privilege for Rebais, dated 635, the first Frankish charter to regulate a monastery's relations with the diocesan (Pertz, *M.G.H., Dipl.*, I, no. 15, p. 16). F. Beyerle's view that this famous charter is a forgery modelled on Marculf can be accepted without casting doubt on the fact that a grant of this kind was made ('Das Formularbuch des westfränkischen Mönchs Markulf und Dagoberts Urkunde für Rebais a. 635', *Deutsches Archiv*, 9, 1952, pp. 43–58).

[3] By L. Van der Essen, '*Le Siècle des Saints, 625–739* (1948). See also W. Levison, *England and the Continent*, esp. chap. 3, and Ewig, *Teilreiche* pp. 99 ff.

[4] The charter does not survive but the matter is discussed in a letter from St Boniface to Pope Stephen II (M. Tangl, *Die Briefe des Heiligen Bonifatius und Lullus*, no. 109, p. 235).

prosperity lay, and how they might take their share of it. A stronghold here, a church or monastery there, witness clearly to Merovingian interest in fresh territory. The development of seventh-century coinage equally points to growing prosperity. The presence in graves of private scales and sharp stones (to test coins by scratching) warn us that, in northern Gaul at least, coins were still thought of as bullion;[1] but over a wider field, gradual replacement of gold coinage by silver in the course of the seventh century, with a transitional coinage about the mid-century, is nowadays looked upon as a healthy recognition that silver was better able than gold to finance the growing trade of northern Europe.[2] If gold had still a use in this direction, it was for fiscal purposes: its scope, because of its value, was limited. But little enough is yet known about Merovingian gold, and Pirenne was probably misled about its significance in his assessment of royal wealth. The effect of the spread of Catholicism in the north, of gifts to the Church and the withdrawal of bullion in the form of Church ornaments, might well have led to some impoverishment of the crown, even while the melting-down of imperial coin would have kept up quality for a time.[3] But there is evidence of Dagobert's direct interest in coinage,[4] and it is reasonable enough to guess that part of the treasure he left at his death he owed to an increase in the movement of trade in and through his domains.[5] Nobody can say how much of his, or his successors', wealth was accumulated in this way; how much *telonea* contributed to the stock; to what extent coinage and trade were associated in a barbarian king's mind; whether bullion, apart from its value as ornament and treasure, mattered to any king, and whether it was a yardstick against which to measure his wealth in lands and service.[6]

[1] Cf. J. Werner, 'Waage und Geld in der Merowingerzeit', *Sitzungsb. d. Bay. Akad., Phil.-Hist. Kl.* (1954).

[2] In particular, P. Le Gentilhomme, *Mélanges de numismatique mérovingienne* (1940), esp. pp. 19, 69.

[3] Cf. Philip Grierson, 'Visigothic Metrology', *Numismatic Chronicle*, sixth series, 13 (1953), who considers these points in relation to Visigothic coinage.

[4] Cf. Le Gentilhomme, op. cit. p. 55, and F. Lot, *Nouvelles recherches sur l'impôt foncier* (1955), p. 142.

[5] Fredegar describes the division of the treasure (*Chron.*, IV, 85).

[6] The reaction against the association of coins with trade is forcibly put by Philip Grierson, 'Commerce in the Dark Ages: a critique of the evidence', *Trans. R. Hist. Soc.*, 5th series, 9 (1959).

However accumulated, Dagobert commanded riches greater than those of any other man in his kingdom, though probably one or two religious foundations were already creeping up towards parity with the royal house. The unrivalled prestige of Merovingian kingship in the earlier seventh century rested on good service; and this service was anchored to gold and to lands, as well as to unquestioning acceptance of Merovingian right to rule.

Saint-Denis had been the burial-place of an infant Dagobert, son of Chilperic and Fredegundis:[1] just possibly his grave has been identified.[2] Dagobert himself was buried there and, after him, his queen Nantechildis. The abbey-church had become the royal burial-ground, thus sealing a Merovingian preference for Paris and its neighbourhood that had not escaped the notice of the Burgundian Fredegar.[3] This drawing-together of Saint-Denis (and monasteries generally) with the dynasty had no discernible effect on the Merovingian way of life. It was not long since St Columbanus had rounded on Theuderic and Brunechildis, castigating their debauchery, their view of how monasteries should be run and their presumption in seeking to interfere with his own rule of life.[4] Jonas' long, vivid account of their clashes was taken over almost without change by Fredegar.[5] One would like to know how the reading of this affected contemporaries, and in particular how it affected Frankish churchmen linked in one way or another to the dynasty. A gentler means than Columbanus' of persuading the Merovingians to lead better lives was to draw their attention, and the attention of others, to the saints of the dynasty. Hence, we get *Vitae* of St Sigismund, St Chrotechildis, St Chlodovald, St Radegundis, and St Balthildis. These *Lives* of Merovingians, or of Merovingians by connection, form a group that is of

[1] The 'infantulus iunior' of Gregory of Tours, *Hist.*, V, 34. The harking-back of Venantius Fortunatus' epitaph is of interest:

> Belligeri veniens Chlodovechi gente potenti,
> Egregii proavi germen honore pari,
> Regibus antiquis respondens nobilis infans,
> Chilpericique patris vel Fredegunde genus.
> (*M.G.H., Auct. Antiq.*, IV, i. Carm. IX, 5, p. 211).

[2] It is no. 17 in E. Salin, 'Les tombes gallo-romaines et mérovingiennes de la basilique de Saint-Denis', *Acad. des Inscriptions*, 44 (1958), p. 50.

[3] *Chron.*, IV, 60.

[4] Jonas, *Vita Columbani*, I, chap. 18.      [5] *Chron.*, IV, 36.

more than literary interest. Bruno Krusch, who edited them, had the instinct to group them (together with some Carolingian *Lives* and the *Gesta Dagoberti*) under the title *Vitae Sanctorum generis regii*,[1] though he never investigated their possible relationship – a task that the extant manuscripts would make very difficult. Do they reveal a common ideal of sanctity? Is this ideal distinguishable from ideals informing non-royal *Vitae*? Which monasteries were interested in them? Only when these questions have been faced will it be possible to go on to inquire whether these *Lives* reflected Merovingian notions of Frankish kingship,[2] and how far they helped in forming the Frankish picture of what good Merovingians should be like.

Did the Church pray for the Merovingians? There are grounds for holding that some monasteries did, or were expected to. We can go a little further, and point to an early seventh-century prayer based on 2 Maccabees i. vv. 24–25, which is a petition for God's help against the king's enemies:

> prista francorum rigibus victuriam ut liberati a rebelli suo salventur quia tu sulus pius omnipotens eternus qui liberasti israhel de omnibus malum egipto . . .[3]

This is a general prayer for victory over the king's enemies, and, as has been pointed out, it has some affinity with the regal formulas in Merovingian sacramentaries of this and the following century. As contrasted with comparable Carolingian prayers, it seems impersonal, though this does not make it vague or insignificant. Nor can one infer that none of the royal *benedictiones* of the Carolingian age would have been possible for the Merovingians because they were personal.[4] There is enough to show of general prayers for peace and victory, involving king and people,

[1] *M.G.H., S.R.M.*, II.

[2] Cf. the extremely suggestive comments of Chanoine É. Delaruelle, in *Études Mérovingiennes* (1953), p. 66.

[3] On fol. 16 of Carlsruhe Landesbibliothek MS Reichenau 253. I have not seen this, and I quote from C. A. Bouman, *Sacring and Crowning* (Groningen, 1957), pp. 92–93. The manuscript, of the first half of the eighth century, belonged to Reichenau at latest by 782, and is described by E. A. Lowe as 'written doubtless in the Frankish kingdom' (*C.L.A.*, VIII, 1101). See also E. Ewig, *Das Königtum*, pp. 23, 4.

[4] I cannot agree with Bouman that the sentiments of the prayer 'Prospice' are un-Merovingian.

to make it seem likely that the Frankish Church was finding room for the king in its liturgies by the seventh century. There is already some association of Merovingian business with church ritual; in particular, the king's business of war is his Church's business.

Fighting bulks large in all Dark-Age history, and perhaps exceptionally large in Merovingian history. From this, it is a step to the conclusion that the main business of Merovingian kingship was the business of war.[1] But fighting is one thing, war another. The daily brawling and feuding of barbarian warriors that stands out from the final chapters of Gregory of Tours gives way, in Fredegar's, to campaigning. There were campaigns, indeed, of a traditional flavour, as when Dagobert intervened in Visigothic and Breton affairs: the treasure-hunt motive was still active, and warriors needed exercise. But Merovingian activity over the Rhine, Merovingian relations with Bavarians, Alamans, Franconians, Saxons and Frisians falls outside any possible definition of treasure-hunts, at least in the seventh century. It could be claimed that this marked a revival of the spirit of 'Heerkönigtum', of warrior-kings leading their peoples to one victory after another. We have the song the people sang about a victory of Chlotar II over the Saxons, or at least the beginning and the end of a later version of it:

> De Chlothario est canere rege Francorum
> Qui ivit pugnare in gentem Saxonum . . .[2]

If these words, or something like them, could be sung of Chlotar, how much more of Dagobert? Dagobert was a man who knew how to move armies about: he sped a mission to secure the surrender of the ruler of Brittany with a threat that failure to submit would cause him to send against the Bretons the Burgundian army that had been in Gascony.[3] This military activity in the marches of Francia is undeniable. Yet, from the Frankish point of view, it was also unforeseeable. The stirring-up of Slavs and

---

[1] It is certainly the conclusion of Bodmer, *Der Krieger der Merowingerzeit*.

[2] *Vita Faronis*, chap. 78 (*M.G.H., S.R.M.*, V, p. 193). The authenticity of this song has been much disputed (cf. Wattenbach-Levison, *Geschichtsquellen*, I, pp. 118–19). I am only concerned to say that the sentiment seems right to me for the seventh century.

[3] Fredegar, *Chron.*, IV, 78.

Avars and northern peoples was not the work of the Merovingians, who rather dealt with situations created by these peoples.
From Fredegar and the *Liber Historiae Francorum*, from the *Vitae
Sanctorum* and correspondence and legal records, one does not get
an overwhelming impression of 'Heerkönigtum' come into its
own again. The day-to-day authority of the Merovingians, the
authority that kept them on their thrones, was more commonly
seen in judgement, ratification of other men's business, the disposal of land, appointments to offices, control of officials; in a
word, administration.[1] Thus, if we wish to know what seventh-
century Merovingians did when they were not fighting, we can
form a reasonably clear impression.

## V · THE ROIS FAINÉANTS

After Dagobert came the kings whom Fredegar saw as 'lesser
beasts',[2] and whose rule, though Fredegar did not know this,
was to last from the death of Dagobert in 638 to the deposition of
Childeric III in 751. There can be no question about the reality of
the decline, and historical tradition is in the main correct in label-
ling the kings of this century the 'rois fainéants'. Even when
allowance is made for the extreme difficulty of interpreting the
surviving sources, and equally for the probability that Pippin III
erased some at least of the traces of their rule, the later Merovingians counted for little, and their decline, though not progressive,
was marked enough in terms of power. Several of them failed to
survive boyhood, while others met early and violent ends. Degeneracy may be suspected, though it cannot be proved, and is,
in any case, unnecessary to account for their eclipse.

The first chapter of Einhard's *Vita Karoli Magni*, written some
eighty years after the fall of the Merovingians, reads as follows:

> The *gens Meroingorum*, from which the Franks used to choose
> their kings, is reputed to have lasted till King Childeric was
> deposed, tonsured and confined to a monastery on the orders of

---

[1] E. Lesne, *Histoire de la propriété ecclésiastique*, I, pp. 420 ff., gives many examples.
Royal concessions of land in the form of *beneficium*, *largitio* or *munificentia* can even
be seen as a method of facilitating local government – as concessions, namely, not
of property so much as of public service yielding its own salary (Immink, *At the
roots of medieval society*, chap. 4).

[2] *Chron.*, III, 12.

Pope Stephen. However, even if the dynasty did seem to end with him, it had long since lost all its strength and was no longer distinguished except by its vain title of king. Wealth and power of rule were in the hands of the chief officers of the household, who were called mayors of the palace and who exercised ultimate authority. The king had nothing remaining to him beyond the enjoyment of his title and the satisfaction of sitting on his throne, with his long hair and his trailing beard, there to give the impression of rule and to grant audience to ambassadors from all parts; and he would charge these, at their departure with answers given in his name, but in fact sketched out for him or even prescribed for him. Apart, then, from the empty name of king and the bare subsistence allowed him by the mayor of the palace, he had nothing left of his own but one poor estate with a house and a few servants to look after his wants and carry out his orders. Wherever he travelled, he went in a bullock-cart in charge of a drover, country-fashion. Thus would he journey to a *palatium*, thus to the general assemblies held annually to deal with public affairs; and thus would he go home. The running of the country and all decisions, internal and external, were the exclusive concern of the mayor of the palace.

Here are the last Merovingians as the Carolingians saw them. One would hardly expect the picture to be flattering; should one expect it to be funny? The long-haired kings in their bullock-wagon might have been culled from some work of Carolingian propaganda,[1] or they might be no more than an innocent misunderstanding of some book-illustration. The bullock-wagon itself might have been a slighting reference to the Minotaur, begetter of the Merovingians. But the point of poking fun at a dynasty so long defunct is hard to imagine. We may do better to interpret Einhard's evocation of the Merovingians as a serious attempt to illustrate, so far as his materials allowed, the political consequences of weakness in kings. The grandsons of Charlemagne

[1] In which Halphen believes (*Éginhard, vie de Charlemagne*, 1947, p. 10). The language of certain of Einhard's contemporaries is, as Halphen says, analogous, but it does not argue the existence of any 'opuscule de propagande' on which all drew. Einhard's chief source for this chapter was the Royal Annals (second redaction).

would have seen the point. However looked at, his words raise more questions than they answer. For example, what royal power did Einhard think the Merovingians might have exercised? For how long, before Childeric III, did Einhard suppose them to have been powerless? Of what, if anything, did tonsuring deprive Childeric III? What should be understood by the 'orders' of the pope? Can we infer the same picture without Einhard's help? In brief, any consideration of the last Merovingians must be a commentary upon this famous chapter.

Einhard permits, if he does not invite, the historian to think of the last century of Merovingian rule in terms of a steady decline in royal power and of an equally steady rise in power of the Austrasian clan of the Arnulfings, or Carolingians. The contrast has a fascination of its own, since one cannot help seeing the end of the matter – the quiet removal of the last Merovingian and the anointing of Pippin III. But the Arnulfings cannot have seen this and cannot have known, as the years passed, that the *progenies sancta* of Clovis was doomed to extinction. Nor can they have known that Rome would one day sanction, and in a sense make possible, the transference of royal authority to themselves. All this was unforeseeable. For this reason it is as well to think twice before accepting any account of the 'rois fainéants' in which the Arnulfings struggle ambitiously for the crown through a whole century, and finally achieve it in their moment of triumph.[1] The period of Merovingian decline is not so neat and orderly, nor is it particularly easy to make sense of.

Neustria, and, more loosely, Burgundy went to Dagobert's young son, Clovis II, who ruled these lands under various tutelage till 657, when he in his turn was succeeded by his son, Chlotar III. Austrasia, meanwhile, had been given by Dagobert to his elder son Sigebert III. The youthfulness of Clovis and Sigebert, not any natural incapacity for rule, reveal the ways in which their elders (mothers, for example, and officials such as mayors of the palace) could deputize for Merovingians and, in effect, hold the crown in commission. It would also, inevitably, emphasize the local cleavages of interest between the different parts of Francia. Sigebert

---

[1] I have in mind J. Calmette's *Charlemagne, sa vie et son œuvre* (1945), which is particularly, but not uniquely, misleading in this respect.

spent his entire reign under the supervision of the Arnulfings. They were a family rich in property; but what distinguished them from others not much less rich was their liberality to religious foundations and their encouragement of missionaries. In this, they were at one with the Austrasian Merovingians. We have Sigebert's charter for the house of Stavelot-Malmédy, 'in terra nostra silva Ardenense'.[1] He trusts that his generosity will redound to the credit of his 'regia potestas'. Sigebert was a very young man, and the sentiments as well as the gift itself may have been inspired by his Arnulfing mayor, Grimoald. If they were, they have added significance. But Sigebert was old before his time. Some five years before the Stavelot charter, he had led the Franks into battle against the Thuringian *dux*, Radulf. Fredegar describes the scene.[2] Divided counsels caused the young king to attack his well-entrenched enemy sooner than he should have done: the result was a disastrous defeat. Two magnates, Grimoald and Adalgisel, took special care to protect him from danger; but it was upon him, not upon them, that the humiliation fell: 'Sigebert, like his followers, was seized with wildest grief and sat there upon his horse weeping unrestrainedly for those he had lost'. One is always looking for the beginning of the end of Merovingian power; and here, in 639, is one beginning: a Merovingian leads his Franks against revolt in Thuringia and must, in the end, seek permission from the Thuringians to find his way home, unmolested, from an area where the Merovingians had been sensitive to any sign of insubordination. Fredegar was alive to the significance of his picture of the young king, weeping on the battlefield: if you are a king and choose to fight, your ranks must be loyal, and counsel undivided; you must win.

Sigebert died young, and was buried in the church of St Martin, near Metz. The succession to his rule over Austrasia and the sequence of events in the years 656–62 are obscure. They must always be a matter of conjecture.[3] What is in doubt is whether his successor was his own son, Dagobert II, or the son of Grimoald,

[1] Pertz, *M.G.H., Dipl. I*, no. 21, p. 21.
[2] *Chron.*, IV, 87.
[3] The theories of L. Dupraz, *Le Royaume des Francs et l'ascension politique des maires du palais au déclin du VIIᵉ siècle* (1948), have met with little support. I have examined them in the *Bulletin of the Institute of Historical Research*, XXII (1949).

Childebert III. It can be argued, but not proved, that Dagobert II lost the succession and was sent into exile to Ireland, not by Grimoald but by the Neustrians, and that the elevation of Childebert was a loyal attempt by Grimoald to foil Neustrian ambitions in Austrasia. The plain meaning of the account in the Neustrian *Liber Historiae Francorum*[1] is rather that Grimoald himself sent Dagobert into exile, substituting his own son as king; and to this the Neustrians took exception, to the extent of ambushing and killing both Grimoald and Childebert. There was, in a word, an act of usurpation; but it can be seen in more than one way: either (and commonly) as a premature realization of Arnulfing designs on kingship – premature only because foiled by the Neustrians; or as the consequence of a desperate attempt of Grimoald and his followers to secure themselves against Austrasian rivals about the person of Dagobert II: it proved easier to change the king than to remove the rivals. Seen thus, the protection of his own, local, interests would have mattered more to Grimoald than the supplanting of Merovingians by Arnulfings. The Arnulfing Childebert III was, by name and adoption, a Merovingian. Only his blood could not be changed; and it has not been shown that this weighed overmuch with the Austrasians. Neustrian-Austrasian rivalry, and conflicting ambitions to control the rich territory of the Rémois, also played some part in these events. No love was lost between the two royal courts and the men whose interests supported them. The lesson of the crisis was not so much that the Arnulfings had betrayed their ambitions as that a mayor could make a king, provided he were disguised as a Merovingian. Yet, the swift consequences of that king-making can hardly have taken Grimoald by surprise. They can only confirm the impression that his had been a desperate step in the first place. His clan was by no means assured of undisputed primacy among the Austrasian magnates; events were soon to show that not all the neighbouring German *duces* trusted him; and, when all is said, Grimoald never behaved like a man who felt sure of himself or of his neighbours.

Both Childeric II, imposed by the Neustrians on the Austrasians, and Chlotar III, his brother, were Merovingians with something to say for themselves. They began to reign when they

[1] Chap. 43 (*M.G.H., S.R.M.*, II, p. 316).

235

were minors. Childeric's earliest extant charter, dated 1 August
661, is subscribed by his mother on his behalf:

> et ego, dum propter imbecillem aetatem minime potui sub-
> scribere, manu propria subter signavi et regina subterscripsit,

but he made his 'signum'.[1] He was to reign till 675, and, during
the last few months of this time, over the whole *regnum* of Francia.
There is some indication that he thought of resuming his ancestors' activities in northern Italy and of intervening in the
struggles of the rival Lombard kings;[2] and some, too, that he
was master in his own house and able to resist over-mighty
mayors, the roots of whose tyranny had lain in the opportunity of
a succession of minors. The *Passio* of St Léger of Autun contains
some arresting words on the magnates' anxiety to escape from the
kind of tyranny exercised by one mayor, Ebroin:

> Interea Childerico rege expetiunt universi, ut talia daret decreta
> per tria quam obtinuerat regna, ut uniuscuiusque patriae legem
> vel consuetudinem deberent sicut antiquitus iudices conservare
> et ne de una provintia rectores in aliis introirent neque unus ad
> instar Ebroini tyrannidem adsumeret.[3]

Here, surely, is no new kind of magnate – Neustrian, Austrasian
or Burgundian – struggling for a new kind of freedom against an
ancient tyranny. It is the tyranny that is new; the tyranny of the
parvenu mayor who ignores the customs of the three *patriae*.
These customs should be kept intact by a Merovingian, who will
lose nothing of his authority by ensuring that his *iudices* administer
the provinces 'sicut antiquitus'. The principal chronicler of these
times, the author of the *Liber Historiae Francorum*, had no concern
with the kingship of Childeric II, and we must reconcile ourselves
to knowing nothing more about it. The end, however, is well
enough known. Childeric suffered from 'levitas', a murderous
light-heartedness, which led him to insult one of his Frankish
followers, and subsequently to perish, together with his pregnant
queen, in the inevitable act of vendetta.[4] This has rightly been
seen as the true succession-crisis of the dynasty;[5] what killed it

[1] Pertz, *M.G.H., Dipl. I*, no. 25, p. 26.  [2] Paul the Deacon, *Hist. Lang.*, V, 5.
[3] *M.G.H., S.R.M.*, V, p. 289.  [4] *M.G.H., S.R.M.*, II, p. 318.
[5] e.g. by E. Ewig, *Die fränkischen Teilreiche*, p. 128.

was the absence of a suitable heir at that moment; after this, no Merovingian was ever again to rule in the plenitude of power. Einhard's analysis begins to fit the facts. It was, however, a decline not at once discerned by contemporaries, still less desired by them. If we look for any immediate indication that the day of the Carolingians had at last dawned, we shall look in vain. The *praecepta* and the judgements of a long series of Merovingians stand to warn us of the things that Carolingians could not yet do, and for which Merovingians had to be sustained through many years. From the brothers, Chlotar III and Childeric II, to Childeric III, last of the Merovingians, there survives a series of seventy-five royal instruments, which it would be right to increase in number by accepting as genuine certain of the instruments classified by Pertz as *diplomata spuria*. Their tone is no less authoritative because the kings are often political ciphers, and royal 'largitas' is still exercised from what remains of the Merovingian fisc. It is still the king who adjudges the restoration of hereditaments, confirms the sentences of his counts, allows the exchange of lands between monasteries, settles quarrels that come to his notice,[1] confiscates property from the unfaithful, rewards fidelity, grants exemption from *telonea*, protects orphans and looks back to a long succession of forebears who had done the same. Churches and monasteries everywhere, but particularly the great Neustrian house of Saint-Denis, benefit from these instruments. What stronger inducement to the continuity of rule could there be than the assurance that Merovingians alone would be likely to continue to confirm and to augment gifts made over many years by their own kindred? Emphasis on family in Merovingian charters seems to increase with the passage of time, though without implication of awareness of magical property in the royal blood. Losers by the disappearance of the Merovingians in these last seventy years would have included Saint-Denis, among other houses that Charles Martel despoiled for the provision of supporters. To put it another way,

---

[1] 'Quotienscumque altercantium iurgia palatii nostri nostra nostrorumque fidelium aut aecclesiarum seu sacerdotum pro quarumcumque rerum negotiis noscuntur advenire, oportet nobis in Dei nomine iuxta legum severitatem inquirere, ut deinceps nulla videatur quaestio renovari' (Pertz, *M.G.H., Dipl. I*, no. 41, p. 38). The king goes on to ask to see the documents in the case. Cf. the comment of G. Chevrier in *Études Mérovingiennes*, p. 25.

the interests of the Merovingians were more obviously bound up with the Frankish Church than with their lay magnates. It was a situation for which parallels could be found outside Francia.

Even in these years, there were occasional Merovingians who appeared not to know that their day was done. There is the curious case of Dagobert II, for twenty years an exile in Ireland, till restored to the Austrasians through the good offices of St Wilfrid, in 676.[1] On his way home from Rome in 680, Wilfrid learnt that Dagobert had been assassinated.[2] An irate Frankish bishop explained to him why this had happened: Wilfrid had sent them a king who proved to be a

> dissipator urbium, consilia seniorum despiciens, populos ut Roboam filius Salomonis tributo humilians, ecclesias Dei cum praesulibus contempnens.

This was a king who was not prepared to do as his bishops told him, who would go his own way without the counsel of his *seniores*, who in a year or so had ruined cities[3] and who, above all, was not afraid to impose taxation;[4] and so this Rehoboam met his end, 'per dolum ducum et consensum episcoporum'. Whatever else he was, Dagobert was no 'roi fainéant'; he had fallen foul of a group of magnates who had reason to fear him, though it would be wide of the mark to simplify the situation into a clash between kingship and aristocracy. It is worth observing that Dagobert's violent death made him the object of popular cult.[5]

The later seventh century saw the grip of the Arnulfings tighten upon Austrasia. Mayors or dukes, they got the better of their local rivals.[6] The power of Pippin II and of Charles Martel can be gauged in two ways: first, by the extent of their religious founda-

---

[1] Eddius, *Vita Wilfrithi*, ch. 28.     [2] Ibid., ch. 33.

[3] Does this mean that he pulled down city walls in order to prevent cities being used as centres of resistance to his rule? *Dissipatio* is several times used of the destruction of city-walls in the Vulgate.

[4] F. Lot, *L'Impôt Foncier* (1928), p. 101, insists that taxes continued to be imposed throughout the seventh century, even though they were considered extortionate.

[5] *M.G.H., S.R.M.*, II, p. 519, n. 1; p. 521, n. 2. There may be a parallel here with the popular canonization of the 'martyr' Sigismund of Burgundy.

[6] A. Bergengruen, *Adel und Grundherrschaft*, p. 180, argues that the title of mayor was not known in Austrasia and was used by writers only by analogy with Neustrian practice.

tions and benefactions in Austrasia,[1] and secondly, by their military activity. That pressure upon the Frankish settlements in the Rhineland, once resisted by Dagobert I, had steadily increased. The Saxons were conquering bits of the old Frankish *Volksland* up to the time of Charles Martel's counter-attack in 718. Westphalian Hatterun first became a Saxon possession after 694, perhaps as late as 715.[2] Merovingian kings took no part in holding and reversing this surge of Germans: for the Arnulfings (or Carolingians, as they may by this time be called), the immediate defence of their possessions and of the approaches to the Rhineland was a domestic concern. And they still had their enemies – for example, the Alaman dukes, Merovingian loyalists till their overthrow at Cannstadt in 746[3] – who feared Arnulfing territorial power and influence in the Rhineland. Merovingian kingship was not so deeply rooted or so well endowed in Austrasia as in Neustria. Without meaning to, Pippin II and Charles Martel could have revived memories, at least in Austrasia, of an outmoded kind of kingship. Thoughts of Germanic *Heerkönigtum*, of warrior-kings defending their own against outside attack, and even extending their territories by taking war into the enemy's camp, must have stirred. The chroniclers' accounts of the rise of the Carolingians are accounts of war successfully waged in the northern and the eastern marches of Francia. But they contain no suggestion that the days of the Merovingians were numbered. Historians are willing enough to conclude that the Merovingians still, in an obscure way, mattered to the Franks. Why not, then, also to the Carolingians? It is not at all unlikely that the Carolingians, like other great men, were the *fideles* of the Merovingians, bound to them by an oath of loyalty that they would long have hesitated to break.

One of the remarkable features of the rule of the Carolingian mayors was the way they had of keeping up the façade of Merovingian kingship, and of sheltering behind it. Merovingians were

---

[1] On which see C. Wampach, *Geschichte der Grundherrschaft Echternach*, I, *Textband* (1929), pp. 113-35.

[2] Cf. E. Ewig, *Civitas Ubiorum*, pp. 16 ff.

[3] Fredegar, *Cont.*, 27. Cf. L. Levillain, 'Les Nibelungen historiques et leur alliances de famille', *Annales du Midi*, L (1938), p. 42, and T. Mayer, *Mittelalterliche Studien* (1959), p. 325.

involved in defeat, as at the battle of Tertry in 687, which revealed their weakness in Neustria; they were put to flight, and bargained for; and yet they could not be done without. One may instance the events that followed the death of Chlotar IV, in 719. The author of the *Liber Historiae Francorum*[1] and, following him, the continuator of Fredegar,[2] record them carefully. Charles Martel at once sent to the Duke of Aquitaine and obtained from him his hostage, Chilperic II, who had once been a monk under the name of Daniel. Chilperic was sent to Charles at Noyon, but soon afterwards died. Then

> Franci vero Theudericum, Cala monasterio enutritum, filium Dagoberto iunioris, regem super se statuunt, qui nunc anno sexto in regno subsistit.

The continuator of Fredegar puts it rather more warmly. He says that Theuderic IV 'still reigns over us and looks forward to years of life'. Theuderic, in fact, died in 737. We may see here signs of anxiety to find kings who really were of Merovingian blood; there is no reason to question the genuineness of the claims made for them by Carolingian writers. Still more noticeable is their connection with the Church. The Merovingians find their last refuge in monasteries, from which they are brought out to do their duty. Should we not rather have expected to find them protected by laymen who believed in the efficacy of their sacred blood? This final retreat into the Church in fact makes the circumstances of their deposition easier to explain.

It could not help much towards an understanding of Frankish kingship to recapitulate the campaigns of Charles Martel and Pippin III, whose energetic sorties against pagan enemies, German and Saracen, were slow to give the Franks any sense of unity in crisis. The vendetta-ridden society of the age would have no reason to cherish an ideal of political cohesion. The Merovingians had neither inherited nor propagated such an ideal – which is not to say they lacked a political morality of their own, or that they had no concept of public authority. But if the unity of France was not born in these years of battle, what plainly was born was a communion of interest between the Frankish Church and the Carolin-

[1] Chap. 53.  [2] Chap. 10.

gians. This may be traced back to the early Arnulfing foundations
in the Ardennes and the Rhineland, and to their encouragement
of Anglo-Saxon missionaries in the same area; and it was surprisingly little affected by later Carolingian expropriation of ecclesiastical lands, when need arose. The interesting point is that the
Carolingians won the support of the Merovingian Church, not
that they founded a new Church, in the sense in which, over some
generations, they founded a new aristocracy of landowners. The
Church of St Martin at Tours, not any new-fangled monastery
in the Ardennes, was the gainer by Charles' victory over the
Saracens in October 732: 'Christo auxiliante tentoria eorum sub-
vertit'.[1] To us, this is one in a series of engagements that was to
free Aquitaine and Burgundy of the Saracen conquerors, whose
ways were not uniformly unattractive to those they conquered.
To the religious communities of western Francia, however, it
seemed rather different: it enabled them to stay where they were
and to prosper, until the Viking raids of the next century. The
Saracens were truly a 'gravissima lues'; Bede spoke for churches
everywhere.[2]

The charters of the mayors for Saint-Denis suggest how the
greatest of the monasteries of the pre-Viking age was won by the
Carolingians. In 741, 'annum quintum post defunctum Theoderi-
cum regem', Charles Martel gave to the monastery the old Merovingian villa of Clichy.[3] Six years later, 'anno V Childerici regis',
Pippin III adjudged a disputed property to the house;[4] and, two
years after that, 'anno VIII regni gloriosissime Childerici regis',
he again found a favourable judgement for the house in respect
of an 'oratorium, nomine Crux'.[5] The mayor freely recalls the
Merovingian charters granting and confirming the gift: the abbot
Fulrad had displayed them for his inspection. Twice more, in 750
and 751, in charters the originals of which are extant,[6] Pippin the
mayor adjudged properties to the monastery. On the second
occasion, indeed, it was more like wholesale restitution. Saint-
Denis knew how to preserve its documents: hence our knowledge
of these transactions. There would have been others, of which

[1] Fredegar, *Cont.*, 13.          [2] *Hist. Eccl.*, V, 23.
[3] Pertz, *M.G.H.*, *Dipl. I*, no. 14, p. 101.
[4] Ibid., no. 18, p. 104.          [5] Ibid., no. 21, p. 106.
[6] Ibid., no. 22, p. 107, and no. 23, p. 108.

nothing is now known. They are enough to throw a little light on the drawing-together of Merovingian Saint-Denis and the Carolingians. Certainly, Saint-Denis suffered large losses in the early eighth century, and faced at least one serious threat to its independence from the Bishop of Paris. But it survived its protectors and benefactors, the Merovingians;[1] and it found new protectors in the Carolingians who, in the matter of a decade, drew so close to it that the abbey seemed the right place for the consecration of the family in 751. The abbot Fulrad presided over this metamorphosis of a Merovingian into a Carolingian monastery. He was also a leader in the negotiations at Rome that led to the disappearance of the Merovingians: Saint-Denis had found that it could do without them.

The Carolingians appropriated one dear symbol of Merovingian religious cultus. By 710, the *cappa* of St Martin was in the possession of Grimoald:

> Sic ab ipso viro Grimoaldo fuit judecatum, ut sex homenis de Verno et sex de Latiniaco, bone fideus, in oraturio suo super cappella sancti Marcthyni memorate homenis hoc deberent conjurare.[2]

It is a fair inference that it never again left the possession of the family.[3] By the time of Charles Martel there were *capellani* in the Carolingian circle, keepers of the *cappa* in the Carolingian oratory and already, in effect, Carolingian 'Hofgeistliche'. In due course, they were to take over the running of the Merovingian chancery, which nonetheless retained some life of its own till 751. It was St Denis, however, rather than St Martin who principally attracted Carolingian devotion; though even more than to St Denis, and increasingly, their church-dedications suggest devotion to the cult of St Peter.

A poem, finally, may suggest how the mayors and their kings shared something of the same spirit of religious observance at court. It is preserved in Verona MS XC (85), of the late ninth

---

[1] It survived them but it remembered them: material from Saint-Denis is held to lie behind *Floovant*, the only 'chanson de geste' in which the Merovingians have a part to play.

[2] Ibid., no. 78, p. 69. Better text in Lauer & Samaran, p. 23, plate 32.

[3] Cf. Fleckenstein, *Die Hofkapelle*, I, pp. 13–14, 29–30.

century, and has only recently been deciphered in such a way as to make sense.[1] It is a poem about the celebration of Easter at the royal court:

> Ymnorum sonus modulantur clerici
> ad aulam regis et potentes personae;
> procul exclusit saeculares fabulas,
> memora divae epulae esplendidae:
> flammas exurit defreneta lingua.

The identity of the 'potentis personae' cannot be guessed at, but the editor is surely right to see in him a Carolingian mayor. He is the man who represses worldly talk and worse, as the royal court prepares to celebrate Easter. The situation seems to belong to the eighth century rather than to the seventh, and it is not at all clear that one particular occasion is in the poet's mind. However that may be, it is not implied that the mayor is busying himself about matters his decadent king should have attended to. The court is the court of both men, and the mayor – 'potens' – sees to the decent observance of the Merovingian Easter celebrations.

In all this can be detected the quiet movement of the Merovingian Church into the orbit of the Carolingian mayors. It could be illustrated in other ways. Certainly it calls for more attention than it gets, since it may well be the decisive factor in the transference of rule to the Carolingians. Another aspect, and better understood, is the growth of the Austrasian and German missionary-churches under Carolingian protection. Recent work has shown fairly clearly that the Merovingian Church did not permanently lose touch with Rome, and never ceased to feel some affection for her. But the links between them were not strong, unlike those that held Rome to the Carolingian mayors. St Boniface had cause to know that his Carolingian protectors had ways of communicating with Rome that short-circuited his own mission; and it is not out of the question that we make too much of Anglo-Saxon influence at the courts of the reforming Carolingians. An Englishman, however, accompanied Fulrad of Saint-Denis to the papal court on the embassy of 750 that led to the deposition of the Merovingians;

---

[1] By Dag Norberg, *La poésie latine rhythmique du haut moyen âge*, chap. IV,

and probably English sympathy as well as English practice would
have been behind any step that ensured strong kingship, and
would have had some part in determining the pope's answer to
the question whether a ruler enjoying no power should rightly
continue to bear the title of king. The separation of the function
from the title of ruler was as alien to papal as to Frankish and
English tradition; a 'rex sine potestate' was a monstrosity.[1] 'Rex
enim a regendo vocatur' had been the dictum of St Augustine,[2]
and this, and other thoughts like it, were much in men's minds
in mid-eighth-century Rome,[3] where they expounded a view of
kingly rule, derived from the Bible, that was against the anomaly
so long countenanced by the Franks. Under the impact of Roman
thought, sponsored by St Boniface among others, the Merovingians appeared to men for the anachronism they were. It looked
possible, perhaps for the first time, that the Merovingian creation
of Frankish kingship might be divorced from the Merovingians,
who had lost the habit of exercising it; that it was unnecessary to
pretend that the business of kingship was a Merovingian preserve;
and that there were other ways than shield-raising of making a
Frank their king. The papal *responsum* to Pippin's inquiry thus
incapsulated a sentiment that all shared: kings should be seen to
rule, as kings of the Old Testament had ruled. From this, it was
a short step to equate the Carolingian armies with the columns of
Israel, fighting under a 'Novus David' or 'Novus Moyses'. The
sentiment finds its proper expression in the language of the
Frankish liturgies, and notably in the earliest Frankish *Laudes
Regiae*, the liturgical acclamations of the priest-king.[4] From the
papal viewpoint, kingship was a privilege that depended entirely
on the suitability of each king. A king who ceased to be suitable
broke the bond that held him to God, from whom he believed his
*gratia* derived. He ceased to be 'rex cui dominus regendi curam
commisit' (*Form. Marc.*, 25). Pope Gregory VII, looking back on
the part played in 751 by Pope Zacharias (not Stephen, *pace*

[1] Cf. H. Büttner, 'Aus den Anfängen des abendländischen Staatsdenkens', *Hist.
Jahrbuch*, 71 (1952), pp. 77–90.
[2] *De civit. Dei*, V, 12. See also Isidore, *Etymol.*, IX, 3, I.
[3] The evidence is discussed by Ewig, *Das Königtum*, pp. 44 ff., and by Büttner,
ibid., pp. 160 ff.
[4] Cf. E. H. Kantorowicz, *Laudes Regiae* (1946), *passim.*

Einhard) commented that the last Merovingian was not deposed for moral defects but 'quia non erat utilis.' [1] All the same, the *utilitas* that had departed was envisaged in terms of the Christian nature of Merovingian kingship.

When it came to the point, it was the making, not the un-making, of a *gens regia* that most struck people about the events of 751. Fredegar's continuator says that, as a result of the exchange of views with the pope, Pippin was made king, and Bertrada queen, and that, following the *ordo* anciently required, Pippin was chosen king by all the Franks, consecrated by the bishops – who may or may not have included St Boniface – and accorded homage by his great men. [2] Which is as much as to say that they had made a king, and by implication a dynasty, in a new way; [3] but not that they expected the king to behave differently from an active Merovingian.

The means used to finish off the Merovingians and to create their successors, notably the shearing of the heads of the former and the anointing of the latter, point to the difficulty and danger of the episode. It called for care in preparation. This can lead one to fasten upon the magical property of Merovingian blood as the element creating the difficulty: what else could there have been to warrant so much trouble? But the sources are not clear about this. The Royal Annals (followed, in the second redaction, by Einhard) content themselves with this brief account of King Childeric's end: 'Hildericus vero, qui false rex vocabatur, tonsoratus est et in monasterium missus'. [4] The *rex falsus*, for long indispensable to Pippin, and probably his son, were shorn of their locks and shut up in the monastery of Saint-Bertin, where they presumably spent the rest of their days. These last Merovingians had been no feebler than their predecessors of the past fifty years, and might have prolonged their dynasty indefinitely. This is why it is misleading to think of the Merovingians as gradually petering out. Their end, as a dynasty, if quiet, was sudden. What, then, was the significance of their tonsuring? It may have signified a deprivation

---

[1] *Reg.* viii, 21 (ed. Caspar, p. 554). Cf. W. Ullmann, *Principles of Government and Politics in the Middle Ages* (1961), p. 68.  I am indebted to Dr Ullmann for further elucidation of this point.

[2] *Cont.*, 33.

[3] Cf. Kern, *Gottesgnadentum* (ed. Buchner), p. 78.                    [4] s.a. 750.

of the magic power of their royal race. Such is the opinion of many scholars.[1] The extant seals of the later Merovingians (Theuderic III, Clovis III, Childebert III, and Chilperic II) plainly exhibit them with their long hair.[2] But wherein lies the proof of its magical properties? To be tonsured, as was Tulga in 641[3] and Theuderic (with Ebroin) a few years later,[4] was meant as a humiliation that no ruler could survive. Looking back, once more, to Gregory of Tours, to his account of the tonsuring of Chararic and his son by Clovis, it was not the loss of magic power but the humiliation that brought tears to Chararic's eyes: 'Chararicus de humilitate sua conquireret et fleret'. They were going to make him a priest, and his son a deacon.[5] In the end, Clovis thought it safer to kill them, in case they let their hair grow again, so giving open proof of their intention to resist him. But we cannot tell that tonsuring deprived them of royal power or rank; and, if not them, then much less the infinitely more sophisticated Merovingians of the eighth century. We cannot therefore be sure that the anointing with chrism of the Carolingians was intended to compensate for the loss of magical properties of blood, symbolized by long hair. If it compensated for anything, it was probably for loss of face incurred in breaking an oath of fidelity in a particularly shocking way.[6] The oath-breakers included churchmen; indeed, the sources associate the act of tonsuring with the Church, just as much as the subsequent act of unction; and the act of deposition, if it is right to think in such terms, appears to have lain not in the tonsuring but in the affirmation, presumably by the Church, that King Childeric was

[1] E.g. P. E. Schramm, *Der König von Frankreich* (2nd ed., 1960), I, pp. 150, 271, and, with some modification, by Theodor Schieffer, *Winfrid-Bonifatius* (1954), pp. 258–59.

[2] Cf. Lauer and Samaran, p. 28, plate 43. Should any significance be attached to the very curious hair-style of King Offa of Mercia, as shown on certain of his coins or to the long hair of King Liuvigild, also shown on his coins?

[3] Fredegar, *Chron.*, IV, 82.

[4] *Liber Hist. Franc.*, chap. 45.

[5] *Hist.*, II, 41. Cf. *Regula Ferioli*, 8: '. . . quid humilem est professus in capite'. Tonsuring takes from a man his independent pride.

[6] The difficulties inherent in determining the significance of the unction of 751 are well brought out in the valuable discussion of the paper of Professor José Orlandis Rovira, 'La iglesia Visigoda y los problemas de la sucesion al trono en el siglo VII', *Settimane di studio del centro italiano di studi sull' alto medioevo*, VII (i), pp. 385–404.

no king: he was a *rex falsus*. The Merovingian monarchy in Gaul began with Remigius and ended with Fulrad. Without the lead given by the Church, could it have occurred to Pippin that it was possible to dispossess the Merovingians of the crown that was their private possession?

So far as is known, the revolution of 751 was completely successful. There were no Merovingian loyalists to rescue their king from Saint-Bertin and to restore him, long-haired once again, to his kingship. All the Franks accepted what was done in their name. One is driven to conclude that the sacrosanct blood of the late Merovingian kings was no serious bar to their deprivation, once the *fortuna* of the house had gone. The difficulty of the transition did not rest in that: it was quite easy to put away the Merovingians, once it had been determined, with the help of Rome, how to put the Carolingians in their place. It was easy, then, to be impressed by the drying-up of the wealth of the Merovingians, to note the progressive diminution of the product of royal taxation, aggravated by huge concessions of exemption or immunity, as well as by the wholesale distribution of estates that could not be replaced or resumed. It was easy to see that loyalty and service and wealth stood or fell together. But does it follow that 'les descendants de Clovis étaient voués à disparaître'?[1] The truth is that, for the better part of a century, Merovingian kingship held its course with hardly any of the advantages of estates to bestow or revenues to collect. Bankrupts often do well for themselves. Lack of means, like lack of a fighting force when it was required, marked the end of Merovingian *potestas*, as Einhard understood it. In particular, the Merovingians lacked power in the right places, in the Rhineland and beyond, where the shape of Europe was being determined. But *potestas* is not *auctoritas*. The *coup d'état*, when it happened, happened in Neustria. We may not be so very far from the truth if we see, in that final scene, the awakening of the Neustrian Franks, and especially of churchmen, to the realization that the Austrasians were right; their fortunes could safely be dissociated from the

---

[1] J. Dhondt, *Études sur la naissance des principautés territoriales en France* (1948), p. 5. If J. W. Thompson's picture of the Merovingian fisc is even approximately right (*The Dissolution of the Carolingian Fisc*, 1935, pp. 4–5), its chief losses to the Carolingians were in control of bishoprics.

dynasty that created them. Rome showed the way by providing in unction a king-making rite, of uncertain origin indeed, and only supplementary to traditional Frankish rites; but a rite that somehow cleared the consciences of 'all the Franks', bishops and abbots as well as other great men, who for so long had been the faithful men of a *rex falsus*. It was safe to revert to real kings, and irrelevant what blood flowed in their veins. The Merovingians had made Frankish kingship, but not themselves, irreplaceable.

# Index

*

# Index

bullock-cart, Merovingian, 232
bull's-head, gold, 162, 220 n. 2
Burdunelus, 48 n. 2
Burgundians, Burgundy, 2, 5, 9, 12, 21, 23, 24, 28, 38, 47, 64, 72, 73, 74, 75, 76, 77, 83, 84, 85, 86, 87, 88, 90, 92, 108, 123, 128, 131, 133, 142 ff., 160, 167 ff., 179, 180, 186, 199 ff., 205, 206, 212, 214, 215, 216, 230, 233, 241
Byzantium, Byzantines (Constantinople), 34, 38, 48, 64, 68, 69, 82, 85, 86, 87, 88, 89, 90, 123, 160, 161, 169, 171, 172, 175 ff., 190 n. 4, 191, 198, 205, 209, 211

Cadwalla, 62.
Caesara, wife of Anaulf, 88
Caesarius of Arles, 41, 46
Calais, St, hermit, 207 ff.
*calices, sexaginta*, 190
Cambrai, 152, 159
*Campus Martius*, 103
Cannstadt, battle of, 239
canon law, 11, 17, 114, 177, 193
Cantabria, 89, 90
cantonments, 32, 152, 182
*capella*, Frankish, 174 n. 3, 223
*capellani*, 242
*capitatio humana et plebeia*, 67
*capitatio terrena*, 67
*capitula Angilramni*, 97
capitularies, 16, 18, 109, 111 n. 4, 145 ff.
*cappa*, St Martin's, 6, 52, 174, 223, 224, 242
*capsae, viginti evangeliorum*, 190
Carausius, revolt of, 149
Carcassonne, 32, 174 n. 2
Carloman I, 145
Carolingians, 8, 10, 11, 13, 14, 15, 16, 18, 19, 21, 22, 72, 123, 144 ff., 207, 223, 226, 232, 237, 239, 240 ff., 246
*cartae de rege, regales*, 4, 5, 189
*cartae pagenses*, 5
*cartae securitatis*, 141
Carthage, 79, 133
*casa, casati*, 15
Cassian, John, 38
Cassiodorus, 57, 124, 168 n. 2, 202 n. 2, 221
*castella*, 5, 182, 226
Catalaunian Plain, 34, 47, 159
catholics, catholicism, 35, 37, 39, 44, 45, 46, 56, 57, 58, 64, 65, 70, 163, 167, 169 ff., 172, 227
cattle, 141
cattle-rustling, 124
cemeteries, 31, 60 n. 2, 152
*centena, centenarius*, 193

Chainulf, feud of, 142
Chalon-sur-Saône, 71, 143
chancery, 75 n. 1, 209, 213, 214, 242
characteristics, Frankish, 202
Chararic, tonsuring of, 246
Charente, river, 29
Charibert I, 195
Charlemagne, 10, 14, 15, 18, 20, 24, 98, 117, 120, 145 ff., 186, 188, 207
Charles Martel, 10, 14, 72, 100, 145, 204, 237, 238, 239, 240, 241
Charles the Bald, emperor, 10, 16, 18, 21, 101, 109 n. 2, 118, 119, 202
charters, 207 ff., 210, 224 ff., 234, 236, 237, 241
Châteaudun, 189
Chaubedo, 93, 143
Chelles (*Cala monasterium*), 240
Childebert I, 31, 132, 189 ff., 192, 207 ff.
Childebert II, 9, 67, 86, 129, 130, 133, 134, 141, 196
Childebert III, 224 n. 2, 235, 246
Childebrand, count, 72
Childeric I, 3, 62, 84, 85, 158, 160 ff., 173, 176, 183, 220 n. 2
Childeric II, 235 ff.
Childeric III, 231, 233, 237, 245 ff.
Childeric the Saxon, 138
Chilperic I, 51, 58, 67, 68, 79, 81 n. 3, 130, 134 ff., 137, 157, 195, 215, 228
Chilperic II (Daniel), 240, 246
chlamys, investiture with, 175
Chlodomer, 131
Chlodosind, niece of Guntramn, 133
Chlotar I, 31, 189 n. 2, 192 ff., 215 n. 3
Chlotar II, 73, 76, 91, 92, 93, 94, 99, 135, 205, 206 ff., 212 ff., 220, 224, 230
Chlotar III, 233, 235, 237
Chlotar IV, 240
Chosroes I (Anōsharwān, Anaulf), Persian ruler, 89
Chramnesind, 140 ff.
chrism, 104, 246
Christ, protector and conqueror, 60 n. 2
Chrodin, 129 n. 5
*chronica Gallica*, 28
chronology, 63, 64, 74, 76, 78, 79, 165, 167 n. 1
Chrotechildis, princess, 136
Chrotechildis, queen, 84, 103, 131, 167, 183
church buildings, embellishments, etc., 53, 99, 183, 225
church endowments, property, 178, 190, 197, 217, 221, 225, 234, 241
Church, Gallic and Frankish, 6, 7, 9, 14, 17, 67, 68, 126, 127, 128, 141, 147, 177 ff., 180, 189, 190, 194, 195, 200, 202, 213, 215, 238, 240, 243 ff.

251

# Index

# Index

# Index

# Index

# Index

# Index